The Nation and Nationalism in Europe

The Nation and Nationalism in Europe

An Introduction

Ireneusz Paweł Karolewski and
Andrzej Marcin Suszycki

EDINBURGH UNIVERSITY PRESS

© Ireneusz Paweł Karolewski and Andrzej Marcin Suszycki, 2011

Edinburgh University Press Ltd
22 George Square, Edinburgh
www.euppublishing.com

Typeset in 11/12.5 Sabon by
Servis Filmsetting Ltd, Stockport, Cheshire, and
printed and bound in Great Britain by
CPI Antony Rowe, Chippenham and Eastbourne

A CIP record for this book is available from the British Library

ISBN 978 0 7486 3806 2 (hardback)
ISBN 978 0 7486 3807 9 (paperback)

The right of Ireneusz Paweł Karolewski and Andrzej Marcin Suszycki
to be identified as authors of this work has been asserted in accordance
with the Copyright, Designs and Patents Act 1988.

Contents

Tables

Introduction

Why a book on the nation and nationalism?

The nation and nationalism have long been major research topics in the fields of social sciences, history and anthropology. The research has included describing the different forms and types of nations as well as the search for the causes of nationalism. Nowadays, the subject of the nation and nationalism continues to challenge scholars in their exploration of its significance for people's lives and its role in the justification of government policies as well as in the democratic context. In addition, new forms and types of nationalism are being discussed against the background of globalisation and individualisation. The more recent debates on the nation and nationalism relate to, among other things, the issue of whether national identity serves basic human needs and is compatible with or even necessary for the implementation of liberal ideals of equality and individuality.

Both concepts of the nation and nationalism are still subject to scientific inquiry and exhibit a growing conceptual and theoretical variety with frequently contrasting positions. For instance, concerning the concept of the nation, a controversy has arisen regarding its political connotation. Although the liberal political theory does not centre on nations, it recognises that a modern state depends on some national justification of popular sovereignty. John Stuart

Mill, the classic thinker of liberalism, spoke unmistakably of the feeling of nationality:

> This feeling of nationality may have been generated by various causes . . . But the strongest of all is identity of political antecedents; the possession of national history, and consequent community of recollections . . . Free institutions are next to impossible in a country made up of different nationalities. Among a people without fellow-feeling, especially if they read and speak different languages, the united public opinion, necessary to the working of representative government, cannot exist.[1]

In this context, even some liberal thinkers argue that the nation lies at the heart of the modern nation-state. They highlight the significance of nations for citizens and their role in the justification of liberal policies. In addition, nations are supposed to serve basic individual needs and should not only be compatible with postulates of equality and individuality, but should also be fostered for the liberal-democratic state to function. In contrast, others suggest that nations are prone to being oppressive to minorities and marginalised members, since they view cultures as essentialist and static, thus rejecting the fundamental value of individual rights. In this view, nations have to be reluctantly but pragmatically accepted as a pervasive form of group loyalty, but one should not bestow any ethical significance upon them. Whereas nations are a currently inevitable form of allegiance, their proponents transfer respect and dignity from individuals to nations, a procedure not only theoretically unsatisfactory but also politically irresponsible.

A plethora of approaches and theories has also been developed with regard to what nationalism is and what it is triggered by. Numerous debates on nationalism have produced many controversies and unresolved questions. For instance, there has been an ongoing controversy regarding the very nature of nationalism. While the mainstream of nationalism research conceptualises nationalism as primarily past-orientated and defensive, some new approaches relate nationalism to the creative construction of the nation in an economic perspective. They argue that nationalist mobilisation is not exclusive to actors and ideologies striving for political autonomy. National identity can also become mobilised by non-political national institutions, such as economic development agencies, dealing with strategies of economic development and attempting to reconcile the actual needs of the societies with their material aspirations.[2] Therefore, nationalism can also be regarded as a set of strategic attitudes and developmental aims rather than as a coherent ideology. The rationale of economic nationalism is associated with the expectation that economic modernisation requires a powerful state; simultaneously, the state derives its power from the symbolic meaning of the nation. Therefore, economic development can strengthen the social cement of the nation by fostering mobilisation and communication among citizens. Conversely, protectionism in industrial and trade policy can amplify not only the economy but also nationalism.[3]

These and other controversies will be the topic of this book. The book has been conceptualised as an introduction to the vast and complex research on the nation and nationalism. It has four aims. First, it will review the existing research on the nation and nationalism in a systematic manner. There is a large and growing number of studies on the nation and nationalism that focus on various aspects of the phenomena at hand. Our goal, therefore, is to offer a wide variety of theoretical perspectives not always available in other monographs. Second, the book will introduce the readers to the major controversies of the current research on the nation and nationalism and will discuss them by using specific points of reference. Without aspiring to propose a complete report on the literature, the book offers an overview of the major contending approaches to the nation and nationalism and supplements them with more recent developments in the field. Third, the monograph will critically assess the existing research and demonstrate the authors' own ideas on the nation and nationalism. In particular, we will present our angle on the systematisation of the concept of national identity as well as on the relationship between nationalism, regionalism and European integration. Fourth, the book will discuss research on the nation and nationalism in the empirical context of some selected country cases. Thus, we will enrich the overview of conceptual and theoretical debates with newer empirical findings and up-to-date developments.

This introductory chapter proceeds by offering some common definitions of the nation and nationalism. It will show the conceptual variety of both phenomena and will introduce the readers to this vast field of inquiry. Next, it will discuss some normative, methodological and theoretical controversies in the research. This section is meant as an introductory overview, rather than a pre-emption of what will be presented in the following chapters. We will address, among other things, the *problématique* of bad and good nationalism, the issue of methodological nationalism and the classical dichotomy of civic and ethnic nationalism. Against this background, the structure of the book will be presented.

Common definitions

Defining a nation

Nations can be generally conceived of as large-scale political communities, frequently with a specific cultural background. Even though there are different conceptualisations of the nation, this minimal definition would fit the majority of them. Beyond this, there is not much consensus on what makes the nature of a nation. Let us briefly present the most common definitions.

First, some authors highlight a specific functionality of nations regarding the survival of modern societies and the legitimacy of their political elites. In this view, nations have homogenising effects on the population and promote collective ties, thus fulfilling relevant functions concerning modernisation processes and the legitimisation of mass democracies. The latter function links nations to the realisation of popular sovereignty and equality among the members of a political community, alleviating otherwise existing inequalities in a modern society. In this sense, nations can be viewed as engines of dignity provision for individuals in capitalist societies. Nations are the key to mediation between different aspects of experience of a society and between the members of that society. This mediation enables nations to act as batteries generating popular power.

Second, an alternative conception of the nation regards it as a unique form of social consciousness that has contingently developed and is thus historically anchored. In this understanding, nations have developed from a contingent consequence of unique events such as the invention of the printing press or the translation of the Bible into vernacular languages and are not easily replaced. This historical nature of nations is also highlighted in the approaches arguing that nations have developed from a premodern ethnic core. In this sense, even contemporary nations should be explained against the background of their ethnic origins.

Third, other authors highlight the everyday, unspectacular appearance of nations. In this interpretation, nations are inseparably integrated with our habits of language and thus appear as our natural cognitive environment. As we take nations for granted, we view social reality through their prism. As a result, nations are interpretative templates perpetuated in a barely noticeable way, and they define the context of our everyday life. This perspective of the nation is related to some degree to the concept of 'imagined communities'. In this conception, nations are imagined because the members of a nation will never know most of their fellow-members and thus have to 'construct' the nation in their minds as both inherently limited and sovereign.

Fourth, nations are also explored as any other collective phenomena such as ethnic groups, gender, religion or professional groups. Nations are only different in that the individuals as members of national groups use cultural or legal differences to demarcate themselves from other collectives with the single aim of maximising individual advantages. A nation can therefore be referred to as a large group of genetically unrelated people with a high degree of solidarity. The solidarity of this group reflects its ability to extract contributions of resources from its members. In this rationalist understanding, national groups seek to carry out collective action in order to control a governance unit, which is responsible for providing collective goods to the group. The collective goods such as social order and welfare favour the members of the national group as opposed to non-members.

Defining nationalism

The term 'nationalism' has always enjoyed a significant popularity among scholars of sociology, political science and history. Despite a growing body of literature on the topic, there is little agreement on what exactly nationalism is, or how to make the concept suitable for the purposes of empirical studies. The term 'nationalism' has been mostly associated with several meanings at different levels, such as that of the individual, society or government. The following connotations of nationalism reflect the most important meanings of the term, although this listing is not exhaustive.

First, nationalism has been associated with a profound and intense expression of the atavistic (or primitive) feelings of people attached to a national collectivity. The intensity of the attachment can vary, whereby it can develop into a potentially profoundly destructive feeling towards outsiders of the nation. The tribal and anti-individualistic twist of this understanding of nationalism links it to collective aggressiveness, belligerence and the pathological behaviour of ethnic cleansing, murder and genocide. Here, nationalism belongs to the same group of 'sinister political concepts' as totalitarianism, fascism, racism and chauvinism.

Second, nationalism is used to depict individuals' sentiment of belonging to the nation and their readiness to sacrifice themselves for its wellbeing, security and social welfare. Here, nationalism assumes a higher ethical meaning of patriotism with a republican connotation. In this sense, nationalism reflects the duties of the citizens in a political community of the nation. On the one hand, it follows the idea that nationalism/patriotism is the realisation of human good: patriots are morally richer people than unattached individualists or cosmopolitans. On the other hand, there is a clear moral prescription for citizens to engage in the political affairs of the community. Nationalists are thus primarily 'holders of duties' vis-à-vis the national community. In particular, the readiness to defend one's own country (as embodied by military service in the modern state) is a significant aspect of this conception of nationalism. In this way, the patriotic virtue of the national citizen comes to the fore, as nationalism is a burdensome and dangerous duty even requiring the sacrifice of life. This argument constructs a moral agency of nations, highlighting that even undemocratically organised nations can hold emancipatory potential for individuals participating in the defence and reconstruction of their nations.

Third, nationalism describes a nationalist ideology based on a definition of the genealogy of the nation, the core narratives of the national identity, the political preferences of the nation and the present state of the nation in relation to other nations, as well as suggestions for the way in which national goals could be realised. It is often assumed that the ideology of nationalism can exist even in the absence of a political nationalist movement. The ideology of nationalism frequently rests on two key aspects. On the one hand, it conjures national bonds drawn primarily from the historical memory of the community, which fosters ancestral forms of political obligation. Since the ancestors spilled their blood to build and defend the nation, members of today's nation are believed to inherit an obligation to continue their work. On the other hand, national ideology often rests on the so-called 'grand architecture' of nationalism (Rogers Brubaker), which includes granting national independence to communities striving for such, as nation-states are not only the basic but also the 'natural' organisational units for modern political communities.

Fourth, nationalism depicts political movements aiming at an achievement of goals, which they declare to reflect the will of the nation. It is believed that nationalist political movements are strongly related to nationalist ideology, or even unthinkable without a pre-existing nationalist ideology. The political nationalist movements can have various goals based on integrationist (irredentist), autonomist and secessionist programmes. On the one hand, these nationalist movements can utilise established and recognised identities as a support for their political claims. On the other hand, they can include actions of group leadership to gain recognition on the basis of the supposedly authentic group identity. In the latter case, the political claims of group leaders aim to preserve their specific group culture via special group rights (for instance, autonomy) and can be motivated by the desire to prevent assimilation, which could undermine the power and privilege of leadership. In other words, nationalism as social movement can reflect the motives of the legitimation and preservation of power.

Fifth, nationalism can be understood as a process of constituting and sustaining nations and nation-states (known as nation-building). This usage of the term is the broadest one and refers to the politics of nationalism. In this view, nationalism pertains to the strategies of political elites whose aim is to establish or strengthen national identity in a top-down manner in order to mobilise the population for the nation-building efforts or to legitimise their policies, which otherwise would not gain sufficient political support. This can include the manipulation of political symbols, propaganda and otherwise collective stimulation of shared national ties through mass media and political events designed to spur emotions and therefore to generate feelings of commonness. By creating and manipulating political symbols pertaining to the nation (through the frequent usage of the national flag or national anthem, the building of national monuments and the introduction of national holidays), political nationalist elites construct and perpetuate an order-creating system which functions as a conveyor of national identity. By so doing, they socialise their citizens into bearers of loyalty towards the nation-state and simultaneously present themselves as bearers of the national will.

Sixth and finally, the term nationalism may also refer to a cultural discourse focusing on language and national symbolism, practised first and foremost by the cultural elites of a nation. Nationalism as a cultural discourse is believed to use and continuously perpetuate specific national ideas, symbols and ceremonies, even though it can use broader narratives than those contained in the referential framework of national identity. It usually remains a domain of national cultural elites dominated by intellectuals but it must be at least superficially comprehensible for wider segments of the nation. Nationalism in this sense strengthens a nationalist ideology and nationalist political movements; however, it may also exist in their absence.

Some normative, methodological and theoretical controversies

In this section we will address some selected common normative, methodological and theoretical controversies in the recent research on nation and nationalism. They are meant as a brief introduction to the topic at hand and the issues that surround the contemporary research, rather than as a systematic analysis.

The complexity of the research on the nation and nationalism generates the overarching methodological problem of nationalism research, which is its conceptual and theoretical labyrinth that produces approaches spawning controversial explanatory templates and contradictory results.[4] As argued in the previous section, the concepts of the nation and nationalism relate to various objects of analysis, such as an ideology, a movement, a process of nation- or state-building or an individual's political attitude. As a result, the nation and nationalism seem to be frequently confused with other national orientations, such as national pride or patriotism, which in turn sometimes leads to an unconvincing normative assessment of good and bad nationalism.[5] One of the most controversial issues in the research is precisely the ethical assessment of nationalism. The diverging positions on the ethics of nationalism between communitarians and liberals demonstrate how divergent the normative assessment of the national idea can be. The communitarian position underlines the moral value of nations on the grounds that they matter to their members and defends the right to national self-determination for national communities. The communitarian position defines nationalism above all by its solidaristic drive and believes that nationalism can have a remedial value for reducing ethnic, racial and other animosities. Communitarians believe that inner nationalism is capable of healing collective injuries of the past without igniting cycles of violence and revenge. This is evident in Anthony D. Smith's conceptualisation of nations as historically evolving solidarity groups which form moral communities underpinned by a shared sense of a collective past. Communitarians are suspicious of liberal statehood without national underpinnings, claiming that liberal policies are made possible only against the background of a national and resilient collective identity.

The opposing liberal position focuses on the negative and exclusionary impulses of nationalism. The chauvinistic inclinations of nationalism are regarded as symptoms of collective communities that are made victims by other communities and thereupon turn to murderous devices of revenge and resentment.[6] In this context, the collective past tends to reproduce chains of violence and revenge among nations, leading to an overall understanding of politics which defines national and ethnic collectivities in sociobiological terms of survival. Consequently, solutions to violent clashes based on the right to national self-determination are likely to strengthen the divisions between national and ethnic groups, rather than contribute to their reconciliation. Liberals criticise probably the two most influential approaches to the nation and nationalism, those of Anthony D. Smith and Ernest Gellner. Some authors argue, for instance, that Smith's vision of nations and nationalism represents a historicist, collectivist and idealist aberration, which prevents him from developing a realistic explanation of nation-building.[7] Gellner's theory of nationalism stresses in turn that the industrial mode of production of modernity demands national homogeneity. For liberals, Gellner tends to ignore that homogeneity can often only be achieved by forced integration, ethnic cleansing and genocide. In addition, the very 'nationalisation' of liberal values creates, particularly in the context of immigration, boundary mechanisms that are among the essential features of nationalism. In this sense, nationalised liberal values tend to be interpreted as organic and are as a result governed by a deterministic logic which does not allow for many individual voluntary choices emphasised by liberalism.[8]

These two positions on nationalism are not easy to reconcile. It is, however, possible that they reflect a two-faced nature of nationalism, which is subject to complex processes of inward integration and outward boundary-making. This complexity is not easy to explain nor does it make a normative assessment of nationalism simple. On the one hand, Hitler's Germany and Milošević's Serbia suggest an equation of nationalism with brutality and murder. On the other hand, there seem to be enough nationalist leaders involved in struggles for popular representation.[9]

This leads us to three specific methodological controversies in the research of nationalism: constructivism, methodological nationalism and Olympian distance. Some authors criticise constructivism in the context of the nation and nationalism as a general weakness of contemporary sociological theory. It describes a methodological paradigm regarding ethnocultural identities as constructed by individuals and groups from the cultural resources available to them in their social environment. It can be argued that the constructivist paradigm exaggerates the responsibility of individuals for their own identity and ignores the social and political constraints of ethnic choices. At the same time, it underplays the fact that many minority demands for justice are made through the group prism, rather than in individualist terms.[10] This individualist position resembles the *problématique* of the methodological individualism, which explains social and collective phenomena as based on individual action and neglects the impact of structures such as social norms and socialising processes.

Furthermore, there is the controversy of methodological nationalism, which depicts the frequent equation between the concept of society and the nation-state in nationalism research. Again, it pertains to a general methodological fallacy of social theory, rather than solely to the social phenomenon of nationalism. Methodological nationalism claims, among other things, that the nation-state has become the 'normal' form of society in modernity, rather than a contingent form. Numerous scholars argue in favour of rejecting this reductionist stipulation. Currently, Daniel Chernilo differentiates between its logical and its historical versions. The historical version relates to the rise of methodological nationalism as a consequence of the importance of state nationalism during the twentieth century. The logical version makes the link between society and the nation-state on the basis of the national structure of sociological categories. Chernilo argues that the elusiveness of the nation-state concept mirrors the nation-state's own ambivalence within modernity. Therefore, social theory's ambivalent attempts at conceptualising the nation-state reflect the actual ambivalence of its historical vagueness, its conceptual uncertainty and its normative ambiguity.[11]

The controversy of the 'Olympian distance' refers to Ernest Gellner's theory of nationalism. Gellner has been widely criticised for approaching his subject from a world-historical perspective and for applying an Olympian apoliticism, which highlights the logic of history to the detriment of contextual circumstances and the ideology and psychology of nationalism. Interestingly enough, Gellner argued that nationalism has proven to be an 'astonishingly weak' principle, as many potential nations have failed to achieve the status of nation-state. Geert van den Bossche picks up this thesis and calls for an investigation into whether nationalist claims have ever been put forward in these failed communities.[12] Van den Bossche explores the study of nationalism referring to thus far neglected methodologies and Gellner's intellectual legacy. Gellner's nationalism theory is based on a belief in the rational evolution of history, which could be described in a limited number of successive stages. Van den Bossche suggests that the Gellnerian position can be enriched with a perspective concerned with the meaning of nationalism for political actors, which entails a substantiation of the nation through the study of ideologies and feelings as well as the links between interest and identity. He argues in favour of adopting the methodologies of the so-called Cambridge school of the history of political thought and of social representations in social psychology.[13]

One of the major theoretical controversies pertains to the classical typology of ethnic and civic nationalism, particularly in the regional context of Western and Eastern Europe.[14] However, an increasing number of approaches challenge the assumption that there is an essential difference between the West European 'civic' and the East European 'ethnic' conceptualisation of the nation and nationalism. For instance, by analysing nation and nationalism in Latvia, Poland and Lithuania, Frederika Björklund argues that a distinctive 'ethnic' concept of the nation cannot be traced among the populations of East European countries. Moreover, Björklund concludes that the societies of each country define the nation and nationalism differently. While Latvians tend to embrace an ethnic concept of the nation, Polish and Lithuanian concepts of the nation are far from coherent. Consequently, the author suggests a less rigid distinction of civic and ethnic models of the nation, allowing for different permutations of ethnic and civic arguments.[15] This research challenging the classical division between civic and ethnic nationalism is also supported by Stephen Shulman's work. By employing survey data from fifteen countries to measure mass conceptions of national identity, Shulman analyses attitudes towards criteria for national membership and state policies on assimilation and immigration. The study finds that according to several measures the civic-West/ethnic-East stereotype is false. The data suggests that communist rule has not shifted East European nationhood in a strongly cultural direction while weakening civicness, which has been a widespread conviction among political scientists. While most West European countries have a relatively long tradition of democracy and stable political institutions, cultural conceptions of nationhood are alive, and support for multiculturalism is relatively weak.[16]

The focus and structure of the book

This publication is not a traditional textbook on nationalism, as there are numerous textbooks of this kind. It has a double function. In one aspect, it is an introductory review of classical and contemporary concepts, theories and approaches regarding the nation and nationalism. This review (Chapters 1, 3 and 4) introduces the reader to the research on the nation and nationalism and comments on it critically. Its emphasis lies in the contemporary research on the nation and nationalism, as opposed to many other publications, where the focus is on the classical and established approaches. In addition to this, the authors offer their own positions and present their 'angles of exploration' of the issues at hand (Chapters 2 and 7). More explorative chapters will therefore follow the chapters concerned with reviewing the research. The explorative chapters will highlight specific themes of contemporary research such as national identity (Chapter 2) and the triangle of nationalism, regionalism and European integration (Chapter 7).

The focus of the book is Europe. It is a double focus, since the book looks at the nation and nationalism in Eastern and Western Europe as well as at the Euro-nationalism of the European Union. Regarding the former focus, we aim to show the multiplicity of nationalism in the West and the East and to challenge the afore-mentioned typology of civic (Western) and ethnic (Eastern) nationalism. With regard to the latter focus, we will address the European Union's politics of identity generation, whereby the European Union can be viewed as a quasi-state.

The authors propose several conceptual innovations. First, the book makes a conceptual division between the nation and nationalism and treats them as separate phenomena. One of the main deficits in both the older and the newer research on the nation and nationalism is that these terms are seldom kept separate and are often merged. The division between the nation and nationalism is also visible in the structure of the book, where Chapter 1 is dedicated to nations and Chapters 3 and 4 to nationalism. Second, the book offers its own framework of analysis for nationalism, which is based on the differentiation between four levels of analysis: the micro, meso, macro and supranational levels. This framework of analysis is presented in Chapter 5 and will act as structural brackets for the empirical chapters in this volume. Third, the book's review and explorative sections will be enriched with information on recent empirical developments in selected European countries. The aim of the empirical section of the book (Chapter 6) is to illustrate newer cases of nationalism with some selected material. We demonstrate the recent trends of nationalism in Great Britain, Germany, Poland, Italy, Sweden, Belgium, Latvia and Bulgaria. The cases for Chapter 6 have been selected according to the criterion of 'isolated variety', which allows for a reconciliation of two methodological goals. On the one hand, we intended to reduce the complexity of this field of inquiry through selected case studies. On the other, the goal of the selected case studies is not to exhibit the central tendency as in a large sample of cases, but rather to preserve the variety of the cases using the 'method of difference', where one examines cases with differing general characteristics.

The final chapter of the book (Chapter 8) will present an outlook into further foci in theoretical and empirical research which are likely to be relevant in future research on nationalism.

Notes

1. John Stuart Mill, 'Considerations on representative government', in Geraint Williams (ed.), *Utilitarism, on Liberty, Considerations on Representative Government* (London: J. M. Dent, 2002 [1861]), pp. 188–410 (pp. 391–2).

2. Ross Bond, David McCrone and Alice Brown, 'National identity and economic development: reiteration, recapture, reinterpretation and repudiation', *Nations and Nationalism* 9, 3 (2003), pp. 371–91.
3. Takeshi Nakano, 'Theorising economic nationalism', *Nations and Nationalism* 10, 3 (2004), pp. 211–29; Andreas Pickel, 'Explaining, and explaining with, economic nationalism', *Nations and Nationalism* 9, 1 (2003), pp. 105–27.
4. See Henk Dekker, Darina Malová and Sander Hoogendoorn, 'Nationalism and its explanations', *Political Psychology* 24, 2 (2003), pp. 345–76; Liah Greenfeld, 'Nationalism of the mind', *Nations and Nationalism* 11, 3 (2005), pp. 325–41; Alan Finlayson, 'Psychology, psychoanalysis and theories of nationalism', *Nations and Nationalism* 4, 2 (1998), pp. 145–62.
5. Fred W. Riggs, 'Ethnicity, nationalism, race, minority: a semantic/onomantic exercise (part two)', *International Sociology* 6, 4 (1991), pp. 443–63; Rogers Brubaker, 'The Manichean myth: Rethinking the distinction between "civic" and "ethnic" nationalism', in Hanspeter Kriesi, Klaus Armingeon, Hannes Siegrist and Andreas Wimmer (eds), *Nation and National Identity: The European Experience in Perspective* (Zurich: Rüegger, 1999), pp. 55–72.
6. See Joan Cocks, 'Collectivities and cruelty', *Political Theory* 32, 3 (2004), pp. 419–26.
7. See Siniša Malešević, '"Divine ethnies" and "sacred nations": Anthony D. Smith and the neo-Durkhemian theory of nationalism', *Nationalism and Ethnic Politics* 10 (2004), pp. 561–93; see also Anthony D. Smith, 'History and national destiny: responses and clarifications', *Nations and Nationalism* 10, 1/2 (2004), pp. 195–209.
8. Sune Lægaard, 'Liberal nationalism and the nationalization of liberal values', *Nations and Nationalism* 13, 1 (2007), pp. 37–55.
9. See John A. Hall, 'How homogenous need we be? Reflections on nationalism and liberty', *Sociology* 30, 1 (1996), pp. 163–71.
10. See Stephen May, Tariq Modood and Judith Squires (eds), *Ethnicity, Nationalism and Minority Rights* (Cambridge: Cambridge University Press, 2004).
11. Daniel Chernilo, 'Social theory's methodological nationalism', *European Journal of Social Theory* 9, 1 (2006), pp. 5–22; see also Andreas Wimmer and Nina Glick Schiller, 'Methodological nationalism and beyond: nation-state building, migration and the social sciences', *Global Networks* 2, 4 (2002), pp. 301–34.
12. Geert van den Bossche, 'Is there nationalism after Ernest Gellner? An exploration of methodological choices', *Nations and Nationalism* 9, 4 (2003), pp. 491–509 (p. 505).
13. Ibid. p. 502ff.
14. Ireneusz Paweł Karolewski and Andrzej Marcin Suszycki (eds), *Multiplicity of Nationalism in Contemporary Europe* (Lanham, MD: Lexington Books, 2010).
15. Frederika Björklund, 'The East European "ethnic nation" – myth or reality?', *European Journal of Political Research* 45 (2006), pp. 93–121; see also Iris Marion Young, 'A multicultural continuum: a critique of Will Kymlicka's ethnic-nation dichotomy', *Constellations* 4, 1 (1997), pp. 48–53.
16. Stephen Shulman, 'Challenging the civic/ethnic and West/East dichotomies in the study of nationalism', *Comparative Political Studies* 35, 5 (2002), pp. 554–85.

CHAPTER ONE

The Nation: In Search of a Concept

The term 'nation' is one of the most frequently used and most contested in political science, sociology, history and their adjacent disciplines. Despite this, it is not a simple task to define what exactly a nation is. The last century saw a plethora of developments in the concept of the nation; further, the term has frequently been used interchangeably with notions such as nationality, nationhood, people or even nationalism.

Thus, 'nation' as a term is far from clear. Its meaning changes depending not only on who is using it but also on when it is or was used. We therefore suggest regarding the nation as a concept of experience and expectation, to use the terminology of historian Reinhart Koselleck.[1]

It changes throughout different historical periods and becomes modified by the historical experience. In addition, it means that circumstances in which specific conceptual connotations of the nation are coined influence its future meaning. Therefore, the concept of the nation is anchored in specific experiences as well as in specific expectations. Consequently, concepts such as that of the nation are not only used to describe current social reality, but also transmit certain beliefs where meaning, experience and expectations about the future are set in relation to each other.[2] In this sense, the term 'nation' can connote different meanings and is therefore of reflexive, rather than constant, character.

In 1936 Luis Wirth argued that a nation could be defined as

people who, because of the belief in their common descent and their mission in the world, by virtue of their common cultural heritage and historical career aspire to sovereignty over a territory or seek to maintain or enlarge their political or cultural influence in the face of opposition.[3]

Here, influence and mission in the world seem to be essential in determining the existence of the nation, features which are not necessarily common to every nation nowadays. The missionary zeal is likely to describe some nations of large countries (probably with colonial experience and empire-like structure of power), rather than smaller nations striving for their independence from an empire or against the resistance of more powerful neighbours.

However, there are also other, more common definitions such as that proposed by Anthony D. Smith, according to whom 'nation' includes the territorial boundedness of separate cultural populations in their own 'homelands'; the shared nature of myths of origin and historical memories of the community; the common bond of a mass standardised culture; a common territorial division of labour, with mobility for all members and ownership of resources by all members in the homeland; and the possession by all members of a unified system of common legal rights and duties under common laws and institutions.[4] Here, the economic, legal, cultural and territorial integration appears to be central to this definition. This, however, might not apply to the growing number of multi-ethnic and multicultural nations such as Canada, Belgium or even the US. In addition, in this definition there is a conflation of reasons for the emergence of a nation (a shared historic territory or a common legal system) with the results of the nation-building process (historical memories or a standardised culture).

Four perspectives on nations

Given the dynamic and multiple nature of the concept of the nation we propose to differentiate four major conceptual perspectives: the *functional, constructivist, genealogical* and *rationalist* perspectives. The functional perspective highlights the functionality of the nation regarding, for instance, the survival or growth of societies in the macro-historical view, the legitimacy of political elites or as a system of reference for individuals. This perspective stresses that nations did not develop by accident. They are optimal (or close to optimal) structures or units that fulfil their given functions in a better way than their alternatives, which makes nations functionally indispensable in the context of modern statehood.[5] In this vein, Ernest Gellner stresses that the nation is associated with the development of a homogeneous language facilitating communication and therefore enabling national sentiments to be constructed and preserved. This sort of unity and equality between members of the national community is viewed as a functional requirement for the cognitive and material growth of modern capitalist societies. Therefore, nationalism is believed to be a functional corollary of industrialisation.[6] Gellner argues that states can establish national identity (the process called 'exo-socialisation') via standardised education systems.[7] The standardisation of language is one component of the process, while the production of a mythologised historiography is another. This allows for a communicative centralisation and standardisation of a modern society despite its cultural variety and complexity, which in turn is necessary for the efficient allocation of human resources in the process of the production and allocation of goods.

Other functionalists stress the relevance of nations regarding the generation of civic resources necessary to sustain the democratic legitimacy of contemporary political systems. They presume that the nation not only is the empirically most common form of a modern political community, but that it also implies a normative value of nations. Liah Greenfeld has offered one of the most pronounced arguments in favour of the nation, as she associates it with popular sovereignty and equality, where it becomes an engine for the provision of individuals' dignity in a modern society.[8] The nation is therefore regarded as a unique form of social consciousness that is historically anchored and hence not easily replaced.[9] In the same vein, authors such as David Miller or Yael Tamir argue that national identity is conducive to individual enrichment in the moral and political sense.[10] The collective bond of nations is supposed to deepen commitments and obligations between those who share it by providing an essential motivation behind civic commitments. According to David Miller, 'nations are ethical communities. They are contour lines in the ethical landscape. The duties we owe to our fellow-nationals are different from, and more extensive than, the duties we owe to human beings as such.'[11] This makes democratic regimes contingent on national identity.[12]

Apart from obligations, nations are expected to produce social trust, drawn primarily from the cultural layer of the community, in which deep obligations stem from national identity and relatedness. This argument is applied to the conditions of modern economy, which are regarded as requiring high levels of moral commitment in the form of mutual solidarity. Only against the background of a high level of social trust can democracy function in a sustainable manner, since redistributive measures cannot be otherwise justified.[13]

In contrast, the constructivist perspective on the concept of the nation puts emphasis on the socially constructed nature of nations, where historical contingencies play an important role. In this sense, nations have developed from a contingent consequence of unique events such as the invention of the printing press. Benedict Anderson's analysis of nationalism traces its origins back to the spread of 'print-capitalism', which made the modern nation-state possible by generating an 'imagined community' of nation.[14] National imagined community was produced in the process of dialect suppression while promoting one specific vernacular version of language, which integrated a diversity of vernacular speakers previously unable to communicate.[15]

A nation, Benedict Anderson argues,

> is an imagined political community – and imagined as both inherently limited and sovereign. It is imagined because the members of even the smallest nations will never know most of their fellow-members, meet them, or even hear of them, yet in the minds of each lives an image of their community.[16]

In this perspective nations are represented in the minds of the nationalised subjects and become influential frames of reference with serious and even destructive consequences. Thus, nations are specific forms of social identities that are produced and reproduced by means of language and other semiotic systems.

Anderson distinguishes his understanding of the definition of a nation from Gellner's argument that states can invent nations where they do not exist.[17] In this sense, nations can be fabricated rather than imagined, which makes them comparable to older nations but also less genuine. For Anderson, however, communities are to be distinguished 'not by their falsity/genuineness, but by the style in which they are imagined'.[18] The 'imagined community' of the nation is not 'imaginary', as it becomes reality in the realm of convictions and beliefs through reification in political discourses and mass media as well as dissemination through the education system, militarisation and sports events.[19]

Other constructivists such as Ruth Wodak and Rudolf de Cillia argue in favour of a discursive construction of nations and national identities.[20] This position is mainly associated with the mutual construction of national difference and uniqueness, where unconscious patterns of domination and conscious politics of distinctiveness and domination determine the national sentiment. For some authors, the main platform for the discursive construction of nations is language politics, which can go hand in hand with the suppression of a nation's linguistic variety, as those who are not speakers of the official language are subject to symbolic domination.[21] As Seyla Benhabib argues, 'what is shocking about these developments is not the inevitable dialectic of identity/difference that they display but rather the atavistic belief that identities can be maintained and secured only by eliminating difference and otherness'.[22]

Furthermore, discursive constructivists argue that there is no such thing as one nation but rather that different national identities are discursively constructed according to context, the situational setting of the discursive act and the topic being discussed. In other words, nations are not completely consistent and stable. They are rather dynamic and often incoherent everyday constructions and reconstructions.[23] This conception of nation emphasises its 'momentum', allowing it to unfold as a dynamic notion, subject to change and permanent debate over its precise content and meaning.

Other authors, such as Michael Billig, also highlight the everyday and subcutaneous quality of nations. In this vein, nations are 'near the surface of contemporary life. If this is correct, then routinely familiar habits of language will be continually acting as reminders of nationhood. In this way, the world of nations will be reproduced as *the* world, the natural environment of today.' According to Billig, nations are perpetuated 'with prosaic, routine words, which take nations for granted, and which, in so doing, inhabit them'.[24] As a consequence, nations are perpetuated in a barely noticeable way but define the context of everyday life. The underlying assumption of a nation is secreted routinely in the political and cultural realms of modern societies, resulting in national self-praise.[25] The daily reinforcement of a nation operates through ubiquitous but mostly unnoticed discursive acts such as the words of politicians taking the nation as a given or newspapers addressing their readers as members of the nation. This daily construction of a nation transmits subcutaneously the message to the individuals that the nation not only underpins their personal existence but also possesses a legitimate place in the natural form of the global organisation of other nations.

The genealogical perspective is in turn in search of the route nations have taken in their development over centuries. For instance, Anthony D. Smith, in his ethnosymbolic approach to nations, argues that almost every nation has developed from an ethnic core, and from the description of its long-term development we can better understand the very nature of contemporary nations. Smith argues that any attempt to explain how nations emerged must start from ethnicity, which is the most common origin of nation-states. There are three main arguments pertaining to the genealogical perspective. First, the majority of today's nations were formed on the basis of pre-modern ethnic cores. Therefore, 'being powerful and culturally influential, they provided models for subsequent cases of the formation of nations in many parts of the globe'.[26] In this sense, modern nations were 'efficient' formations, as they used pre-existing forms of social organisation, simply adapting them to the requirements of modernity.

Second, the ethnic model of the nation has become popular, as 'it sat so easily on the pre-modern "demotic" kind of community that had survived into the modern era in so many parts of the world'.[27] Nations became widespread and almost universal in appeal as a result of the sociological 'fertility' of ethnicity. Without the pervasiveness of the ethnic model of social formation, nations would never have achieved contemporary relevance.

Third, ethnic unity is a necessary condition for national survival, since it is hard for a political community to survive without a coherent mythology, symbolism of history and shared culture. In order to survive nations must be able to use the 'raw material' of ethnicity whose prominent element is the myth of common descent.[28] Therefore, nations with no ethnic antecedents or shadowy ethnic ties are forced to fabricate the myths and forge the symbolism of a community of descent. As Craig Calhoun argues,

> where it is recognized that a nation has a founding moment,
> it is still attractive to see this as a consequence not merely of

choice, but of a long narrative of historical development that historically locates the proto-nation in primordial times.[29]

From these three major arguments we can derive four attributes of modern nations, which Anthony D. Smith has formulated:

- a strong emphasis on genealogy, on the fictive tie of ethnic descent defining membership of the community
- the importance of vernacular cultures, including myths of election, linguistic codes, customs and traditions
- a nativist interpretation of history, or 'ethno-history' – the set of authentic tales retold by the community
- a commitment to 'the people', and hence an emphasis on popular mobilisation as the key to authenticity[30]

According to Smith the ethnonational transformation comprises three processes, which depict the path from ethnic communities to nations: vernacular mobilisation, cultural politicisation and ethnic purification. Vernacular mobilisation 'involves a rediscovery by ethnic intellectuals of indigenous traditions, customs, memories, symbols and, especially, languages and their dissemination to wider strata of the designated population'. In this case, the so-called ethnic intelligentsia promote the vernacular culture, as their status and careers are coupled with the success of the vernacular language. In contrast, cultural politicisation is the weapon of the state to treat the community's cultural heritage as a political resource. Cultural heritage is used against both outsiders and the guardians of the tradition. The nationalists see their task as twofold, as they fight against outside enemies as well as with the 'fathers' within. Finally, 'ethnic purification' is associated with a belief in the sanctity of that culture. As the ethnic culture is believed to be irreplaceable, it has to be guarded against alien and contaminating influences. It becomes the subject of purification through the relegation, segregation, expulsion or even extermination of aliens.[31]

Smith's genealogical perspective highlights the continuous and stable nature of nations and their identities. National identity is more meaningful than alternative identities, since it is more stable. As a result of its embeddedness in historic continuity, common descent and shared destiny, nations are likely to be associated with an identity more resilient than gender, class or region. Membership of a nation is supposed to enable an individual to find a place not only in the world in which he or she lives, but also in an uninter-rupted chain of time. Thus, nations promote a sense of identity both among compatriots and across generations. In this sense, nations are believed to endow human action with a meaning that endures over time, thus carrying the promise of immortality. Nations are not therefore pathologies of the modern age but a development of *longue durée*, which can be viewed as 'an answer to its malaise – to the neurosis, alienation, and meaninglessness characteristic of modern times'.[32]

Finally, the rationalist perspective on nations refers to writings applying the rational choice model to ethnic and national collective behaviour. Rational choice theory is based on the assumption that human beings are rational and are motivated by self-interest in their actions, be it everyday decisions or political ones.[33] In this perspec-tive individuals tend to behave as rational, cost-sensitive actors, as their actions are predominantly intentional and have a stable and relatively consistent set of preferences. As a result groups and col-lective behaviour are analysed in terms of the cooperation among actors that is driven by self-interest, where the notion of free riding plays a crucial role.[34]

Against this backdrop, most rational choice theorists consider national or ethnic phenomena as similar to class, gender, religion or status. Nations and ethnic groups are only different in that the individuals use the cultural or legal differences of the nations to demarcate themselves from other collectives with the single aim of maximising individual advantages.[35] According to Hechter, ethnic and national groups fulfil two major functions. First, they are relevant sources of the advantages and disadvantages that moti-vate actors to participate in collective action. Second, ethnic and national groups deliver relevant information on the probability of individuals' success in the collective action.[36]

Hechter's theory holds that

> the members of any ethnic group will engage in collective action only when they estimate that by so doing they will receive a net private benefit. In this view ethnic collective action does not depend on a group's desire to attain a public good. Instead, its likelihood is a function of two different kinds of structural constraints: the group's organizational resources (which can serve to reward potential participants regardless of the outcome of the collective action), on the one

hand; and the ability of its antagonists (sometimes including the state) to sanction potential participants, on the other.[37]

This theory has some consequences for the concept of the nation. In his major work, *Containing Nationalism*, Hechter defines a nation as a 'relatively large group of genetically unrelated people with high solidarity'.[38] The solidarity of the group is measured by the extent to which the group is able to successfully demand contributions of resources from its members. Moreover, national groups seek to design collective action 'to render the boundaries of the nation congruent with those of the governance unit'.[39] The nations strive for control of the governance unit, since it is responsible for providing collective goods such as social order, justice and welfare to its members.[40] However, the governance unit does not have to be a state; the term may also refer to local government organisations or kinship groups. In this sense, nations can strive for independence, secession or autonomy. Hechter's main prescription for containing nations engaging in violent collective action is granting them limited self-government rights within larger states.

Other rationalists, such as James Fearon and David Laitin, use the rational choice tool of game theory to analyse intra-ethnic and inter-ethnic relations or language politics of nation-states.[41] For instance, Fearon and Laitin argue that inter-ethnic relations are frequently characterised by tensions that are relatively absent in intra-ethnic relations. Since ethnic and national groups exhibit better developed social networks and interactions, individuals have easier access to information about their co-ethnics or co-nationals than they do about ethnic and national others. This information, rather than solidarity-based argument, is, however, congruent with Hechter's position on nations, since it also focuses on the rational calculation of costs and benefits by individuals. Better information and more frequent interactions allow individuals to develop and maintain reputations for cooperative behaviour that are more difficult to sustain in inter-ethnic interactions. In addition, thanks to cultural familiarity, people are better able to distinguish opportunists from among co-ethnics and co-nationals, which facilitates peaceful interaction within and impedes it across ethnic and national groups. In other words, ethnic and national groups are more effective in solving the problem of opportunism. In contrast, in inter-ethnic relations Fearon and Laitin identify two basic institutional approaches to resolving problems of opportunism, i.e. cheating and free riding. In the parlance of game theory they are both equilibriums, as they tend to be self-fulfilling and self-sustaining. In one type of equilibrium, individuals expect that if cooperation collapses because of an accident or mistake, members of each group will punish each other indiscriminately for some time. In this 'spiral equilibrium', violence and non-cooperation quickly expand beyond the initial tension. In contrast, in the 'in-group policing' equilibrium individuals expect that someone who defects against an ethnic other will be identified and sanctioned by members of his or her own group. This institutional arrangement makes the punishment visible to the offended group and thus makes that group refrain from carrying out revenge violence against any member of the opposing group.[42]

Beyond the issue of violence among ethnic and national groups, David Laitin explores in his work the so-called language regimes.[43] This work is also a part of the rationalist perspective on nations, as Laitin focuses on what is known as the tipping game for the analysis of individual decision-making and collective results regarding language and national identity. The tipping game analyses the decision either to use ethnic/national language or to concentrate on English. Alternatively, it can be applied in different ethnic contexts, for instance in Estonia where the tipping game refers to the use of Estonian versus Russian. The tipping game can be described as a diagram consisting of two curves, a horizontal S-shaped curve and its mirror image. While the x-axis shows the percentage of the population engaging in speaking either Russian or Estonian, for instance, the y-axis represents the payoffs for speaking either language. Laitin's focal point lies on the twenty-five million Russian-speaking residents in the ex-Soviet states that became independent after 1991. Dominant in the Soviet Union, the Russian speakers turned into minorities in non-Russian-speaking states that underwent a nation-building process of their own. In the Soviet Union the payoff for speaking Russian exceeded, for example, that for speaking Estonian. However, after the collapse of the Soviet Union increasingly more people shifted to Estonian and the payoff for Russian declined. At the tipping point, which is the intersection of the two curves, the payoff for Estonian begins to surpass that for Russian, and a cascade towards speaking Estonian may be expected. In this analysis, the choice for a nation, whose essential component is the language, is determined by the rational calculation of costs and benefits. Individuals can switch between languages if the incentives are high enough or can stay with the status quo.

Some points of critique

These different perspectives on the concept of the nation have spawned debates on topics including the accuracy of the conceptions of the nation, their theoretical consistency and their empirical usefulness. We can thus observe a scholarly 'communication' between the perspectives.

The functional perspective on nations suggests that national identity has become the dominant collective identity in modern human societies because it was first and foremost associated with the establishment of states as powerful identity-making agents. Therefore, even today other identities are significantly less institutionalised and have a less statist character, even in federal or multicultural states, compared with national identities.[44] More strongly than any other political organisations, nation-states are expected to pursue a policy of identity construction and reconstruction as the major agents of identity politics. However, scholars postulating the 'new transnationalism' have become increasingly critical regarding the unquestioned role of the nation-state, postulated, for instance, by Ernest Gellner. In this perspective, there are ongoing processes of transnationalisation due to global mobility and growing multiculturalism, in particular in multinational global cities. As a result, nations become denationalised and repositioned in a new context of social interactions.[45] It also implies that the hitherto legal, political and social aspects of nations, such as citizenship, assume post-national or extra-national forms.[46] For instance, transnational citizenship becomes located in multiethnic cities, where new ethnic and social boundaries are forged[47] and non-national forms of political belonging are constructed.[48] Apart from the transborder mobility as a booster for transnationalism, recent technological inventions such as the internet are also regarded as crucial for the development of alternatives to the nation. In this context, civil society is believed to play an important role by organising itself at a transnational level. It is expected to deal with political and social issues beyond the boundaries of the nation and thus allow citizens to engage with 'unbounded' issues and to create a transnational public sphere.[49]

With regard to other functionalists, such as Greenfeld, who argues that nations mitigate status differences in democratic societies through equal membership, there can be also some points of critique. Yael Tamir, for instance, criticises the 'equality via nation' argument by suggesting that the equality of membership in nations is not necessarily contingent on democratic politics. While nations may convey the 'feeling of belonging and a sense of mutuality', they do not eliminate divisions of class, gender and status, which often make national equality a mere formality. Tamir argues that this renders nations similar to families that grant all members equal standing qua members, while often remaining hierarchical.[50] In this way, Greenfeld conflates democracy and nationalism.

Regarding the constructivist perspective, Anderson's conception of a nation as an 'imagined community' has in particular provoked a debate about whether nations are real communities (a group of people) or just images of a community. The term 'imagined' suggests that political entrepreneurs could easily invent nations, which questions the positions highlighting the realness of nations. In this vein, Alexander J. Motyl argues that imagining is not sufficient to turn nations into communities, as it is based on a serious exaggeration of the power of imagination.[51] He suggests that the belief that 'nations, unlike other entities such as classes and electorates, are especially susceptible to imagination, seems wrong. And that nations are, like all socially constructed entities, imagined seems trivial.'[52] This questions the term as conceptually not sufficiently clear-cut to be empirically tested. Furthermore, the lack of clarity of the term 'imagined community' does not answer the question of whether it concerns a specific set of people or a specific idea about this set of people. For Motyl the difference between these two positions is crucial, since the former associates Anderson with modernist approaches to the concept of the nation (supporting the realness of nations) and the latter postmodernist approaches (supporting the imagery of invention and fluidity of nations).[53]

The modernist reading of Anderson's concept would require distinguishing between the different styles of how communities are imagined and what these styles might consist of. In this way, we could better explore the differences in the realness of communities. Thus, the concept of the 'imagined community' could contribute in a more substantial way to the analysis of national communities by distinguishing various identity politics and their impact on people's minds and actions, as in some cases identity politics are likely to be consequential for imagined communities as opposed to other cases. Furthermore, Tamir suggests that national imagined communities have to be somehow distinguished from other imagined communities based on age, gender, race, income or place of birth.[54] This would in turn make the concept more specific and sharpen its conceptual edges. In the same vein, David Miller argues that nation is real, as it is 'constituted by mutual belief, extended in history, active in character, connected with a particular territory, and thought to be marked off from other communities by its members' distinct traits – served to distinguish nationality from other collective sources of personal identity'.[55]

The postmodern reading of Anderson's concept would in turn highlight the fluidity of imagined communities. Recent research in this field highlights multiple or hybrid identities of individuals, and it has become common to underline the process of making and claiming identities, in which identities are not attributes but rather resources that people use.[56] An example of that is the work of Zygmunt Bauman, in which the individualisation of identity is viewed against the background of 'liquid' modernity, in which the traditional collective identities, first and foremost the national one, lose their grip on individuals. However, individualisation does not necessarily imply a shift towards self-centredness as opposed to collectivities such as nation, but rather a choice of identity or its permanent change depending on context and necessity. Thus, as the concept of liquid modernity suggests, nations become undermined as a result of rapidly changing social order that weakens all notions of durability. The 'rootlessness' and fluidity of identities suggest that nations cannot be 'imagined' in a stable manner.[57]

However, this theoretical position is also criticised by other scholars. The theory that identities are fluid and contextual does not just stress the new freedom of choice for individuals.[58] New identity conflicts emerge as identities clash with each other because of the new multi-ethnicity, which reproduces ethnic, religious and socioeconomic cleavages.[59] In this vein, some authors argue that the globalisation of the economy and human affairs has made individuals ontologically insecure and existentially uncertain. Therefore, we might expect as a response to such insecurity attempts to reaffirm self-identity by approaching any collectivity (including nations) that is expected to decrease insecurity and existential anxiety. Consequently, we should expect a rise in collectivism as an 'identity signifier', particularly in the form of national sentiment as a reaction to ontological insecurity associated with cultural fluidity, mobility and contextuality.[60] This would suggest that despite the hopes for liquid modernity and the end of the nation-state, fluid identities might be prone to 'chronic' identities, which tend to freeze and become conflictive rather than flexible, hybrid and multi-compatible. 'Chronic group identities' would always be potentially accessible; therefore, they have an impact on the self-categorisation of individuals across diverse social contexts.

With regard to the genealogical perspective on nations, the writings of Anthony D. Smith have become a target for criticism. In his multi-aspect definition Smith argues that a nation is a named human population sharing a historic territory, common myths and historical memories, a mass public culture, a common economy and common legal rights and duties for all. However, Smith does not differentiate between the relevance of the factors nor does he explain which of them are necessary conditions and which are merely sufficient conditions for nation-building. As Yael Tamir argues, Smith's

> conditions can, but do not necessarily, give rise to national feelings. Individuals may share a territory and even historical memories without seeing themselves as members of the same nation, as is usually true for nations competing for the same piece of land.[61]

Furthermore, Smith's work is criticised for focusing on subjective differences between ethnies and nations in order to distinguish between them. Alexander Motyl makes the criticism that it is not sufficient to insist that ethnic groups are not nations since they possess little or no collective self-awareness or sense of community.[62] As all groups have some sense of collective self-awareness, even if a rudimentary one, 'insistence that groups can be nations only if they call themselves by that name confuses the etymology of a term with the defining characteristics of a concept'.[63]

Moreover, Smith's argument that only nations as the largest communities can enforce the loyalty and sacrifice of their members appears to be empirically unconvincing. Given the multiple identities, 'long-distance nationalism' as perennial identity does not have to be congruent with 'on-the-spot' nationalism, which becomes activated when necessary.

A further critique concerns the teleology of the nation inherent in the genealogical perspective. This teleology has two aspects. First, the world order is a nationalist one, as nations are believed to be perennial, which makes hopes for a non-national global order appear naive. This kind of teleology embraces a vision of history that inevitably culminates in the triumph of the world of nations. Such almost religious belief regards complicating factors such as the regional integration of nation-states or existing empires as short-lived obstacles to the realisation of the national vision. Second, should the obstacles to the national world order turn out to be more persistent, one should correct the 'grand architecture', as the nation-states are natural and optimal units of inter-national relations. Rogers Brubaker calls this concept 'architectonic illusion', arguing that:

> This is the belief that if one gets the 'grand architecture' right – if one discovers and establishes the proper territorial and institutional framework – then one can conclusively satisfy legitimate nationalist demands and thereby resolve national conflicts.[64]

The 'architectonic illusion' is based on a 'correspondence theory of justice', which postulates that nations are entitled to govern their own affairs and to establish their own states. Once justice is done, we should observe a diminishing number of national conflicts. Against this background, the proces of redrawing state boundaries and delegitimising the existing ones can follow. This can, however, increase the likelihood of border conflicts rather than reducing them.

We can also point to some deficiencies and omissions debated in the scholarly literature on the subject of the rationalist perspective. Siniša Malešević, for instance, argues that the application of rational choice to ethnic and national relations is built on false assumptions and is explanatorily irrelevant.[65] First and foremost, the rationalist perspective delivers circular explanations. According to Malešević:

> If we assume that every individual action is rational and motivated by self-interest, then what is the point of analysis when we already know what our research results will be? In other words [rational choice] explanations seem often to resemble some die-hard Marxist and feminist analyses that presuppose

their findings by simply looking for and then finding their explanans and explanandums in patriarchy and capitalism.[66]

As a result, the rationalist finding that national and ethnic group behaviour is a product of individual rationality suffers from explanatory sterility. As the rationalist perspective uses a circular form of reasoning, its models rationalise events only in an *ex post* manner, rather than offering genuine explanations of real-world phenomena.

Furthermore, many rationalist studies use economic rationality as their methodological tool. For instance, ethnic mass killings are explained by referring to group competition in imperfect markets, where individuals participate in genocide, since it is the least costly option. For instance, Michael Hechter[67] argues that ethnic cleansing in Bosnia is a result of rationally calculated 'land-grab' by stronger Serbs and Croats against their weaker Muslim neighbours. As there is no state authority capable of enforcing social order, grabbing land, looting and theft become rational.

In a further statement Hechter claims that 'there is ample evidence that nationalist groups employ violence strategically as a means to produce their joint goods'.[68] However, he tends to ignore the fact that 'in most ethnic wars and large-scale conflicts violence comes as a chaotic end and a very last resort to the long process of historically changing relations between ethnic groups'.[69]

For Malešević this reductionist position remains psychologically uninformed, ignoring human behaviour under extreme circumstances. However, the application of rationalist explanations to less extreme situations shows serious deficiency. Psychoanalytical approaches to nationalism highlight the fact that strife for group membership occurs regardless of cost-benefit calculations and is anchored in early socialisation experiences. The need for group belonging can be analysed as being based on ego-weakness, for instance, which is the product of social conditions having an effect on child-rearing practices.

The research on nations by other rationalists is also questioned. For instance, the model of the tipping game used by David Laitin raises some doubts. Here again, the criticism of explanatory reductionism weighs heavily. While Laitin insists that tipping games really do motivate people, one can doubt whether individual choices regarding language and identity actually reflect a rational application of the tipping game model. Rather, the model assumes a hyper-rationalised idea of the individual decision-making process in which people act primarily on the basis of the model trade-offs. It is likely that individuals in question are not even aware of these trade-offs and that the tipping game explores an artificial world that it has created. Methodologically, it is insufficient to merely argue that the model is plausible, as it is supposed to explain complex real-world phenomena, rather than solely reflecting plausibility and methodological elegance.[70]

Furthermore, Alexander Motyl suggests that Laitin's focus on language games overestimates the role of language in collective (including national) identity. Laitin argues that language is the most important aspect of complex individual identity and subsequently language shifts (as in the tipping game) imply a formation of identity without giving sufficient empirical support to this assumption. Therefore, the focus on language oversimplifies the process of identity formation and thus can lead to faulty conclusions concerning individual choices. A choice to switch a language may very well have an impact on people's national identity. However, many other choices can have a similar or even greater influence, as we do not know to what extent language choices are responsible for generating identities as opposed to other factors.[71]

Finally, the application of rational choice to identity-based phenomena seems to be problematic. For instance, David Laitin argues on the one hand that tipping games reflect language-cum-identity shifts. On the other hand, his explanatory model rests predominantly on the material preferences of the individuals, which leads to an explanatory gap between assumptions about the rational behaviour and the identity formation effects. Therefore, one can argue that a rationalist perspective on nations introduces contradiction into the theoretical core of the model and thus undermines its axiomatic foundations. However, it is uncertain how rationalists could fill this gap without surrendering the methodologically parsimonious nature of rational choice, since potential gap-filling factors such as culture or ideology would destroy the rational assumptions of the model.[72]

Regarding nations in particular, there may be besides rational utilitarian calculations completely non-material motivations for involvement in collective action. Ideal interests or ethical impulses such as righteous indignation can explain the degree of individual involvement with a nation. If we follow David Miller, with his ethical arguments on nation, we could make a case that a nation as an ethical community frequently demands obligations or even sacrifice from its followers rather than promising them rewards.[73] Moreover, in the psychological view the numerous expected sacrifices are the main 'pull factor' that attracts individuals to nations, rather than the benefits promised by political elites. As Heribert Adam argues, 'the self-imposed discipline and sacrifice allows followers to feel superior compared with the normal selfishness of ordinary free riders. It gives the true believer a new identity.'[74]

In sum, these four perspectives on nation reflect not only different conceptions of a nation, but also their underlying methods of inquiry, which are frequently incompatible with each other. As suggested at the beginning of the chapter, we regard the nation as a concept of experience and expectation, which changes throughout different historic periods, and becomes modified by historic experience. As a consequence, we should view the concept of nation through the lens of contemporary society in order to uncover the relevance of nations in today's social and political context. Against this background, in the following chapter we will move away from the four perspectives on the nation and try to pin down the concept of the nation with reference to national identity.

Notes

1. Reinhart Koselleck, 'Linguistic change and the history of events', *Journal of Modern History* 61, 4 (1989), pp. 650–66; Anders Schinkel, 'Imagination as category of history: an essay concerning Koselleck's concepts of Erfahrungsraum and Erwartungshorizont', *History and Theory* 44, 1 (2005), pp. 42–54; Reinhart Koselleck, 'Begriffsgeschichte and social history', *Economy and Society* 11, 4 (1982), pp. 409–27.
2. Reinhart Koselleck, '"Erfahrungsraum" und "Erwartungshorizont" – zwei historische Kategorien', in Reinhart Koselleck, *Vergangene Zukunft: Zur Semantik Geschichtlicher Zeiten* (Frankfurt am Main: Suhrkamp Verlag, 1979), pp. 352–3.
3. Luis Wirth, 'Types of nationalism', *American Journal of Sociology* 41, 6 (1936), pp. 723–37 (p. 723).
4. Anthony D. Smith, 'National identity and the idea of European unity', *International Affairs* 68, 1 (1992), pp. 55–76.
5. See Margaret Canovan, 'Sleeping dogs, prowling cats and soaring doves: three paradoxes in the political theory of nationhood', *Political Studies* 49 (2001), pp. 203–15.
6. Ernest Gellner, *Nations and Nationalism* (Ithaca, NY: Cornell University Press, 1983), p. 40; Ernest Gellner, 'Nationalism', *Theory and Society* 10, 6 (1981), pp. 753–76; Ugo Pagano, 'Nationalism, development and integration: the political economy of Ernest Gellner', *Cambridge Journal of Economics* 27 (2003), pp. 623–46.
7. Ernest Gellner, 'The importance of being modular', in John Hall, *Civil Society* (Cambridge: Cambridge University Press, 1995), p. 50.
8. Liah Greenfeld, 'Is nation unavoidable? Is nation unavoidable today?', in Hanspeter Kriesi, Klaus Armingeon, Hannes Siegrist and Andreas Wimmer (eds), *Nation and National Identity: The European Experience in Perspective* (Zurich: Rüegger,

1999), pp. 37–54; see also Paul Gilbert, 'Ethics or nationalism', *Journal of Applied Philosophy* 19, 2 (2002), pp. 185–7; Bernard Yack, 'Popular sovereignty and nationalism', *Political Theory* 29, 4 (2001), pp. 517–36.

9. Liah Greenfeld, *The Spirit of Capitalism: Nationalism and Economic Growth* (Cambridge, MA: Harvard University Press, 2001), p. 2; see Rogers Brubaker, 'In the name of the nation: reflections on nationalism and patriotism', *Citizenship Studies* 8, 2 (2004), pp. 115–27.

10. Yael Tamir, *Liberal Nationalism* (Princeton, NJ: Princeton University Press, 1993); Albert W. Dzur, 'Nationalism, liberalism, and democracy', *Political Research Quarterly* 55, 1 (2002), pp. 191–211; see also Arash Abizadeh, 'Liberal nationalist versus postnational social integration: on the nation's ethnocultural particularity and concreteness', *Nations and Nationalism* 10, 3 (2004), pp. 231–50; Andrew Vincent, 'Liberal nationalism: an irresponsible compound?', *Political Studies* XLV (1997), pp. 275–95; Sune Lægaard, 'Liberal nationalism and the nationalization of liberal values', *Nations and Nationalism* 13, 1 (2007), pp. 37–55; Pierre-Yves Bonin, 'Libéralisme et nationalisme: où tracer la ligne?', *Revue Canadienne de Science Politique* 30, 2 (1997), pp. 235–56.

11. David Miller, 'In defence of nationality', in David Miller, *Citizenship and National Identity* (Cambridge: Polity Press, 2000), p. 27.

12. Margaret Moore, 'Normative justifications for liberal nationalism: justice, democracy and national identity', *Nations and Nationalism* 7, 1 (2001), pp. 1–20.

13. David Miller, *On Nationality* (Oxford: Clarendon Press, 1995), p. 26; Catherine M. Frost, 'Survey article: the worth of nations', *Journal of Political Philosophy* 9, 4 (2001), pp. 482–503; Bo Rothstein, 'Trust, social dilemmas and collective memories', *Journal of Theoretical Politics* 12, 4 (2000), pp. 477–501.

14. Benedict Anderson, *Imagined Communities: Reflections on the Origin and Spread of Nationalism* (London: Verso, 1991); Tim Phillips, 'Imagined communities and self-identity: an exploratory quantitative analysis', *Sociology* 36, 3 (2002), pp. 597–617.

15. See Will Kymlicka, *Politics in the Vernacular: Nationalism, Multiculturalism, and Citizenship* (Oxford: Oxford University Press, 2001).

16. Anderson, *Imagined Communities*, p. 6.

17. Ernest Gellner, *Thought and Change* (London: Weidenfeld and Nicolson, 1971), p. 169.

18. Ibid. p. 6.

19. Rudolf de Cillia, Martin Reisigl and Ruth Wodak, 'The discursive construction of national identities', *Discourse & Society* 10, 2 (1999), pp. 149–73.

20. Ruth Wodak and Rudolf de Cillia, 'Commemorating the past: the discursive construction of official narratives about the "Rebirth of the Second Austrian Republic"', *Discourse & Communication* 1, 3 (2007), pp. 337–63; Ruth Wodak, Rudolf de Cillia, Martin Reisigl and Karin Liebhart, *The Discursive Construction of National Identities* (Edinburgh: Edinburgh University Press, 2009).

21. Adrian Blackledge, 'The discursive construction of national identity in multilingual Britain', *Journal of Language, Identity, and Education* 1, 1 (2002), pp. 67–87.

22. Seyla Benhabib, 'The democratic movement and the problem of difference', in Seyla Benhabib (ed.), *Democracy and Difference: Contesting the Boundaries of the Political* (Princeton, NJ: Princeton University Press, 1996), p. 3.

23. De Cillia et al., 'The discursive construction of national identities', p. 154.

24. Michael Billig, *Banal Nationalism* (London: Sage, 1995), p. 93.

25. Alex Law, 'Near and far: banal national identity and the press in Scotland', *Media, Culture & Society* 23 (2001), pp. 299–317; Kathryn Crameri, 'Banal Catalanism', *National Identities* 2, 2 (2000), pp. 145–57.

26. Anthony D. Smith, *National Identity* (London: Penguin Books, 1991), p. 41.

27. Ibid. p. 41.

28. Walker Connor, 'The timelessness of nations', *Nations and Nationalism* 10, 1/2 (2004), pp. 35–47; John Hutchinson, 'Ethnicity and modern nations', *Ethnic and Racial Studies* 23, 4 (2000), pp. 651–69.

29. Craig Calhoun, 'Nationalism and ethnicity', *Annual Review of Sociology*, 19 (1993), pp. 211–39.
30. Anthony D. Smith, 'When is a nation?', *Geopolitics* 7, 2 (2002), pp. 5–32 (p. 9).
31. Anthony D. Smith, 'The ethnic sources of nationalism', *Survival* 35, 1 (1993), pp. 48–62.
32. Yael Tamir, 'The enigma of nationalism', *World Politics* 47, 3 (1995), pp. 418–40 (p. 432).
33. Edward N. Muller and Karl-Dieter Opp, 'Rational choice and rebellious collective action', *American Political Science Review* 80, 2 (1986), pp. 471–88; Elinor Ostrom, 'A behavioral approach to the rational choice theory of collective action', *American Political Science Review* 92, 1 (1998), pp. 1–22.
34. Erich Weede and Edward N. Muller, 'Rebellion, violence and revolution: a rational choice perspective', *Journal of Peace Research* 35, 1 (1998), pp. 43–59; Douglas D. Heckathorn, 'The dynamics and dilemmas of collective action', *American Sociological Review* 61, 2 (1996), pp. 250–77.
35. Michael Hechter, Debra Friedman and Malka Appelbaum, 'A theory of ethnic collective action', *International Migration Review* 16, 2 (1982), pp. 412–34; Michael Hechter, 'The dynamics of secession', *Acta Sociologica* 35 (1992), pp. 267–83.
36. Michael Hechter, 'The politcal economy of ethnic change', *American Journal of Sociology* 79, 5 (1974), pp. 1,151–78.
37. Michael Hechter and Debra Friedman, 'Does rational choice theory suffice? Response to Adam', *International Migration Review* 18, 2 (1984), pp. 381–8 (p. 381).
38. Michael Hechter, *Containing Nationalism* (Oxford: Oxford University Press, 2000), p. 11.
39. Ibid. p. 7.
40. Ibid. p. 9.
41. James D. Fearon and David D. Laitin, 'Explaining interethnic cooperation', *American Political Science Review* 90, 4 (1996), pp. 715–35; James D. Fearon and David D. Laitin, 'Violence and the social construction of ethnic identity', *International Organization* 54, 4 (2000), pp. 845–77.
42. Fearon and Laitin, 'Explaining interethnic cooperation', p. 730.
43. David D. Laitin, 'The game theory of language regimes', *International Political Science Review* 14, 3 (1993), pp. 227–39; David D. Laitin, *Identity in Formation: The Russian-Speaking Populations in the Near Abroad* (Ithaca, NY: Cornell University Press, 1998).
44. See Furio Cerutti, 'Can there be a supranational identity?', *Philosophy & Social Criticism* 18 (1992), pp. 147–62.
45. See Bronislaw Szerszynski and John Urry, 'Visuality, mobility and the cosmopolitan: inhabiting the world from afar', *British Journal of Sociology* 57, 1 (2006), pp. 113–31; Noel Cass, Elizabeth Shove and John Urry, 'Social exclusion, mobility and access', *The Sociological Review* 53, 3 (2005), pp. 539–55; Saskia Sassen, 'Territory and territoriality in the global economy', *International Sociology* 15, 2 (2000), pp. 372–93; Luke Desforges, Rhys Jones and Mike Woods, 'New geographies of citizenship', *Citizenship Studies* 9, 5 (2005), pp. 439–51.
46. Linda Bosniak, 'Citizenship denationalized', *Indiana Journal of Global Legal Studies* 7 (2000), pp. 447–509; Saskia Sassen, 'The repositioning of citizenship: emergent subjects and spaces for politics', *The New Centennial Review* 3, 2 (2003), pp. 41–66; Saskia Sassen, 'Globalization or denationalization?', *Review of International Political Economy* 10, 1 (2003), pp. 1–22.
47. Eric Fong and Kumiko Shibuya, 'Multiethnic cities in North America', *Annual Review of Sociology* 31 (2005), pp. 285–304; Ayse S. Çaglar, 'Constraining metaphors and the transnationalisation of spaces in Berlin', *Journal of Ethnic and Migration Studies* 27, 4 (2001), pp. 601–13; Justus Uitermark, Ugo Rossi and Henk van Houtum, 'Reinventing multiculturalism: urban citizenship and the negotiation of ethnic diversity in Amsterdam', *International Journal of Urban and Regional Research* 29, 3 (2005), pp. 622–40; Mark Purcell, 'Citizenship and the right to the global city:

reimagining the capitalist world order', *International Journal of Urban and Regional Research* 27, 3 (2003), pp. 564–90; Marisol García, 'Citizenship practices and urban governance in European cities', *Urban Studies* 43, 4 (2006), pp. 745–65. For a rather critical view of transnational citizenship, see Monica W. Varsanyi, 'Interrogating urban citizenship vis-à-vis undocumented migration', *Citizenship Studies* 10, 2 (2006), pp. 229–49.

48. 48. See Anne McNevin, 'Political belonging in a neoliberal era: the struggle of the sans-papiers', *Citizenship Studies* 10, 2 (2006), pp. 135–51; Linda Bosniak, 'Universal citizenship and the problem of alienage', *Northwestern University Law Review* 94, 3 (2000), pp. 963–84.

49. See Bart Cammaerts and Leo van Audenhove, 'Online political debate, unbounded citizenship and the problematic nature of a transnational public sphere', *Political Communication* 22 (2005), pp. 179–96; Agnes S. Ku, 'Beyond the paradoxical conception of civil society without citizenship', *International Sociology* 17, 4 (2002), pp. 529–48; Maurice Roche, 'The Olympics and global citizenship', *Citizenship Studies* 6, 2 (2002), pp. 165–81.

50. Tamir, 'The enigma of nationalism', p. 435.

51. Alexander J. Motyl, 'Imagined communities, rational choosers, invented ethnies', *Comparative Politics* 34, 2 (2002), pp. 233–50.

52. Ibid. p. 235.

53. Ibid. p. 235.

54. Tamir, 'The enigma of nationalism', p. 421.

55. David Miller, 'The nation-state: a modest defense', in Chris Brown (ed.), *Political Restructuring in Europe: Ethical Perspectives* (London: Routledge, 1994), p. 141.

56. See Dahlia Moore and Baruch Kimmerling, 'Individual strategies of adopting collective identities: the Israeli case', *International Sociology* 10, 4 (1995), pp. 387–407.

57. See Zygmunt Bauman, 'Identity in the globalizing world', *Social Anthropology* 9, 2 (2001), pp. 121–9; Zygmunt Bauman, *Liquid Modernity* (Cambridge: Polity Press, 2000); see also Sanford F. Schram, 'Postmodern policy analysis: discourse and identity in welfare policy', *Policy Sciences* 26, 3 (1993), pp. 249–70; Peter Abrahamson, 'Liquid modernity: Bauman on contemporary welfare society', *Acta Sociologica* 47, 2 (2004), pp. 171–9; Vince Marotta, 'Zygmunt Bauman: order, strangerhood and freedom', *Thesis Eleven* 70, 1 (2002), pp. 36–54.

58. See Steven Seidman, 'The end of sociological theory: the postmodern hope', *Sociological Theory* 9, 2 (1991), pp. 131–46; John W. Murphy, 'Making sense of postmodern sociology', *British Journal of Sociology* 39, 4 (1988), pp. 600–14.

59. See Steven Vertovec, 'Transantionalism and identity', *Journal of Ethnic and Migration Studies* 27, 4 (2001), pp. 573–82; Henry A. Giroux, 'Living dangerously: identity politics and the new cultural racism: towards a critical pedagogy of representation', *Cultural Studies* 7, 1 (1993), pp. 1–27; Pnina Werbner, 'Divided loyalties, empowered citizenship? Muslims in Britain', *Citizenship Studies* 4, 3 (2000), pp. 307–24; Feyzi Baban, 'From Gastarbeiter to ausländische Mitbürger: postnational citizenship and in-between identities in Berlin', *Citizenship Studies* 10, 2 (2006), pp. 185–201; Gershon Shafir and Yoav Peled, 'Citizenship and stratification in an ethnic democracy', *Ethnic and Racial Studies* 21, 3 (1998), pp. 408–27.

60. Catarina Kinnvall, 'Globalization and religious nationalism: self, identity, and the search for ontological security', *Political Psychology* 25, 5 (2004), pp. 741–67.

61. Tamir, 'The enigma of nationalism', p. 424.

62. Motyl, 'Imagined communities', p. 244.

63. Ibid. p. 244.

64. Rogers Brubaker, 'Myths and misconceptions in the study of nationalism', in John Hall (ed.), *The State of the Nation: Ernest Gellner and the Theory of Nationalism* (Cambridge: Cambridge University Press, 1998), pp. 272–306 (p. 274).

65. Siniša Malešević, 'Rational choice theory and the sociology of ethnic relations: a critique', *Ethnic and Racial Studies* 25, 2 (2002), pp. 193–212.

66. Ibid. p. 202.

67. Michael Hechter, 'Explaining nationalist violence', *Nations and Nationalism* 1, 1 (1995), pp. 53–68 (p. 54).
68. Ibid. p. 62.
69. Malešević, 'Rational choice theory', p. 205.
70. Motyl, 'Imagined communities', p. 238.
71. Ibid. p. 238.
72. Ibid. p. 239.
73. Miller, 'In defence of nationality', p. 27.
74. Heribert Adam, 'Rational choice in ethnic mobilization: a critique', *International Migration Review* 17, 3 (1983), pp. 546–50 (p. 547).

CHAPTER TWO

The Nation and National Identity

Since there are numerous perspectives of what constitutes a nation, we suggest applying a derivative method, which defines a nation as a political community endowed with a collective identity. The basic understanding of a nation pertains to its nature as a community whose members are citizens, that is individuals with claims to political self-determination. In contrast to local identities, nations assume a highly abstract form of collective identity.[1] Even though the majority of citizens will never encounter each other, they assume that they belong to the same group as other citizens. However, this understanding goes further than Anderson's concept of imagined community. The focus on the political dimension of national identity implies that the nation impinges directly on individuals' sense of political inclusion, as it shifts its focus from the social to the political domain.[2] In this sense, a nation relates to a collective identity in the context of a polity, a political system and political decision-making. This associates the nation with political collective identity, distinguishable from other social identities and social roles.[3]

However, the exact nature of the nation as a community endowed with a political collective identity remains variable, as we can refer to different sources of the political bond among citizens and of the feeling of national we-ness. In this regard, national identity frequently fluctuates between creating a community and constituting a community with a fuzzy relationship to individual membership. In some conceptions of nations citizens constitute the nation; in others the nation makes the citizens.[4] Despite this variability nations are frequently conceptualised as an integrative device bridging differences of a social nature. Such shared nationhood is expected to supersede rival identities and differences in social status. Such national identity can assume different forms, allowing for varying degrees of multiplicity (unitary versus multiple) and bonding (individualist versus collectivist).[5]

In sum, national identity represents an integrating category, despite the fact that individuals can feel that they belong to various groups or social units at the same time. Even though multiplicity and variability are features of contemporary societies, national identities are supposed to integrate idiosyncrasies of individuals and differences of social status into group behaviour. However, this does not imply a uniformity of individual behaviour under the influence of national identity. National identities frequently operate under the circumstances of societal pluralism that makes recombination of identities necessary. As every society is in need of integration, this is provided by an overlapping national identity sustained by various mechanisms.[6]

Three aspects of national identity

At the abstract level, we can define national identity as a three-tiered concept, the criteria of which are: internal cohesion or thickness; the principle of exclusion; and the dynamics of identity in form of the We–I balance.

First, national identity can be analysed in terms of the degree of internal integration, which translates into the 'thickness', or resilience, of nations in times of crisis and external shock. National identity facilitates the construction of the nation as an abstract community and structures non-face-to-face interactions. As a consequence, citizens assume that significantly more individuals belong to the same nation as they do and act upon this assumption. In other words, without national identity members of the nation would have to rely on an ad hoc situational and contextual provision of collective identity based on the face-to-face experience. However, the situational context does not suffice to construct the nation as a stable pattern of reciprocity and recognition among the members of the national group. Therefore, reciprocity and recognition among participants requires a specific set of institutionalised national values and national symbols, which can convey the specifics of the nation to its members.[7] Furthermore, nations become ethical communities, as defined by David Miller, when they uphold normative claims, whereby members of the nation define themselves as such and develop a sense of obligation towards their fellow-nationals.[8] How demanding and extensive these obligations are depends on the type of nation in question. The obligations can relate to a thin collective identity found in a shared rationality, a thick collective identity stemming from mutual demanding obligations and specific responsibilities or a specific collectivism of shared perception of threat and danger.

Second, we can explore national identity with reference to the mode of exclusion of non-citizens, the issue of access to the political community as well as the assimilation of new citizens.[9] This, again, is a matter of what type of nation it is, as various types apply different exclusion and assimilation mechanisms. In this sense, nations are a double-coded phenomenon, since they are associated with bonding among fellow-nationals yet at the same time give rise to boundaries excluding the non-nationals (bonding/bounding). This double-edged functioning of nations is essential for their effectiveness as integrating mechanisms, as they have to mediate between collectivisation impulses inherent in any collective identity and fragmentation tendencies of the functionally differentiated modern societies.

With regard to the mode of exclusion, numerous scholars have examined the 'othering' as a device for national identity formation. Nations tell 'us' who 'we' are by relating 'us' to 'them'.[10] By so doing, nations respond to the needs of societies to create and recreate their own 'Others'. The category of 'Others' is also subject to dynamic processes of redefinition, since national identity must constantly deliver a relevant psychological framework for new societal circumstances. In this sense, the construction of 'Others' reacts to the changing symbolic or affective needs of the nation members.[11] Particularly in times of crises, the significant Other becomes activated in the national identity of individuals, since the binary construction of 'us' versus 'them' helps in overcoming the crises by, for instance, using blaming and scapegoating strategies.[12] The significant Other unites the nation in front of a common enemy by highlighting that the nation is different and unique. Therefore, what matters is not merely the image of the 'Other' as such, but the perceived attributes of the 'Other'. The initial step of 'othering' includes the decision either in favour of recognition of otherness or in favour of its negation. However, the nature of representing the 'Other' is also significant for the consequences of collective identity. First, there can be significant and insignificant Others, but only the significant Other can become the relevant reference for collective identity formation. Second, if the Other is constructed as threatening qua an enemy-accentuating political rhetoric, it may create xenophobia and lead to (verbal and physical) violence against the Others. The Other, however, can also be constructed as inferior, which boosts the feeling of supremacy and grandeur of a given nation and might lead to the stigmatisation of Others, particularly if the Other can be found within the collectivity as a minority.[13]

Third, we can analyse national identity by referring to the notion of the We–I balance, proposed by Norbert Elias in his discussion of societal civilisation processes. The We–I balance of national identity can account for identity formation in different societies, where the relational aspect of identity between minority and majority collective identity appears to be central. According to the optimal distinctiveness theory, individuals define themselves as much in terms of their group membership as in terms of their individual achievements.[14] As individuals can identify with different social groups, they do so in order to achieve and maintain a stable self-concept. Since an individual's self-concept is shaped by two opposing needs – the need for assimilation (collective identity) and the need for differentiation (individual identity) – people aspire to become part of larger social entities, while at the same time wanting to feel unique and original. However, too much of either identity generates the opposite motivation, which provokes efforts to change the current level of social identification. This mixture of individual and collectivist needs is likely to produce a momentary balance between the opposing needs – the We–I balance. Consequently, we might face not only waves of collectivisation and individualisation in one society (as Norbert Elias suggested) in a diachronic comparison but also differently collectivistic and individualistic types of national identity. Furthermore, the optimal distinctiveness theory would suggest that a pervasive and intense forging of national identity (especially in individualist societies) could prompt an opposing effect on individuals, thus rendering efforts of identity construction counterproductive. When individuals become assigned to a majority group, they need to differentiate themselves in some way from this group, and thus tend to highlight their individuality with regard to the group. This would also imply that identification with a negatively valued group (with certain nations, for example) could have a positive value, if such identification helped to restore homeostasis, thus achieving a greater balance between the opposing needs for assimilation and differentiation.

The three-tiered understanding of national identity, including internal cohesion or thickness of identity, the principle of exclusion and the internal dynamics of identity can describe any nation regardless of the conceptual controversies surrounding it. In this sense, it is a parsimonious approach, as it does not answer the question about the actual substance of a nation, which scholars of the nation and nationalism have made numerous attempts to address. As we argued above, the nation is also a concept of expectation which changes according to the historical experience of nations and the expectations associated with it. We therefore suggest approaching the concept of the nation in less of a substantial manner but rather through its workings or effects. In the next chapter, we will try to systematise the expected effects of nations and national identity.

Effects of national identity

We can identify four main effects of national identity: cognitive effects, self-esteem booster effects, legitimacy effects and solutions to collective action dilemmas.[15] In contrast to the four perspectives on nation here we draw heavily on the literature from psychology, in particular social psychology. As mentioned above, the lack of reference to psychological research was one of the major points of critique regarding mainstream research on nations.

Cognitive effects of national identity

The research on cognition suggests that nations are mental and social constructs which allow individuals to perceive themselves as group members. Thus, even under the circumstances of high social complexity and uncertainty individuals can identify themselves and make sense of their problems and interests. A further cognitive effect of nations is that political authorities can use the boundaries indicated by nations as a powerful tool for recognising and classifying people, thus reducing cognitive complexity. In this sense, nation-states construct both similarity (fellow-nationals) and difference (others), which they use as templates for organising perceptions and cognitions as well as frames for social comparisons.

A number of psychological theories discern cognitive effects that can be ascribed to national identity. Their point of departure is that human relations are arranged through the ongoing definition of collective self-categories, through which individuals manage their social relations. Collective self-categorisation indicates that individuals regard themselves as members of groups, whereby nations are examples of such groups.[16] This perception reduces social complexity for individuals by rendering it comprehensible. As a consequence, the reduction of perceived social complexity decreases individual uncertainty with regard to social relations, which appear less chaotic.[17] Once collective self-categorisation has occurred, the individuals start identifying themselves as similar to other members of the nation. As a result of this depersonalisation process, the perceived importance of the individual's personal identity is diminished, and the importance of the person's national identity is increased. The result is collective self-stereotyping, during which the individual acquires the characteristics of the group: the person assumes that the attributes stereotypical of the group are also characteristic of the self. While depersonalisation delineates the inclination of a person to act as a member of a group (and thus refers to the internal aspect of national identity), the so-called 'entitativity effect' pertains to the nature of in-group and out-group impressions in terms of their perceived and expected unity (and the external aspect of collective identity).[18] However, the entitativity effect means also that the perception of the in-group unity depends on the perception of the out-group.[19]

Against this backdrop, we can identify at least two cognitive effects of national identity: different interpretations of who represents the genuine nation by the very members of the national group and the potential discriminatory effects of nations regarding non-members.

First, if nations are fluid, as suggested by discursive constructivists, the national identity cannot be considered a completely stable and static mental structure. Rather, the national identity of individuals is an outcome of a process of activation and categorisation, which includes social judgement and social recognition of identity claims. This perspective corresponds to the postmodern difference-accentuating conceptions of a nation, which renounces the national claim of homogeneity in favour of a cognitive fragmentation of nations.[20] In this view, nation disintegrates into a number of separate groups that lay political claims to public recognition as the representatives of a genuine nation. In this view, the nation ceases to be an integrative concept for society as a whole, as different groups not only present their claims of being true representatives of the nation but also have diverging conceptions of what constitutes the nation. Therefore, diverse social identities become politicised, leading to a contextual nation of competing group claims, where the demarcation lines between groups are fluid. The question remains, however, whether the nation as an integrative meta-identity still can provide a sort of primary identity framework of reference, able to transcend all other competing identities, or whether the nation instead becomes a platform for permanently fragmented and conflictive claims to nationhood.[21]

Second, the entitativity effect relates to the perceived homogeneity of other national groups that occurs when out-group members are viewed as similar to each other in comparison to in-group members, who are viewed as more diverse than they are. This effect is further strengthened when there is a perception of an identity threat to their own national group. The threat makes other national groups appear more unitary, or 'groupy', than their own nation and therefore more dangerous. Consequently, the dangerous out-group is perceived as more unitary and can be more easily categorised in pejorative terms, thus depersonalising its members.[22] As other nations can be viewed as threats, they can be reacted to with bias and discrimination.[23] Since other national groups are evaluated negatively, discrimination might ensue as a valid norm of behaviour towards the out-group.[24] In this view, nations are primarily boundary-drawing instruments, establishing a categorisation that distinguishes primarily between nationals and non-nationals. In an extreme form it can foster prejudice against non-nationals, particularly if a nation rests on ascriptive and ethnic traits of group membership. In his seminal work on 'cognitive prejudice', Henri Tajfel indicated that the 'blood-and-guts model' could even lead to the dehumanisation of out-groups.[25]

However, the discrimination processes can occur within the same nation. Even though the modern conception of a nation can be associated with the claim of citizen equality, most nation-states categorise and therefore discriminate within their citizenries, distinguishing at least between minors and adult citizens, prisoners and free citizens, naturalised and native citizens.[26]

Moreover, nations can further the 'othering' of immigrants by the majority of nationals. As Joanna Goodey argues, there is a tendency in some European nation-states of public stereotyping of migrants as 'undesirables' or as potential criminals. This criminalisation of migrants may be based on the selective focus on some offences or crimes committed by migrants and on the simultaneous ignoring of the criminality of the majority group.[27] This can lead to stigmatisation, perpetuating new images of the 'Other' as a basis for national identity.

On the one hand, the line between nationals and non-nationals is becoming less distinct as the latter gain increasing civil and social rights and as access to citizenship becomes liberalised.[28] Particularly in the context of the EU, it is argued that the policies of universal human rights endowed immigrants with virtually all the privileges associated with formal citizenship.[29] Therefore, instead of a national/non-national dichotomy, we should rather distinguish a membership continuum including national citizens, residents, asylum seekers, and so on. In this sense, as access to citizenship becomes less difficult, citizens are confronted with a perception of devalued national citizenship, which might entail a stronger need for boundary-making vis-à-vis incomplete citizens. The incomplete citizens or non-citizen members might in turn react to the stigmatisation processes with anger, stress, aggression and isolation from the majority.

On the other hand, despite the liberalisation and differentiation of citizenship, national governments increasingly demand affirmation of belonging and loyalty from non-nationals or naturalised citizens. They seek to restrict foreign, particularly diasporic, identities and to attach them to the core identity of the nation-state. While notions of fluidity and multiplicity of identities are found in academic discourses on globalisation, increasingly determined demands for exclusive loyalty and belonging to national cultures and polities make the unattached citizens and non-citizen residents appear suspect to national governments. In particular, citizens and residents of differing religions such as Islam are expected to conform to the core identity and to assert their commitments to the nation-state of their residence.[30]

Self-esteem booster effect

This effect of national identity refers to the need of individuals to acquire and uphold a positive image from membership of a social group such as a nation. Comparing oneself favourably to other nations drives the process by which one's self-esteem is produced and maintained.[31] Consequently, if one identifies with a negatively valued group, the self-stereotyping will create a negative impact on one's current level of self-esteem. Therefore, the underlying motivation for membership in groups such as nations is the enhancement of self-esteem.[32] In this perspective, nations are social resources used by individuals for their psychological benefits, but in a less conscious manner than is stipulated by the rationalist perspective on nations.[33]

Against this background, individuals have two major strategies to improve their collective status. On the one hand, an individual can attempt to leave the collectivity and become a member of a more positively evaluated group. However, the permeability of the boundaries is a relevant criterion in this context, since some groups (especially communities) are difficult to abandon not only in light of frequently ensuing social sanctions but also in terms of practicability. In fact, nations still belong to this category despite increasing global migratory trends, as cross-border mobility is limited to a minority of the world population. On the other hand, individuals may attempt to redefine the inter-group comparison process by selecting other reference points or standards of comparison.[34] Here, collective memory seems to play a central role with regard to nations. A sense of shared continuity and shared memories of the past not only gives the individual the feeling of greater durability and meaning, but also presents a list of potential points of reference for a redefinition of the intra-group comparison, compensating to some extent for the immobility of nationals. This allows for a recurrent production of self-esteem through belonging to the same group, particularly in cases in which leaving the nation is not an option. Thus, a collective memory of past experiences supplies a resource container from which individuals can derive their sense of uniqueness, unity and continuity. This continuity is directed both at the past (in memories and routines) and at the future (in expectations and aspirations). We might even argue that this feeling of continuity generated by collective identity is one of the main features attracting individuals to groups, since it can be conceptualised as an immortality strategy, as individuals become part of something surpassing human life.[35]

The role of collective memory is also stressed in the research on collective identity in social psychology, where scholars point out that national identity can be forged first and foremost against the background of common history – a point also strongly highlighted by the genealogical perspective.[36] This is also in tune with other research on nations pointing to the role of the myths of origin and highlighting the role of historiography. However, we can argue that it is not the mere existence of common experiences, but also the relevance of commemorative rituals, which appears relevant for the nations. Commemorative rituals are conducive to a revitalisation of a group's social heritage, cause a reaffirmation of its bonds and entail a reinforcement of the in-group solidarity.[37] Collective memory is essentially social in nature and is located not in history itself, but in social rules, laws, routines and records. In this sense, it is a strategic resource that can be transformed into a reliable source of collective identity for the present.[38] Periodic commemorations are significant for the renewal of the sentiment of national unity by vitalising social energy and arousing emotions by means of a shared deliberation of a mythical past. Therefore, commemorative rituals and their symbolism become a condition for continuity of national identity. In this sense, commemorative rituals function as 'mnemonic devices', used also by national communities to encourage emotions of unity, the goal being to boost people's feeling of belonging.[39]

Let us turn to some expected effects of the self-esteem booster of nations. First, viewed through the modernist prism of the nation-state, nations either delineate the differentiation between citizens and non-citizens or respond to the social differentiation of various social groups with an integration concept. For some authors, the most worrisome aspect is the competitive nature of collective self-esteem, which implies that citizens feel better when their collectivity does better than others. This can lead to outright hostility, particularly when groups compete for resources and political power. In the context, nations might be viewed as devices for production of tensions rather than for solution of conflicts.[40] Once nations develop a national identity, social routines and commemorative rituals that maintain in-group loyalty and solidarity can acquire a character of moral authority. Consequently, nations tend to establish their own moral order, which may be incompatible with a tolerance for difference. When out-groups within the nation (for instance, national groups other than the titular nation) do not subscribe to the same moral rules as the in-group, indifference can be replaced by deprecation and disrespect. As Marilynn Brewer argues, moral superiority provides justification or legitimisation for domination or active subjugation of out-groups.[41]

Second, the issue of collective memory has implications for the national identity in diverse societies. If the bonds of collectivity in nations are drawn primarily from the historical memory of the community, it fosters ancestral forms of political obligation leading the aforementioned 'blood-and-guts model' of a nation. Since the ancestors spilt their blood to build and defend the nation, citizens are believed to inherit an obligation to continue their work.[42] However, this conception of commemoration-based nations fails to explain why non-national immigrant citizens should have duties towards their national citizens, since they should have obligations towards their communities of origin rather than their communities of residence. Therefore, a commemoration-based nation tends to isolate immigrants rather than integrating them into the nation. As a result, ancestral conception of a nation leaves open the possibility that the public culture of commemoration might be illiberal or unjust and hence prone to oppression towards minorities.[43]

Legitimacy effects of nations

One of the standard insights of political science is that every political system, irrespective of its form or institutional configuration, can be analysed with regard to its legitimacy, which is needed for the system to be preserved. The issue of legitimacy pertains to national identity insomuch as it plays a decisive role in legitimising the political decisions of a national community. This legitimacy can be mainly nurtured from two sources. On the one hand it is legitimacy by output, drawn from the quality of the results of the political process. However, assessment of what is a good political decision depends on the expectations of the citizens, which are modulated by their collective identity.[44] On the other hand it is the participation of citizens in the process of political decision-making, which is expected to result from a common will of the citizenry (based on the national identity).[45] Therefore, both dimensions should ideally be fulfilled in order to legitimise modern political systems. However, the measurement of how far a political authority generates its legitimacy via input, output or both depends on the collective identity. This relates to the question of whether political decisions, generated by the political authority, correspond to the collective will of the population (national identity) as opposed to the will of the majority.

Furthermore, the legitimacy effect of national identity pertains to so-called national identity politics.[46] The notion of identity politics refers to political action and political measures using national identity as a basis for political mobilisation by political authorities. Therefore, we can identify two types of collective identity. First, there is the bottom-up approach of strategic essentialism, which utilises on the one hand established and recognised identities of the nation-state as a support for their political claims. On the other hand, it includes actions of group leadership to gain recognition on the basis of the supposedly authentic national identity.[47] Political claims of group leaders to preserve their specific group culture via special group rights can be motivated by the desire to prevent assimilation, which could undermine the power and privilege of leadership. In other words, the political claim of collective identity has the function of legitimating and preserving power.[48] Second, identity politics also pertains to a political strategy of political elites whose aim is to establish new collective identity or strengthen the existing weak national identity in a top-down manner in order to legitimise their policies, which otherwise would not gain sufficient political support. This can include manipulation of political symbols, propaganda and collective brainwashing through mass media and political events designed to spur emotions and therefore generate feelings of national commonness. Each of these approaches subordinates national identity to political interests.[49]

From the perspective of the elites, the promotion of national identity is an instrument to achieve two fundamental goals. On the one hand they claim legitimacy (and hence monopoly) in representing the collective concerns of the group, and on the other they control the 'deviant' behaviour of their political opponents within the group by interpreting what genuine national identity is.[50] Identity politics relies on the fact that the majority of group members are unlikely to have any direct contact with each other.[51] Nonetheless, they draw on a horizontal feeling of belonging, which is expected to be sufficiently powerful to mobilise and legitimise political actions. This feeling of belonging is supported and stabilised by an ideology of 'we-ness', which holds that the defining characteristics of the group establish authentic boundaries towards other groups and at the same time generate a legitimate basis for laying political claims of either special treatment or collective self-determination. In order to support their political claims, group leaders emphasise and manipulate shared myths, symbols and cultures associated with a particular territory or a particular good way of life as factors that help to consolidate and maintain collective identity. As there is no face-to-face communication among the majority of the group members, national identity is transported via images and representations such as the national soccer team.

Approaches to national identity politics oscillate between the voluntarism of authentic groups and the constructionism of collective identity by political elites. Both perspectives suffer from certain weaknesses. Oliver Zimmer proposes distinguishing between the mechanisms that social actors use for the reconstruction of the collective identity boundaries at a particular point in time and the symbolic resources upon which they draw in order to reconstruct these boundaries. Employing the Swiss example, Zimmer argues that the reliance solely on a voluntarist vision of the political community posed considerable problems for nation-building elites. According to nationalism's core doctrine, nations have to be 'natural' communities to be authentic. The national ideologues of multi-ethnic Switzerland were therefore at pains to demonstrate that their nation was organically determined rather than merely a product of human will.[52] In contrast, constructivism is criticised by some authors as a general weakness of contemporary sociological theory. It describes a methodological paradigm regarding ethnocultural identities as constructed by individuals and groups from the cultural resources available to them in their social environment. However, the constructivist paradigm exaggerates the responsibility of individuals for their own identity and ignores the social and political constraints of ethnic choices. At the same time, it underplays the fact that many minority demands for justice are made through the group prism, rather than in individualist terms.[53]

Solution of collective action dilemmas

Finally, we shall identify an effect of national identity that relates to what is well known in social sciences as 'dilemmas of collective action'.[54] These dilemmas delineate types of social situations in which the individual rationality of interdependent actors leads to collectively irrational outcomes.

These dilemmas are analysed by mainly rational choice approaches, as shown in our discussion of the rationalist perspective on nations. For instance, in a collective-good dilemma, each actor benefiting from the provision of a collective good such as pollution control does not have any incentive to contribute to the production of the good at hand, since he or she cannot be excluded from its consumption.[55] A similar problem of free riding can be found in collective action literature on political participation, since political protesters also aim for collective goods. As soon as such goods are produced, they are obtainable by everyone regardless of whether that individual has participated in the protests that made the goods possible. Simultaneously, the production of collective goods is rarely determined by the contribution of a single person. Therefore, rational and socially unencumbered individuals would refrain from participating in political protest or production of other collective goods, as they can enjoy the benefits regardless.

There is a variety of solutions to collective action dilemmas, discussed in the debates on cooperation problems. For the prisoner's dilemma there exist various models of game iteration[56] or of information provision.[57] Regarding the solution to the free-riding problems, models of threshold, selective incentives, critical mass concepts or social norms, among others, are proposed and examined.[58]

However, collective identity, including national identity, is increasingly debated as one of the possible explanations to the anomaly of collective action.[59] In fact, there is growing evidence that rationality is too limited as a theoretical framework to account for participation, cooperation and other forms of collective action where there should be none. We have already suggested this in the criticism of the rationalist perspective on nations, but some approaches in sociology and social psychology go even further and apply the concept of collective identity as a solution to dilemmas of collective action.

For instance, group identification is viewed as a significant factor in the explanation of participation in protest, whereby identification is expected to foster participation. Bert Klandermans argues that of three types of identity – cognitive, evaluative and affective – the latter appears to be the most relevant for protest behaviour.[60] He includes an additional behavioural component pertaining to group membership and stresses that group identification becomes visible in organisations that encompass members of a specific social category. Therefore, both the affective and the behavioural components of identity appear to have an impact on the readiness of individuals to engage in protect actions. Klandermans argues that the relationship between identification and protest participation is a double-edged one, since identity promotes participation, and participation reinforces identification.[61]

Furthermore, social identity approaches to collective identity suggest that members of in-groups are likely to cooperate with other in-group members, rather than with out-group members, both in continuous and binary-choice versions of the prisoner's dilemma. Even though many social psychologists would agree that collective identity has an impact on cooperation, they differ in their explanations of the mechanism of the influence. Brent Simpson argues, for instance, that collective identity is likely to reduce actors' responses to the 'greed component' in the prisoner's dilemma (the motivation to 'free-ride' on others' cooperation), but it does not have an effect on the responses to the 'fear component' (the motivation to avoid being 'exploited').[62]

In addition, literature on social movement highlights that collectively defined grievances can generate a sense of 'we-ness' directed at 'them', who are deemed responsible for the grievances in question. If political authorities become regarded as the culprits in a given context, collective identity will be politicised, leading to the overcoming of a collective action dilemma. This is especially the case when political authorities are unresponsive or react in repressive ways. Collective identity produced in a social movement can even tip over to produce a revolutionary mobilisation.[63] Consequently, the concept of collective identity in the literature on social movements primarily involves shared representations of the group based on common interests and experiences, but also pertains to a process of shaping and creating an image of what the group stands for and how it wants to be viewed by others. In this sense, collective identity is conceptualised as an achievement of collective efforts.[64]

Other scholars examining social movements stress the cultural background of collective action, as actors pull elements from their cultural repertoire and adapt them to their movement's purposes. Consequently, collective grievances would not be the only source of collective identity, but rather the hitherto existent wider cultural repertoire of the given social movement. In this sense, collective identity is explained structurally, rather than as a consequence of individual rationality.[65]

Notes

1. See Ian Hacking, 'Between Michel Foucault and Erving Goffman: between discourse in the abstract and face-to-face interaction', *Economy and Society* 33, 3 (2004), pp. 277–302; Velina Topalova, 'Individualism/Collectivism and social identity', *Journal of Community & Applied Social Psychology* 7, 1 (1997), pp. 53–64.
2. See Leonie Huddy, 'From social to political identity: a critical examination of social identity theory', *Political Psychology* 22, 1 (2001), pp. 127–56; Chantal Mouffe, 'Citizenship and political identity', *October* 61 (1992), pp. 28–32.
3. See Bernd Simon and Bert Klandermans, 'Politicized collective identity: a social psychological analysis', *American Psychologist* 56, 4 (2001), pp. 319–31; see also Margarita Sanchez-Mazas and Olivier Klein, 'Social identity and citizenship', *Psychologica Belgica* 43, 1/2 (2003), pp. 1–8.
4. See Charles Tilly, 'International communities, secure or otherwise', in Emanuel Adler and Michael Barnett (eds), *Security Communities* (Cambridge: Cambridge University Press, 1998), pp. 397–412; see also Katherine Fierlbeck, 'The ambivalent potential of cultural identity', *Canadian Journal of Political Science* 29, 1 (1996), pp. 3–22.
5. See Liah Greenfeld, 'Is nation unavoidable? Is nation unavoidable today?', in Hanspeter Kriesi, Klaus Armingeon, Hannes Siegrist and Andreas Wimmer (eds), *Nation and National Identity: The European Experience in Perspective* (Zurich: Rüegger, 1999), pp. 37–54; José Medina, 'Identity trouble: disidentification and the problem of difference', *Philosophy & Social Criticism* 29, 6 (2003), pp. 655–80.
6. See Niklas Luhmann, 'Differentiation of society', *Canadian Journal of Sociology* 2, 1 (1977), pp. 29–53.
7. See Anne Warfield Rawls, 'Language, self, and social order: a reformulation of Hoffman and Sacks', *Human Studies* 12, 1 (1989), pp. 147–72; Ulises Schmill, 'The dynamic order of norms, empowerment and related concepts', *Law and Philosophy* 19, 2 (2000), pp. 283–310.
8. Jeremy Waldron, 'Special ties and natural duties', *Philosophy and Public Affairs* 22, 1 (1993), pp. 3–30.
9. See Rogers Brubaker, 'The return of assimilation? Changing perspectives on immigration and its sequels in France, Germany, and the United States', *Ethnic and Racial Studies* 24, 4 (2001), pp. 531–48.
10. Michael Billig, *Banal Nationalism* (London: Sage, 1995), p. 78.
11. Anna Triandafyllidou, 'National identity and the Other', *Ethnic and Racial Studies* 21, 4 (1998), pp. 593–612.
12. Arash Abizadeh, 'Does collective identity presuppose an Other? On the alleged incoherence of global solidarity', *American Political Science Review* 99, 1 (2005), pp. 45–60.
13. See Pille Petersoo, 'Reconsidering otherness: constructing Estonian identity', *Nations and Nationalism* 13, 1 (2007), pp. 117–33.
14. See Steven J. Sherman, David L. Hamilton and Amy C. Lewis, 'Perceived entitativity and the social identity value of group memberships', in Dominic Abrams and Michael Hogg (eds), *Social Identity and Social Cognition* (Oxford: Blackwell, 1999), pp. 80–110.
15. See Ireneusz Paweł Karolewski, *Citizenship and Collective Identity in Europe* (London: Routledge, 2010).
16. See Stephen Reicher, 'Psychology and the end of history: a critique and a proposal

for the psychology of social categorization', *Political Psychology* 22, 1 (2001), pp. 383–407.

17. Michael A. Hogg, 'Subjective uncertainty reduction through self-categorization: a motivational theory of social identity processes', *European Review of Social Psychology* 11 (2000), pp. 223–55.

18. Rupert Brown, 'Social Identity Theory: past achievements, current problems and future challenges', *European Journal of Social Psychology* 30 (2000), pp. 745–78; Kathleen M. McGraw, 'Contributions of the cognitive approach to political psychology', *Political Psychology* 21, 4 (2000), pp. 805–32.

19. Lowell Gaertner and John Schopler, 'Perceived ingroup entitativity and intergroup bias: an interconnection of self and others', *European Journal of Social Psychology* 28 (1998), pp. 963–80; Emanuele Castano, Vincent Yzerbyt and David Bourguignon, 'We are one and I like it: The impact of ingroup entitativity on ingroup identification', *European Journal of Social Psychology* 33 (2003), pp. 735–54.

20. See Joan W. Scott, 'Multiculturalism and the politics of identity', *October* 61 (1992), pp. 12–19.

21. See Isis H. Settles, 'When multiple identities interfere: The role of identity centrality', *Personality and Social Psychology Bulletin* 30, 4 (2004), pp. 487–500; Richard J. Crisp and Miles Hewstone, 'Multiple identities in Northern Ireland: hierarchical ordering in the representation of group membership', *British Journal of Social Psychology* 40 (2001), pp. 501–14; Anna Melich, 'The nature of regional and national identity in Catalonia: problems of measuring multiple identities', *European Journal of Political Research* 14 (1986), pp. 149–69.

22. See Paul Hutchison, Jolanda Jetten, Julie Christian and Emma Haycraft, 'Protecting threatened identity: sticking with the group by emphasizing ingroup heterogeneity', *Personality and Social Psychology Bulletin* 32, 12 (2006), pp. 1,620–32.

23. Julian A. Oldmeadow, Michael J. Platow, Margaret Foddy and Donna Anderson, 'Self-categorization, status, and social influence', *Social Psychology Quarterly* 66, 2 (2003), pp. 138–52.

24. Amélie Mummendey and Michael Wenzel, 'Social discrimination and tolerance in intergroup relations: reactions to intergroup difference', *Personality and Social Psychology Review* 3, 2 (1999), pp. 158–74; Michael Wenzel, 'A social categorization approach to distributive justice: social identity as the link between relevance of inputs and need for justice', *British Journal of Social Psychology* 40 (2001), pp. 315–35.

25. Henri Tajfel, 'Cognitive aspects of prejudice', *Journal of Biosocial Sciences* Supplement No. 1 (1969), pp. 173–91; Michael Billig, 'Henri Tajfel's cognitive aspects of prejudice and the psychology of bigotry', *British Journal of Social Psychology* 41 (2002), pp. 171–88; Geoffrey J. Leonardelli and Marilynn B. Brewer, 'Minority and majority discrimination: when and why?', *Journal of Experimental Social Psychology* 37 (2001), pp. 468–85; Emanuele Castano and Vincent Y. Yzerbyt, 'The highs and lows of group homogeneity', *Behavioral Processes* 42 (1998), pp. 219–38.

26. Charles Tilly, 'A primer on citizenship', *Theory and Society* 26, 4 (1997), p. 601.

27. Joanna Goodey, 'Non-EU citizens' experiences of offending and victimisation: the case for comparative European research', *European Journal of Crime, Criminal Law and Criminal Justice* 8, 1 (2000), pp. 13–34.

28. Christian Joppke, 'Transformation of citizenship: status, rights, identity', *Citizenship Studies* 11, 1 (2007), pp. 37–48; Christian Joppke, 'How immigration is changing citizenship: a comparative view', *Ethnic and Racial Studies* 22, 4 (1999), pp. 629–52; Christian Joppke, 'Asylum and state sovereignty: A comparison of the United States, Germany, and Britain', *Comparative Political Studies* 30, 3 (1997), pp. 259–98.

29. See Yasemin Nuholu Soysal, 'Citizenship and identity: living in diasporas in post-war Europe?', *Ethnic and Racial Studies* 23, 1 (2000), pp. 1–15; Suzanne Shanahan, 'Different standards and standard differences: contemporary citizenship and immigration debates', *Theory and Society* 26, 4 (1997), pp. 421–48.

30. Eleonore Kofman, 'Citizenship, migration and the reassertion of national identity', *Citizenship Studies* 9, 5 (2005), pp. 453–67.

31. Brown, 'Social Identity Theory', pp. 745–78.

32. See Riia Luhtanen and Jennifer Crocker, 'A collective self-esteem scale: self-evaluation of one's social identity', *Personality and Social Psychology Bulletin* 18, 3 (1992), pp. 302–18.

33. Joshua Correll and Bernadette Park, 'A model of the ingroup as a social resource', *Personality and Social Psychology Review* 9, 4 (2005), pp. 341–59.

34. Kristen Renwick Monroe, James Hankin and Renée Bukovchik Van Vechten, 'The psychological foundations of identity politics', *Annual Review of Political Science* 3 (2000), pp. 419–47; Michael Hogg, Deborah J. Terry and Katherine M. White, 'A tale of two theories: a critical comparison of identity theory with social identity theory', *Social Psychology Quarterly* 58, 4 (1995), pp. 255–69. Mathias Blanz, Amélie Mummendey, Rosemarie Mielke and Andreas Klink, 'Responding to negative social identity: a taxonomy of identity management strategies', *European Journal of Social Psychology* 28 (1998), pp. 697–729.

35. See Emanuele Castano and Mark Dechesne, 'On defeating death: group reification and social identification as immortality strategies', *European Review of Social Psychology* 16 (2005), pp. 221–55.

36. Marilynn B. Brewer, 'The many faces of social identity: implications for political psychology', *Political Psychology* 22, 1 (2001), p. 119.

37. See Maurice Halbwachs, *The Collective Memory*, trans. F. J. Ditter and V. Y. Ditter, intro. by M. Douglas (London: Harper, 1950, orig. pub. 1926).

38. Barbara A. Misztal, 'Durkheim on collective memory', *Journal of Classical Sociology* 3, 2 (2003), pp. 123–43; Bo Rothstein, 'Trust, social dilemmas and collective memories', *Journal of Theoretical Politics* 12, 4 (2000), pp. 477–501.

39. Misztal, 'Durkheim on collective memory', p. 126. Even though Misztal uses the commemorative rituals and emotion-loaded practices with regard to early societies, they are equally true for any mass society, in which they fulfil an integrative and mobilisation function.

40. See Jeff Spinner-Halev and Elizabeth Theiss-Morse, 'National identity and self-esteem', *Perspectives on Politics* 1, 3 (2003), pp. 515–32.

41. Marilynn B. Brewer, 'The psychology of prejudice: ingroup love or outgroup hate?', *Journal of Social Issues* 55, 3 (1999), pp. 429–44.

42. David Miller, *Citizenship and National Identity* (Cambridge: Polity Press, 2000), p. 29.

43. Laura Andronache, 'A national identity Republicanism?', *European Journal of Political Theory* 5, 4 (2006), pp. 399–414.

44. Peter A. Kraus, 'Cultural pluralism and European polity-building: neither Westphalia nor Cosmopolis', *Journal of Common Market Studies* 41, 4 (2003), pp. 665–86.

45. See David Easton, 'A re-assessment of the concept of political support', *British Journal of Political Science* 5, 4 (1975), pp. 435–57; David Easton, 'Theoretical approaches to political support', *Canadian Journal of Political Science* 9, 3 (1976), pp. 431–48.

46. A good and comprehensive review of literature on identity politics is offered by Mary Bernstein. Mary Bernstein, 'Identity politics', *Annual Review of Sociology* 31 (2005), pp. 47–74.

47. Joan W. Scott, 'Multiculturalism and the politics of identity', *October* 61 (1992), pp. 12–19; see also Jonah Goldstein and Jeremy Rayner, 'The politics of identity in late modern society', *Theory and Society* 23, 3 (1994), pp. 367–84.

48. Claus Offe, 'Homogeneity and constitutional democracy: coping with identity conflicts through group rights', *Journal of Political Philosophy* 6, 2 (1998), p. 133.

49. For a discussion of strategic essentialism see Dietmar Rost, 'Social science approaches to collective identity, essentialism, constructionism and strategic essentialism', in Dietmar Rost, Erhard Stölting, Tomasz Zarycki, Paolo Pasi, Ivan Pedrazzini, Anna Tucholska, *New Regional Identities and Strategic Essentialism: Case Studies from Poland, Italy and Germany* (Münster: LIT Verlag, 2007), pp. 451–503.

50. See Erich Goode and Nachman Ben-Yehuda, 'Moral panics: culture, politics, and social construction', *Annual Review of Sociology* 20 (1994), pp. 149–71; Emanuele Castano et al., 'Protecting the ingroup stereotype: ingroup identification and the man-

agement of deviant ingroup members', *British Journal of Social Psychology* 41 (2002), pp. 365–85.

51. See Hacking, 'Between Michel Foucault and Erving Goffman', pp. 277–302.

52. Oliver Zimmer, 'Boundary mechanisms and symbolic resources: towards a process-oriented approach to national identity', *Nations and Nationalism* 9, 2 (2003), pp. 171–93.

53. See Stephen May, Tariq Modood and Judith Squires (eds), *Ethnicity, Nationalism and Minority Rights* (Cambridge: Cambridge University Press, 2004); see Dietmar Rost, 'Social science approaches to collective identity, essentialism, constructionism and strategic essentialism', in Dietmar Rost et al., *New Regional Identities and Strategic Essentialism*, pp. 451–503.

54. Mancur Olson, *The Logic of Collective Action. Public Goods and the Theory of Groups* (Cambridge, MA: Harvard University Press, 1968); John Chamberlin, 'Provision of collective goods as a function of group size', *American Political Science Review* 68, 2 (1974), pp. 707–16; Mancur Olson, *The Rise and Decline of Nations: Economic Growth, Stagflation and Social Rigidities* (New Haven, CT: Yale University Press, 1982).

55. See Elinor Ostrom, 'A behavioral approach to the rational choice theory of collective action', *American Political Science Review* 92, 1 (1998), pp. 1–22.

56. See Jianzhong Wu and Robert Axelrod, 'How to cope with noise in the iterated prisoner's dilemma', *Journal of Conflict Resolution* 39, 1 (1995), pp. 183–9; Robert Axelrod, *The Complexity of Cooperation* (Princeton, NJ: Princeton University Press, 1997).

57. See Otto Keck, 'The information dilemma: private information as a cause of transaction failure in markets, regulation, hierarchy, and politics', *Journal of Conflict Resolution* 31, 1 (1987), pp. 139–63.

58. Chien-Chung Yin, 'Equilibria of collective action in different distributions of protest thresholds', *Public Choice* 97 (1998), pp. 535–67; Mark Granovetter, 'Threshold models of collective behavior', *American Journal of Sociology* 83, 6 (1978), pp. 1,420–43; Gerald Marwell, Pamela E. Oliver and Ralph Prahl, 'Social networks and collective action: a theory of critical mass III', *American Journal of Sociology* 94, 3 (1988), pp. 502–34; see also Douglas D. Heckathorn, 'The dynamics and dilemmas of collective action', *American Sociological Review* 61, 2 (1996), pp. 250–77; Steven E. Finkel et al., 'Personal influence, collective rationality, and mass political action', *American Political Science Review* 83, 3 (1989), pp. 885–903; Elinor Ostrom, 'Collective action and the evolution of social norms', *Journal of Economic Perspectives* 14, 3 (2000), pp. 137–58; Jon Elster, 'Rationality, morality, and collective action', *Ethics* 96, 1 (1985), pp. 136–55.

59. See Amartya Sen, 'Goals, commitment, and identity', *Journal of Law, Economics, and Organization* 1, 22 (1985), pp. 341–55; Arieh Gavious and Shlomo Mizrahi, 'Two-level collective action and group identity', *Journal of Theoretical Politics* 11, 4 (1999), pp. 497–517.

60. Bert Klandermans, 'How group identification helps to overcome the dilemma of collective action', *American Behavioral Scientist* 45, 5 (2002), pp. 887–900.

61. Ibid. p. 898; see also Bert Klandermans, Jose Manuel Sabucedo, Mauro Rodriguez and Marga de Weerd, 'Identity processes in collective action participation: farmers' identity and farmers' protests in the Netherlands and Spain', *Political Psychology* 23, 2 (2002), pp. 235–51; Bert Klandermans and Dirk Oegema, 'Potentials, networks, motivations, and barriers: steps towards participation in social movements', *American Sociological Review* 52, 4 (1987), pp. 519–31.

62. Brent Simpson, 'Social identity and cooperation in social dilemmas', *Rationality and Society* 18, 4 (2006), pp. 443–70; Marilynn B. Brewer and Roderick M. Kramer, 'Choice behavior in social dilemmas: effects of social identity, group size, and decision framing', *Journal of Personality and Social Psychology* 50, 3 (1986), pp. 543–9; Brent Simpson and Michael W. Macy, 'Power, identity, and collective action in social exchange', *Social Forces* 82, 4 (2004), pp. 1373–409.

63. Steven Pfaff, 'Collective identity and informal groups in revolutionary mobilization:

East Germany in 1989', *Social Forces* 75, 1 (1996), pp. 91–117; see also Timur Kuran, 'Sparks and prairie fires: a theory of unanticipated political revolution', *Public Choice* 61 (1989), pp. 41–74; Erich Weede and Edward N. Muller, 'Rebellion, violence and revolution: a rational choice perspective', *Journal of Peace Research* 35, 1 (1998), pp. 43–59; Edward N. Muller and Karl-Dieter Opp, 'Rational choice and rebellious collective action', *American Political Science Review* 80, 2 (1986), pp. 471–88; Sidney Tarrow, 'National politics and collective action: recent theory and research in Western Europe and the United States', *Annual Review of Sociology* 14 (1988), pp. 421–40.

64. See Francesca Polletta and James M. Jasper, 'Collective identity and social movements', *Annual Review of Sociology* 27 (2001), pp. 283–305.

65. Rhys H. Wlliams, 'Constructing the public good: social movements and cultural resources', *Social Problems* 42, 1 (1995), pp. 124–44; Jeffrey Berejikian, 'Revolutionary collective action and the agent-structure problem', *American Political Science Review* 86, 3 (1992), pp. 647–57.

CHAPTER THREE

Nationalism: A Problem of Definition?

Main research foci on nationalism

The multiplicity of meanings of the term 'nationalism' is reflected in the plethora of theories of and approaches to nationalism. Our goal in the following section is not to account for all theories and approaches but to systematise the research around the main research foci. First, we will discuss three major research foci on nationalism. We shall consider the relationships between nationalism and modernity, nationalism and democracy, and nationalism and social justice. Here, we do not hesitate to discuss older approaches to nationalism, especially with regard to the recent writing, which seems to believe that it invented the study of nationalism while often it only perpetuates the original ideas and explanations. Further, we will discuss other important research interests, such as the relationship between nationalism and religion, nationalism and gender, nationalism and globalisation, and nationalism and regional integration, especially European integration. Since this last aspect will be broadly analysed later in the book, in this section we will only give a brief description.

Table 3.1 Main research foci on nationalism

Relationship	Relationship	Relationship
Nationalism and modernity	Nationalism and democracy	Nationalism and distributive justice

Nationalism and modernity

The relationship between nationalism and modernity has been the traditional and dominant research focus of several theories of nationalism. Within this research focus there are three major schools of thought.

The first school of thought confirms a complete causality between nationalism and modernity. Within this scholarship, we can distinguish two perspectives. The first, which can be called modernist-nationalist and which contains socioeconomic, sociophilosophical and social-constructionist approaches, suggests that nationalism is a product of modernity. The second, which can be defined as nationalist-modernist, claims that the rise of modernity was made possible by nationalism.

The second school of thought confirms a partial causality between nationalism and modernity. It claims that modernity was necessary for the outbreak of nationalism but the roots of nationalism lie before modern times. Within this school we can find a sociohistorical and an ethno-symbolic perspective.

The third school of thought denies any causality between nationalism and modernity. Within this scholarship we can distinguish two perspectives. The first, which can be called perennialist, argues that although nationalist ideologies and movements are a recent phenomenon, nations have existed in every period of history and several nations have existed from time immemorial.[1] Further, it is believed that nationality represented one of the most stable principles of social organisation in human history. The second perspective, usually defined as primordialist, holds that nations have deep roots in 'the first order of time' and that these roots are the source of subsequent processes and developments.[2]

Table 3.2 Relationship between nationalism and modernity

Full causality		Partial causality		No causality	
Modernist-nationalist perspective	Nationalist-modernist perspective	Socio-historical perspective	Ethno-symbolic perspective	Perennial perspective	Primordial perspective

Full causal relation between nationalism and modernity

Within the scholarship believing in full causality between nationalism and modernity, the perspective regarding nationalism as a product of the modern era is clearly dominant. It contains socioeconomic, sociophilosophical and social-constructionist approaches.

Ernest Gellner, one of the most prominent scholars of nationalism, represents the socioeconomic approach. Gellner rejects the assumption of the naturality of nationalism and that political units for most of history were animated by nationalist principles. He departs from the assumption that pre-modern political units rarely, and only accidentally, coincided with the linguistic and cultural boundaries of 'nations'.[3] Gellner sees nationalism as a phenomenon derived from sociopolitical, socioeconomic and sociocultural modernisation, which has taken place especially since the eighteenth century. Literacy, social mobility and modern industrial societies' need for human groups to be organised into large, centrally educated, culturally homogeneous units are the key concepts here:

> ... nationalism is not the awakening of an old, latent, dormant force, though that is how it does indeed present itself. It is in reality the consequence of a new form of social organization, based on deeply internalized, education-dependent high cultures, each protected by its own state.[4]

According to Gellner, in agrarian societies occupations were hereditary and work processes were simple. The need for social mobility was low. Literacy was not a precondition for social mobility and high culture – the codified and standardised written language – could remain a domain of the elite strata. This situation changed in industrial societies, in which all occupations ceased to be hereditary and production processes became more and more technical. The need for social mobility grew significantly. A labour force was required which would be capable of understanding the orders of the rulers, reading the instructions for the work tools, signing work contracts and – at least as significant – moving from its place of origin and maintaining these capabilities in other places. Hence, literacy was no longer a specialism but was now a precondition of all other specialisations. Consequently, there grew a need for impersonal, context-free communication and a high degree of cultural (and in particular linguistic) standardisation and homogenisation. This need could be met by an expansion or a universalisation of high culture to the whole of society.

The conditions for this expansion existed only within a national polity that corresponded to high culture and was in most cases clearly distinct from other national polities. Where the borders of cultural units did not coincide with the borders of political units, striving to make them congruent became a sociologically necessary phenomenon; thus there arose the functional necessity for nationalism. As Gellner argues, 'Nationalism has been defined . . . as the striving to make culture and polity congruent, to endow a culture with its own political roof, and not more than one roof at that.'[5]

In contrast to the socioeconomic approach, the sociophilosophical approach claims that the emergence of nationalism was made possible by the mainstream political philosophy of enlightenment. For instance, Elie Kedourie, one of the most prominent representatives of this approach, saw the origins of nationalism in Kant's philosophical individualism.[6] Kedourie suggested that even if Kant did not invent nationalism, his philosophy gave supporters of nationalist solutions important arguments. Kant's emphasis on continual efforts to invent and strengthen the autonomy of the individual and to make the will of the individual a source of all moral imperatives, as well as his demands for the right to self-determination of every individual, were misinterpreted by broad circles of European intellectuals as a demand for making the national collective the only source of moral imperatives as well as a demand for collective rights, such as the right of nations to self-determination. Kant's original ideas thus became transmuted into a doctrine under which membership of a nation, and the transformation of this nation into an independent state, became the only true form of freedom.[7] Conversely, nationalism could also emerge as a consequence of an interpretation of Kant's philosophy. In this sense, it was as a reaction to Kant's cosmopolitan thought, his dismissal of all existing communal ties and his suggestion that common moral commitments such as family, locality or communal law could function as moral imperatives. Nationalism thus arose from an 'attempt to escape the awful loneliness of the Kantian individual by inventing the comforting identity of "the nation"'.[8] This invention was necessary because of Kant's idea that the existing, historically established social identities were unsatisfactory. According to Kedourie, the need for such a comforting identity was particularly acute for 'rootless, half-educated intellectuals subject to the strains of autocracies such as Prussia'.[9] The paradox of nationalism thus was that Kant's celebration of the individual will had resulted in the submission of the individual to the demands of the nation and freedom was reinterpreted as a submission and sacrifice to the 'organic' whole.[10] In sum, the German Romantic followers of Kant elevated nationalism at the beginning of the nineteenth century to the most important source of legitimacy, to a new sacrum.

The socioconstructionist approach stresses the socially constructed character of nations and nationalism. Cornelius Castoriadis suggested that nations, national identity and nationalism are no more than imaginary meanings or discursive formations which can be compared to other imaginary cultural formations. According to Castoriadis, the national substratum was built on conventions, symbols and images and as such had a subjective character.[11] In a similar vein, Eric Hobsbawm argues that modern political actions such as elite appropriation, manipulation and justification form the basis of subsequent nationhood and that there is no connection between pre-modern religious, linguistic or ethnic communities and the modern phenomenon of nationalism expressed in the quest for a territorial nation-state.[12] Benedict Anderson, another prominent scholar of this approach, proposes regarding nations as imagined political communities. They are imagined because while the members of even the smallest nation will never know all their fellow-members, meet them or even hear of them, they still believe in their unity and community.[13] They are imagined as communities because, regardless of the actual inequality and injustice that may characterise some nations, every nation is always conceived as a deep, horizontal comradeship. According to Anderson, it is this comradeship that has made it possible for millions of people over the past two centuries to willingly die for such imaginary concepts.[14] Anderson adds that these communities are imagined as both inherently limited and as sovereign. They are imagined as limited since even the largest nation has finite boundaries beyond which lie other nations and as sovereign since the idea of nations emerged during the Enlightenment and the French Revolution, which destroyed the legitimacy of the previous divinely ordained hierarchical dynastic world.[15]

The second school of thought, called here nationalist-modernist, reverses the order of precedence and causality. It not only claims that the rise of modernity was made possible by nationalism but also asserts that nationalism is regarded as the constitutive element of modernity. Liah Greenfeld summarises it thus: 'Rather than define nationalism by its modernity, I see modernity as defined by nationalism.'[16]

The relevant factors here are status, pride, self-respect and dignity. According to Greenfeld, nationalism can be traced to the structural traits of the society of orders. In the pre-national society of orders, pride and self-respect were a privilege of the elites, while other segments of the society were confronted with humility and abnegation and could not see themselves as represented in and by the power wielded over them. However, in the society of orders, nobody was safe from degradation, and preoccupation with status was permanent, since status was dependent on the maintenance of rigid distinctions between orders and the strict observance of the rules of pre-eminence.[17] Against this background, nationalism should be understood as an action of individuals affected by these traditional structures and preoccupations. It was invented by English commoners as they ceased to accept the situation in which the society of orders significantly limited their upward mobility. They substituted the idea of a homogeneously elite people – the nation – for the traditional image of society.[18] The idea of common nationality raised all members of the community and gave them pride and self-respect as well as the claim to the respect of others, bestowing on them a previously unknown dignity.[19] Moreover, the idea of common nationality also guaranteed a previously unknown stability with regard to social status since it made status independent of the preservation of the distinctions. Nationalism led to the modern principle of the fundamental equality of membership, which allowed for the open class system of stratification based on achievement, rather than ascription, and in which transferable properties, such as wealth and education, rather than birth were the basis of status distinctions.[20] In this way, nationalism diminished the significance of detrimental distinctions and, at the same, secured all members of the community from ultimate economic and sentimental degradation. As Greenfeld argues, 'Within a nation, status (and, with it, sense of pride and self-respect) can never be totally lost. One still can rise and fall, but never fall so low that it would break one's heart.'[21]

In sum, the nationalist-modernist school of thought believes that the political and economic structures of the modern world are to a considerable extent a product of nationalism and that nationalism emerged from the preoccupation with status.[22]

Partial causal relation between nationalism and modernity

Within the school of belief in partial causality between nationalism and modernity we can find a sociohistorical and an ethnosymbolic perspective.

The sociohistorical perspective asserts, on the one hand, that nationalism is a modern phenomenon, in general dating back no further than the French Revolution with some precursors in the mid-eighteenth century. Hans Kohn, one of the most prominent representatives of this approach, claimed:

> Nationalism as we understand it is not older than the second half of the eighteenth century. Its first great manifestation was the French Revolution, which gave the new movement an increased dynamic force. Nationalism had, however, become manifest at the end of the eighteenth century almost simultaneously in a number of widely separated European countries.[23]

According to Kohn, nationalism is not a natural phenomenon, a product of 'eternal' or 'natural' laws. Rather, it is an artificial product of the growth of social and intellectual factors at a certain stage in history.[24] Nationalism is inconceivable without the core ideas of modernity, such as the idea of popular sovereignty, which led to a complete revision of the power relations between the rulers and the ruled as well as between the social classes and made possible the process of the integration of the masses of the people into a common political form.[25] Furthermore, nationalism presupposed the existence of a centralised form of government over a distinct and large territory. This form was created by the absolute monarchs, who were the pacemakers of modern nationalism; the French Revolution inherited and continued the centralising tendencies of the previous power-holders, at the same time filling them with a new spirit and giving them a high degree of hitherto unknown cohesion. Nationalism was thus unthinkable before the emergence of the modern state in the period from the sixteenth to the eighteenth centuries.[26] Once emerged, it spread because of such modern phenomena as the rise of print capitalism, mass education systems and new information and propaganda techniques, as well as the intensification of international relations, international trade and cultural interactions.

On the other hand, however, this approach maintains that although the French Revolution or the Enlightenment and Romantic philosophy were powerful factors in the emergence and spread of nationalism, they were not responsible for its coming into existence in the first place:

> Like all historical movements, nationalism has its roots deep in the past. The conditions which made its emergence possible had matured during centuries before they converged at its formation. These political, economic, and intellectual developments took a long time for their growth and proceeded in the various European countries at different pace.[27]

Kohn believed that nationalism used in its growth some of humankind's oldest and most primitive feelings which throughout history constituted important factors in the formation of social groups:

> There is a natural tendency in man – and we mean by 'natural tendency' a tendency which, having been produced by social circumstances since time practically immemorial, appears to us as natural – to love his birthplace or the place of his childhood sojourn, its surroundings, its climate, the contours of hills and valleys, of rivers and trees. We are all subject to the immense power of habitude, and even if in a later stage of development we are attracted by the unknown and by change, we delight to come back and be at rest in the reassuring sight of the familiar.[28]

Therefore, even if the sociohistorical perspective assumes that modernity transformed the meaning of territory, common language and common descent and embedded them in a broader context, it also asserts that these factors constituted the 'natural elements' out of which nationalism was formed.[29]

In a similar vein, the ethnosymbolic perspective suggests, on the one hand, that modernity was the framework within which nationalism could emerge, as without the institutions of the strong, centralised state, there would still be only an 'untutored' and largely unselfconscious ethnicity of pre-modern life.[30] On the other hand, instead of conceptualising nations in terms of a structural rupture that occurred between the seventeenth and eighteenth centuries which provided the political and sociocultural framework for increased social mobility and facilitated the rise of trans-class cultural identities, the ethnosymbolic perspective argues for an essential element of continuity between earlier forms of cultural identity and newly emerging nations. As claimed by Anthony D. Smith, 'The nation may be a modern social formation, but it is in some sense based on pre-existing cultures, identities and heritages.'[31]

Nations are not to be conceived in modernist terms as collectivities that emerge suddenly *ex nihilo* but rather as social entities that have been gradually built around pre-modern ethnic cores (ethnies).[32] The ethnosymbolic perspective therefore relates modern national identities and contemporary political behaviours to deep-rooted ethnic ties and argues that subjective elements which emerged or are believed to have emerged in pre-modern times, such as shared symbols, traditions, myths and memories or sentiments, helped to sustain the relationship between various elites and the lower strata. They made it possible for the elites to be seen as legitimate representatives of 'the people', and 'the people' influenced their political leaders and upper classes as well as the intelligentsia by delimiting the frameworks of their political and cultural goals and instruments. Consequently, in many cases, the prior existence of linguistic, ethnic and religious communities and the continuing emotional attachments of many people to these communities formed the basis of subsequent nationhood and endowed it with its 'everyday' qualities. For instance, as demonstrated by Smith, Great Britain, France and Spain were formed over the centuries around 'ethnic cores' (the English, northern French and Castilians) with their particular cultures and symbolisms. Hence, without the particular pre-modern ethnic elements, it would have been difficult, if not impossible, for modern states, however strong and efficient, to have forged the nation.[33]

No causal relation between nationalism and modernity

The third school of thought, which contains the perennialist and primordial perspectives, denies any causality between nationalism and modernity.

The perennialist perspective argues that nations, though they may have spread more rapidly in the modern period, did not emerge at the time of the French and American revolutions and nor were they the product of modernity. As claimed by Hugh Seton-Watson, 'The doctrine of nationalism dates from the age of the French Revolution, but nations existed before the doctrine was formulated.'[34]

The perennialist perspective argues that the origins of a large number of European nations (and their nationalisms) can be traced back to the Middle Ages, or even to antiquity. In this regard, Seton-Watson distinguished between 'old' and 'new' nations. He maintained that 'the old nations of Europe in 1789 were the English, Scots, French, Dutch, Castilians and Portuguese in the west; the Danes and Swedes in the north; and the Hungarians, Poles and the Russians in the east' and that these nations had a 'continuous' character, as they acquired national identity or national consciousness before the formulation of the doctrine of nationalism (even if some of them needed an independence movement to assert themselves as sovereign states). 'New' nations such as Germany, Italy or Ireland acquired national consciousness only in the nineteenth century – at the same time as their nationalist movements were created.[35] Another perennialist, Adrian Hastings, stressed the premodern and Christian provenance of nations and nationalism.[36] According to Hastings, nations and nationalism were products of the spread of Christianity in Europe, because Christianity sanctioned the use of vernacular languages in biblical translations and in the liturgy, and nations were founded on literary languages. Hastings also asserted that since Christianity had adopted the Old Testament, it also adopted the Old Testament ideal of a polity. As a result, the biblical ideal of the ancient Israelite polity, with its unification or merger of land, people and religion, which Christianity later spread throughout Europe, was mono-national. Hastings suggested that since other religious traditions have not had such a political prototype, nations and nationalism are exclusively Judaeo-Christian and European phenomena.

The perennialist perspective emphasises that all nations have a history, some of them a long and brilliant one, even though not all of them had a national consciousness in the symbolic year of 1789. It also claims that the terms 'state-building' and 'state sovereignties' are decoupled from the terms 'nation' or 'nationalism' and that the disappearance of state sovereignties has not caused the disappearance of nations, any more than the emergence of new states has sufficed to create new nations.[37]

The primordialist perspective also denies that there is any causality between nationalism and modernity. It argues that nations have deep roots in 'the first order of time', have especially deep-rooted cultural ties and that genetically determined individual or kin behaviour contributed to the development of nations. For instance, Edward Shils asserts that primordial ties always persisted alongside the secular, civil ties and that personal identity is based on the continuing strength and hold of attachments to kin, race, language, religion, customs and territory:

> As I see it . . . modern society is . . . no Gesellschaft, soulless, egotistical, loveless, faithless, utterly impersonal and lacking any integrative forces other than interest or coercion. It is held together by an infinity of personal attachments, moral obligations in concrete contexts, professional and creative pride, individual ambition, primordial affinities and a civil sense . . .[38]

According to the sociobiological approach of Pierre Van den Berghe, nations (and races) can be seen as a consequence of the primary reproductive drive of people. Van den Berghe maintains that myths of ethnic origins correspond to real biological origins as 'culture acts on genes and genes act on culture'.[39] In this regard Van den Berghe speaks of the 'enlightened self-interest' of individuals, which includes their striving for better 'genetic fitness' through extending their gene pool beyond the nuclear or larger family (lineages or clans) to wider kin groups defined in racial, ethnic, linguistic, religious or national terms, but, in most cases, not beyond these wider kin groups. Cultural symbols such as language, religion or skin colour are used as markers of biological affinity. That is the reason why people who are not directly related treat unknown co-ethnics as kin and are ready to care for them:

> Kin-selection theory says in effect that our altruism is proportional to the number of genes we share with the beneficiaries

of our altruism. By increasing the reproductive fitness of those who share some of our genes, we indirectly, and to the extent that we are related, enhance our own fitness or, more precisely, that of our genes.[40]

Nationalism and democracy

In terms of the number of analyses, the relationship between nationalism and democracy has been rather a minor and more recent research focus. Nonetheless, we can distinguish two main streams of research interest within this scholarship.

The first refers to the significance of nationalism for the emergence of modern democratic systems, while the second refers to the function nationalism has in the framework of democratic systems, especially in socially stratified, economically differentiated and culturally plural polities. Here, in turn, we can find two arguments. The first is of normative character and suggests that nationalism is instrumental to a well-functioning democracy; it may even be indispensable since it provides social solidarity and relations of mutual trust required by democratic institutions and helps to develop and sustain a structure of coercive institutions with a capacity to make political decisions and to enforce them by limiting people's liberty. The second argument denies this importance and maintains that civic ties between citizens engaged in the public discourse have more relevance for addressing the functional needs of democratic systems.

Table 3.3 Relationship between nationalism and democracy

	Functions of nationalism for democracy	
Nationalist basis of democracy	Normative instrumentalist perspective	Non-national public deliberation perspective

Few scholars have represented the thesis that democracy emerged with nationalism, or even through nationalism. Nonetheless, we can resort to some interesting theoretical and empirical findings. According to Liah Greenfeld, the core elements of nationalism, which are the location of sovereignty within the people and the recognition of fundamental equality among the various strata of the people, constitute at the same time the basic tenets of democracy. Hence, democracy was born with the sense of nationality. Greenfeld asserts that democracy and nationality are inherently linked, and democracy cannot be understood other than in the context of nationality.

> Nationalism was the form in which democracy appeared in the world, contained in the idea of the nation as a butterfly in a cocoon. Originally, nationalism developed as democracy; where the conditions of such original development persisted, the identity between the two was maintained.[41]

England was the first place where democracy emerged together with nationalism in the sixteenth century as the borders between the nobility and the commoners were replaced by the construction of the English people, which, in turn, replaced the king as the bearer of sovereignty. As nationalism spread all over the world and the emphasis of the idea of the nation changed from the sovereignty of the people to the uniqueness of the people, the original sameness between nationalism and democracy was lost. Greenfeld suggests that democracy might be an inherent predisposition in some nations, since it is inherent in their own self-understanding as nations, whereas it might be alien to other nations, and the capability to adopt and maintain it would require a change of national identity. One of the most important consequences of this is, therefore, that democracy may not be exportable.[42]

Greenfeld's thesis seems, however, to be of limited range, for instance when it comes under scrutiny with regard to several democratic systems in the pre-modern era. We might think of democracies that developed without the elements of nationality during the classical period of Ancient Greece in the city-state of Athens and other Greek cities, in the Northern Italian city-states or in the Polish Nobles' Democracy.

The second research stream focuses on the functions of nationalism for democratic systems. The normative instrumentalist argument is a domain of scholars representing liberal nationalism. We can find the intellectual precursors of this scholarship in Rousseau's and Mill's work. Rousseau argued that a corporate identity was needed to maintain the people's unity and the stability of the democratic system and that the process of nation-building which generated a common (national) identity would lead to the mutual trust necessary to secure loyalty and sacrifice.[43] Mill also argued that democracy could only flourish under the condition of the coincidence of the 'boundaries of government' with those of nationality.[44] Contemporary proponents of this argument claim that, in this sense, a shared national identity and nationalism, both terms being used synonymously, are instrumental to securing a communicative competence of the citizens, to creating and maintaining trust between different societal groups with possibly conflicting interests as well as to strengthening a collective sentiment among the citizens. Communicative competence refers to the ability to communicate with each other and to interpret the behaviour of other people by means of linguistic homogeneity and cultural similarity.[45] Trust means that participants abide by the decisions that are reached even in cases of electoral losses and they believe that the arguments others put forward are sincerely expressed and justified.[46] Linguistic and cultural communication codes, trust and a collective sense of belonging are, in turn, instrumental to building up a high level of 'organic' identification with the polity in the sense that people know where their democracy comes from and what its ideational basis is, and that they accept and internalise this knowledge. They are also instrumental to achieving two constituent elements of democracy: representation and participation.[47] From identification, representation and participation results, in turn, the legitimacy of a democratic system – the moral obligation of those legitimately ruled by the ruler to obey, and the moral immunity of the ruler from coercive interference in the exercise and enforcement of legitimate rule[48] – and, with the legitimacy, the stability and endurance of a democratic system.

As far as identification with the polity is concerned, the normative instrumentalist perspective claims that a common nationality and nationalism provide the narrative basis for this identification with a set of 'historical myths'. These 'historical myths' provide reassurance that there exists a continuity between generations and that the national community to which a person now belongs is based in history and also stretches forward into the future. At the same time, they forge a community in which citizens have obligations to one another arising from sacrifices made in the past by some members of the community on behalf of other members.[49] As David Miller argues:

Because our forebears have toiled and spilt their blood to build and defend the nation, we who are born into it inherit an obligation to continue their work, which we discharge partly towards our contemporaries and partly towards our descendants.[50]

Since this community stretches back and forward across the generations, it is not one that the present generation can renounce.[51] Hence, with regard to democracy, the present generation feels obliged to maintain the democratic institutions that its ancestors created, and this maintenance belongs to the most important national sainthoods.

With regard to representation, the normative instrumentalist perspective argues that a shared national identity and nationalism provide a basis for the unity of the people which is important to the idea that members of a political community can and are willing to elect others to be their representatives and that the elected can take binding decisions, including the fundamental foreign and domestic issues of the state, on behalf of the people. Hence, the action of the representatives must be seen as legitimate and genuine expression of collective will. Besides, members must trust that others are willing to respect their interests and those who lose in one election are likely to abide by the results only if they believe that they might win in the future and that others will abide by the results if this is this case.[52] However, in societies with ethnic or national divisions, the rule of majority vote is a mechanism of exclusion, since different national communities always vote for nationality-aligned parties and the elections are similar to a census, with minority groups being permanently excluded from power.[53] What is more, since the majority is never afraid to change to minority status, in which it would be in need of a majority self-restraint, it has no incentives to refrain from oppressing the minority. As a whole segment of the population can never participate in the process of decision-making in the state in which it lives, the basic conditions for responsible democracy are not fulfilled. Further, the normative instrumentalist perspective claims that there is little trust between the different nationalities and the members of the minority are reluctant to address their problems to representatives of the governing majority, since they know that the government has been elected by votes of the other nationality and will always be re-elected by voters from the other nationality. Hence, vertical dialogue between the national minority and the governing majority is difficult, if possible at all, and the particular interests of the national minority cannot be realised, often even remaining unnoticed.[54]

With regard to participation, scholars such as Will Kymlicka assert that democratic politics takes place 'in the vernacular'. Real democratic processes can take place only in communities that share a common language since citizens feel comfortable discussing important political issues in their own language and territorialised linguistic political units are regarded as the best and possibly the only sort of forum for genuinely participatory and deliberative politics.[55] In a similar vein, Brian Barry argues that even liberal states need to have a cultural commonality and their citizens need to speak one language since political communities are bound to be linguistic communities and politics is linguistically constructed:

> We can negotiate our way across language barriers but we cannot deliberate together about the way in which our common life is to be conducted unless we share a language. Where historic communities based on language exist already, there is no satisfactory alternative to recognizing them as political communities as well . . .[56]

This is also characteristic for states that promote bilingualism or multilingualism, for instance Canada or Belgium, where the necessary fluency in more than one language is usually limited to the elites. Extensive translation facilities amongst people of different languages are possible but they are extremely expensive and difficult to manage.[57] Therefore, horizontal dialogue between the different nationalities is barely possible. Consequently, the formation and formulation of collective will is extremely difficult, and democratic politics in multinational states can function only if it is limited to political elites and only if these elites are not adversarial towards each other – a rarely fulfilled condition.

In contrast, the non-national public deliberation perspective, which has generated a number of hybrid positions such as 'discursive democracy',[58] 'procedural democracy',[59] 'post-national politics'[60] or 'constitutional patriotism'[61] agrees with normative instrumentalists that a shared public culture is important for the functional needs of democratic systems, but it denies that public culture depends upon a network of specifically national ties and sentiments. It asserts that trust, communicative competence and collective sentiment are not scarce resources that nation-states have inherited from previous generations but are goals to be continuously promoted and advanced – often slowly over time – by a plurality of actors through widespread participation in public deliberation marked by the rules of political equality and reasonableness. The non-national public deliberation perspective turns to the procedures of the democratic politics itself; it emphasises democratic practices, which motivate citizens to participate and behave in a rational way and reach mutually acceptable collective decisions, and, at the same time, discourage political inequalities and egoistic bargaining. Jürgen Habermas, one of the most prominent representatives of this school of thought, speaks in this sense of an 'ideal speech situation' in which each person is fully informed and has equal power and in which all essential issues of the polity are subjected to real discussion to which all reasonable persons would then assent.[62] Treating other fellow citizens with respect and recognising their equal political and moral rights provides an instructive way of avoiding resort to national bonds. According to Habermas, it is possible to integrate new citizens into a liberal state without requiring of them assimilation to the culture of the national majority. New members of the polity must only recognise and support the principles of the constitution. Habermas suggests that the fusion in most European countries between the culture of the national majority and the general political culture should be dissolved and the 'post-national' shared political culture should be uncoupled from the subcultures and their 'pre-political' roots.[63]

Nationalism and distributive justice

The third main research focus is the relationship between nationalism and distributive justice. The most important question here is the significance of nationalism for the emergence and maintenance of egalitarian political and social systems.

Table 3.4 Relationship between nationalism and distributive justice

Communitarian perspective	Cosmopolitan perspective

Within this stream of scholarship we can distinguish two major schools of thought. The point of departure of the first school of thought, which can be called communitarian – and which to a great extent overlaps with the normative instrumentalist perspective on the relationship between nationalism and democracy discussed above – is that a system of justice, in order to be successfully implemented, must be one with which the participants can identify and that the idea of distributive justice presupposes a bounded world – the national political community – within which distributions takes place: a group of people committed to dividing, exchanging and sharing social goods, first of all among themselves. Members of this bounded world distribute power to one another and try to avoid sharing it with non-members.[64] Without strong social support every distributive system is condemned to collapse.

In this sense, representatives of the communitarian school of thought see a common nationality and nationalism, with both terms being used synonymously, as an indispensable instrument to sustain egalitarian principles of national social citizenship and social justice and they regard the persistence of nationalism as something justified and desirable under normative points of view. Nationalism is considered to be unavoidable not only because it serves to bind members of a community to the place they consider their homeland and supports their overall cooperation but, even more important, it encourages them to recognise that they have special ties to their compatriots, and that they owe their compatriots more than they owe to non-members, including even greater personal sacrifices.[65] Hence, co-nationals are bound in a double way, as they owe humanistic obligations to each other as human beings as well as political and social obligations to each other as members of a historically grown collective project.[66]

Common nationality and nationalism have these effects on individuals and communities because they help to generate trust and a strong specific feeling of solidarity and loyalty, which are seen as the most important preconditions for a just distribution of welfare.[67] What is more, the communitarian perspective emphasises that trust, solidarity and loyalty can only be achieved within the borders of clearly delineated national communities:

> Language, history, and culture come together . . . to produce a collective consciousness. National character, conceived as a fixed and permanent mental set, is obviously a myth but the sharing of sensibilities and intuitions among the members of a historical community is a fact of life.[68]

It is believed that, because of a shared nationality and nationalism, in modern complex societies, which recognise many separate spheres of distributional justice, inequalities in one sphere can be compensated for by inequalities in other spheres. Consequently, it is because of nationalism that the overall equality of members as well as the stability of the political and social system can be sustained.[69] In sum, nationalism is regarded as a valuable political means, under certain circumstances the only available one, to develop and sustain appropriate structures of social justice.

Whereas the communitarian perspective argues that in homogeneous nation-states, especially liberal states, distributive justice would not pose severe problems, it maintains, on the other hand, that in states divided in terms of national identities and national loyalties, or in states with a weak sense of common nationality, social justice is extremely precarious over a longer period of time. Even the very presence of sizeable ethnic diversity erodes the welfare state, regardless of what sorts of policies governments adopt to manage that diversity. Kymlicka and Banting sum up this argument as follows:

> That ethnic diversity as such makes it more difficult to sustain expansive social programs and to achieve substantial redistribution toward the poor through taxes and transfers. This is said to be true because it is difficult to generate feelings of national solidarity and trust across ethnic lines. We can formulate this as the hypothesis that the greater the size of ethnic minorities as a percentage of the population, the harder it is to sustain a robust welfare state.[70]

For this reason, as illustrated by David Miller, one of the most prominent representatives of communitarian thinking, social citizenship must have a communitarian background, since people who no longer consider themselves vulnerable to the socioeconomic risks against which they used to be protected by traditional insurance models of the welfare state would withdraw their support for redistributive institutions. To avoid this social desertion, which would be based on egoistic but – admittedly – rational grounds, the rights of citizenship must necessarily be embedded in the moral relationships of shared nationality. Hence, the legitimacy of political rights and social institutions requires the deeper, and prior, mutual ethical obligations that can exist only between co-nationals.[71] Attempts made by national governments, especially Western ones, to manage ethnical diversity by accommodating it by means of multiculturalism policies, rather than ignoring or suppressing it – are believed only to aggravate the problem. The communitarian perspective holds that the 'multiculturalism policies'

> adopted to recognize or accommodate ethnic groups tend to further undermine national solidarity and trust. Such policies . . . include multicultural education, legal exemptions, and funding of ethnic groups. We can formulate this as the hypothesis that the more a country embraces the multicultural politics of (ethnic) recognition, the harder it is to sustain the politics of (economic) redistribution . . .[72]

Communitarian theorists not only explore the relationship between nationalism and social justice but they usually tend to make ideological statements in defence of nationalism. They strongly privilege the right of national communities to determine the rules of membership according to their cultural norms and their will to remain in a majoritarian position within the structures of the state. They also deem the obligations, which members of the community have to compatriots, the most significant and demanding moral commitments, even though they are not always based on free choice.[73]

The second perspective on the relationship between nationalism and distributive justice is cosmopolitan. It has its precursors in ancient Greece and especially in the eighteenth-century philosophy of Kant. Being a broad intellectual mainstream and academic paradigm, it is not an explicit research on nationalism; rather it treats nationalism as a normative adversary and an analytical opposite. The cosmopolitan perspective is strongly normative. In general, we can distinguish two versions of the cosmopolitan counter-arguments with regard to distributive justice. The point of departure for the strong cosmopolitan argument is that there is no good reason to privilege the nation-state as a focus of solidarity, a domain of mutual responsibility and a locus of citizenship. The nation-state is seen as a morally arbitrary community, with membership determined, for the most part, by the lottery of birth or parentage. Therefore, the strong version of cosmopolitanism rejects the importance of nationalism and maintains that egalitarian institutions and welfare systems can and should also be achieved beyond the borders of the nation-state.[74] It does so by using three main arguments, in the moral, political and cultural dimensions.[75] In moral terms, strong cosmopolitanism assigns priority not to groups but to the dignity, moral status and interests of individuals and it denies favouritism of every kind. It affirms the equal moral worth of each individual, regardless of his or her race, ethnicity, nationality, religion or other forms of group membership. It thus demands that each person's rightful claims are given a fair consideration. In political terms, strong cosmopolitanism asserts that nationalism and the selfish behaviour of nation-states are responsible for the failure to achieve a just global social order. It suggests that political authority should be shifted from individual states to supranational political institutions in order to overcome disadvantages created by the traditional world model of nation-states. Hence, it is committed to reforms of political, economic and social institutions at the national and international level, which are blocked by nationalist state actors. In cultural terms, strong cosmopolitanism rejects the nationalist assumption that individuals can be committed to share burdens and sacrifices only with their compatriots and within one particular culture. It claims that individuals can conduct a satisfactory life both within and beyond the confines of particular cultural spaces. In this sense, it believes that individuals can have multiple identities shaped by various cultures, and that they would be ready to share their welfare with other human beings. In sum, the very ideal of the strong version of the cosmopolitan perspective is – according to Martha Nussbaum – the person whose allegiance is to the worldwide community of human beings, not to his or her nation, and the person who does not emphasise national pride, which is morally dangerous and subversive of the worthy moral ideals of global justice and equality.[76]

The point of departure also for the weaker version of the cosmopolitan argument is that the boundaries of the nation-state should not set limits to our moral responsibility and political commitments.[77] The weaker cosmopolitanism also argues that most of the problems arise from the processes of growing global flows of money, people, goods, services and that global effects of pollution, diseases and communication undermine the distinctions between the 'internal' sphere – local, regional or national – and the 'external' sphere – transnational or international – that have previously been central to the creation and practices of nation-states. Therefore, it also maintains that it is necessary to construct new guarantees of universally valid human rights and thus to approach a more just global distribution of goods and life chances rather than to perpetuate the existing patterns of the distribution of social and economic resources. However, the weaker cosmopolitan argument highlights both the practical and the ethical limitations of cosmopolitan democracy and distributive justice and suggests, in response to these limitations, a more 'secure stepping-stone towards the cosmopolitan goal of alleviating global injustices'.[78] It regards its own validity not as absolute but rather as relative to other forms of inter-societal relations, including those of the nation-states.[79] It does not make any assumption that cosmopolitan social forms should supersede the world of nation-states.

> The core of the argument is that cosmopolitan democracy needs to be reframed and practiced, in the first instance, as a national rather than international or global project. This means that, instead of welcoming the weakening of nationalism as a force that constrains cosmopolitan goals, cosmopolitans should be searching for ways to rescue, reframe and harness nationalism so that it takes on a more cosmopolitan character.[80]

The weaker cosmopolitan perspective asserts that the realisation of the liberal cosmopolitan project of turning the international law of states into a cosmopolitan law of individuals needs to be accepted by nation-states. Hence, it suggests exploring what kind of nation-states would serve as the basis for a new cosmopolitan global order.[81] In sum, it assumes that processes of change from nationalist to cosmopolitan forms of political, economic and cultural relations will require a 'reconciliation' between different interests at several levels and can take place only in a longer-term perspective.

Other important research foci

As a complex phenomenon, nationalism can be studied from several perspectives. Besides the aforementioned research foci of nationalism regarding modernity, democracy and distributive justice we can identity four additional research foci of nationalism research: those regarding regionalism, globalisation, religion and gender. We will refer to these in more detail in Chapter 7 and Chapter 8.

The first focus relates to regionalism in terms of both subnational regionalism and supranational integration, such as in the European Union. Regarding subnational regionalism, some scholars speak of a scalar turn in political and economic geography, which involves an emphasis on the changing interrelationships between institutions at different spatial levels of region, nation and Europe. This restructuring is expected to have implications for nation-state political and economic functions and their shift to a plethora of subnational institutional entities, which questions the empirical validity of nationalism; understood is the claim that only the nation-states offer the optimal framework for political and economic activity. This position draws on comparative studies of regionalism and explores the tensions present in the new regionalist territorial settlements. These tensions crystallise around the contending efforts to construct regional identities.[82] In addition, scholars begin focusing on a horizontal reorganisation between various subnational and regional units, which in turn form boundary-crossing networks. These conceptions of regions stress flexibility and elasticity in contrast to the traditional state-centric perspective of fixed and static nation-states and their nationalisms. Consequently, the disintegration of the international system into new regional units leads to calls for new mechanisms of political control beyond the nation-state. Hence, ideas of international management via international regimes or new governance structures without government are developed with the goal of solving global and regional collective problems.[83] The trend moves from nationalism and the hierarchical control by the states over their citizens and societies to a horizontal constructivism and transactionism. According to this trend, the notion of nationalism becomes devalued, since new regional units become free to promote new political solutions that are alternatives both to the international hegemonic structure and to the politics of discipline of the nation-state. This development seems to lead scholars away from studying military and political issues and towards those involving society, economy and culture.[84] This research focus is based on the idea that late capitalism promotes regional and subnational conflicts rather than international ones. In this perspective, the term 'self-determination' as the basis for nationalism ceases to be a sensible notion, since nations are no longer the exclusive units for the collective processes of 'self-determining'. For instance, scholars exploring Catalan and Basque identities argue that the collective identity in both cases is cultural rather than economic. Precisely because it has been challenged by the powers of the central Spanish state, it has led to crisis and military dictatorship. Therefore, only democratisation was capable of producing guarantees of autonomy for the regions, showing that these cannot be abolished in the name of the Spanish nation.[85]

Concerning the latter meaning of regionalism as supranational integration, this has been increasingly regarded in the context of European integration. The issue of nationalism and supranational integration has been discussed in relation to several aspects. One of them, for instance, is the question of whether the EU strengthens the nation-state by mitigating the negative effects of globalisation or whether it weakens it even further.[86] Further, how far the European Union questions the traditional relationship between nation and state by undermining traditional sovereignty and weakening the need for statehood has been increasingly discussed. According to Michael Keating, minority nationalist movements have in many cases adopted European integration as a part of their ideology and strategy to resist majority nationalism. Therefore, they apply 'new regionalist' postulates to provide new opportunities for political action below and above the nation-state. Since the European Union constructs opportunity channels for territorial movements and grants minority protection rights, it encourages minority nationalism of a regional range and weakens the traditional nationalism of nation-states.[87]

The relationship between nationalism and the processes of regional integration will be thoroughly examined in Chapter 7. Here, we give a short review of the argument. Frequently, the point of departure for studies on this relationship is the widespread assumption about the erosion of national sovereignty, which entails the parting of the overlapping cultural and political spheres of the nation and the state. It is maintained that we are confronted with a reversion of the Gellnerian principle of nationalism. The invalidation of the Gellnerian principle of integration between culture and political authority within the modern nation-state has significant consequences at the level of national identity and the politics of nationalism. The issue is, however, a complex one, since new identities do not necessarily replace national identity or make nationalism redundant. Therefore, as we argue in Chapter 7, the question rather pertains to the new complexity of regionalism, nationalism and European integration. It should deal with the semantic triangle of regionalism, nationalism and European integration as the concept of regionalism becomes semantically intertwined with nationalism and conceptually placed in the context of the EU. While the scholarly debate on regionalism oscillates between nationalism and European integration, it seems to suffer from two fallacies. First, one can observe a tendency to ontologise regionalism in the same way as other collective phenomena, of which nationalism is another example. Second, approaches to regionalism tend to mimic the characteristics of the nation in the analysis of regions and regionalism. In this sense regions are treated as partial nations, or nations on a smaller scale. This mimicry in the study of regionalism arises from the application of categories from the study of nationalism and nation-states to regionalism and regions. As suggested in Chapter 7, this problem can be solved by de-ontologising regions and regionalism through applying the concept of regional identity, in a similar way as scholars approach the concept of a nation by exploring national identity. The ontologisation of regions arises from ascribing agency to regions, ignoring the fact that regional actors, rather than regions, integrate or make decisions. Accordingly, understanding regionalisation is easier through an examination of interactions between regional actors and their regional identity. In many cases regionalism and nationalism mesh into each other so that we are unable to distinguish between regionalism and nationalism and we question whether we are in fact dealing with new phenomena (regional nationalism, minority nationalism). However, regionalism or new nationalism occurs against the background of European integration. Further, as Chapter 7 suggests, we should focus on the issue of collective identity in the EU as a marker of European nationalism, since the EU is at pains to construct collective identity in a way that emulates the integrative logic of national identity. It therefore attempts to generate a national sense of belonging in a non-nation-state environment. Nevertheless, the EU applies identity technologies towards its citizens. The political elites of the EU appear to be aware of the stabilising effects of collective identity and attempt to generate it, albeit in a more subtle manner than the EU member states can do by reverting to nationalism. Therefore, the 'nationalism light' of the EU either uses selected identity technologies of nationalism or uses them at a more subtle level, as the EU cannot exactly emulate nationalism regarding its strength, sacrificial appeal and aggressiveness.

Notes

1. Anthony D. Smith, *Nationalism. Theory, Ideology, History* (Cambridge: Polity Press, 2001), p. 49.
2. Ibid. p. 51.
3. Ernest Gellner, *Thought and Change* (London: Weidenfeld and Nicolson, 1964), p. 152.
4. Ernest Gellner, *Nations and Nationalism* (Ithaca, NY: Cornell University Press, 1983), p. 48.
5. Ibid. p. 18.
6. Elie Kedourie, *Nationalism* (London: Hutchinson & Co., 1960).
7. Alan Beattie, 'Elie Kedourie's philosophical history', *Middle Eastern Studies* 33, 5 (1998), pp. 109–32 (p. 114).
8. Ibid. p. 114.
9. Ibid. p. 114.
10. Ibid. p. 114.
11. Cornelius Castoriadis, *The Imaginary Institution of Society* (Cambridge: Polity Press, 1987).
12. Eric Hobsbawm, *Nations and Nationalism Since 1780. Programme, Myth, Reality* (Cambridge, New York and Melbourne: Cambridge University Press, 1990), p. 47.
13. Benedict Anderson, *Imagined Communities. Reflections on the Origin and Spread of Nationalism* (London and New York: Verso, 2006, rev. edn), pp. 5–6.
14. Ibid. p. 7.
15. Ibid. p. 7.
16. Liah Greenfeld, *Nationalism. Five Roads to Modernity* (Cambridge, MA and London: Harvard University Press, 1993), p. 10.
17. Ibid. p. 487.
18. Ibid. p. 487.
19. Ibid. p. 487, and Liah Greenfeld, 'Is nation unavoidable? Is nation unavoidable today?', in Hanspeter Kriesi, Klaus Armingeon, Hannes Siegrist and Andreas Wimmer (eds), *Nation and National Identity: The European Experience in Perspective* (Zurich: Rüegger, 1999), p. 39.
20. Greenfeld, 'Is nation unavoidable? Is nation unavoidable today?', p. 40.
21. Greenfeld, *Nationalism. Five Roads to Modernity*, p. 488.
22. Ibid. p. 488.
23. Hans Kohn, 'The nature of nationalism', *American Political Science Review* 33, 6 (1939), pp. 1,001–21 (p. 1,001).
24. Ibid. p. 1,004.
25. Ibid. p. 1,002.
26. Ibid. p. 1,002.
27. Ibid. p. 1,001.
28. Ibid. p. 1,002.
29. Ibid. p. 1,004.
30. Anthony D. Smith, 'The limits of everyday nationhood', *Ethnicities* 8, 4 (2008), pp. 563–73 (p. 569).
31. Anthony D. Smith, 'Gastronomy or geology? The role of nationalism in the reconstruction of nations', *Nations and Nationalism* 1, 1 (1995), pp. 3–23 (p. 13).

32. Siniša Malešević, '"Divine ethnies" and "sacred nations": Anthony D. Smith and the neo-Durkhemian theory of nationalism', *Nationalism and Ethnic Politics* 10 (2004), pp. 561–93 (pp. 564–5).
33. Smith, 'The limits of everyday nationhood', p. 569.
34. Hugh Seton-Watson, *Nations and States: An Inquiry into the Origins of Nations and the Politics of Nationalism* (London: Methuen & Co., 1977), p. 6.
35. Ibid. pp. 6–7.
36. Adrian Hastings, *The Construction of Nationhood: Ethnicity, Religion and Nationalism* (Cambridge: Cambridge University Press, 1997).
37. Seton-Watson, *Nations and States*, p. 2.
38. Edward Shils, 'Primordial, personal, sacred and civil ties: some particular observations on the relationships of sociological research and theory', *British Journal of Sociology* 8, 2 (1957), pp. 130–45 (p. 131).
39. Pierre L. Van den Berghe, 'Sociobiology, dogma, and ethics', *The Wilson Quarterly* 1, 4 (1977), pp. 121–6 (p. 124).
40. Ibid. p. 125.
41. Greenfeld, *Nationalism. Five Roads to Modernity*, p. 10.
42. Ibid. p. 10.
43. Jean-Jacques Rousseau, *Discourse on Political Economy and The Social Contract* (New York: Oxford University Press, 2009).
44. John Stuart Mill, *Utilitarianism, On Liberty, Considerations on Representative Government* (London: Everyman, 1993), p. 394.
45. For this argument see Brian Barry, 'Self-government revisited', in David Miller and Larry Siedentop (eds), *The Nature of Political Theory* (Oxford: Clarendon Press, 1983), pp. 121–54 (pp. 144–5).
46. David Miller, 'Democracy's domain', *Philosophy and Public Affairs* 37, 3 (2009), pp. 201–28 (p. 209).
47. Margaret Moore, 'Normative justifications for liberal nationalism: justice, democracy and national identity', *Nations and Nationalism* 7, 1 (2001), pp. 1–20 (p. 7).
48. Arthur Isak Applbaum, 'Legitimacy without the duty to obey', *Philosophy and Public Affairs* 38, 3 (2010), pp. 215–39 (pp. 217–18).
49. See David Miller, *On Nationality* (Oxford and New York: Oxford University Press, 1995), pp. 23–4.
50. Ibid. p. 23.
51. Ibid. p. 24.
52. Will Kymlicka and Christine Straehle, 'Cosmopolitanism, nation-states, and minority nationalism: a critical review of recent literature', *European Journal of Philosophy* 7, 1 (1999), pp. 65–88 (p. 70).
53. Margaret Moore, 'Normative justifications for liberal nationalism: justice, democracy and national identity', *Nations and Nationalism* 7, 1 (2001), p. 9.
54. Ibid. p. 10.
55. Will Kymlicka, *Politics in the Vernacular: Nationalism, Multiculturalism and Citizenship* (New York: Oxford University Press, 2001), p. 324.
56. Brian Barry, *Culture and Equality* (Cambridge, MA: Harvard University Press, 1993), p. 227.
57. Kymlicka and Straehle, 'Cosmopolitanism, nation-states, and minority nationalism', p. 70.
58. John S. Dryzek, *Discursive Democracy: Politics, Policy, and Political Science* (Cambridge: Cambridge University Press, 1990).
59. Joseph M. Bessette, *The Mild Voice of Reason: Deliberative Democracy and American National Government* (Chicago, IL: University of Chicago Press, 1994).
60. Jürgen Habermas, *The Postnational Constellation: Political Essays* (Cambridge: Polity Press, 2001).
61. Ciaran Cronin, 'Democracy and collective identity: in defence of constitutional patriotism', *European Journal of Philosophy* 11, 1 (2003), pp. 1–28.

62. Jürgen Habermas, *The Theory of Communicative Action: Reason and the Rationalization of Society* (Cambridge: Polity Press, 1986), pp. 25–6.
63. Jürgen Habermas, *Die Einbeziehung des Anderen* (Frankfurt am Main: Suhrkamp Verlag, 1996).
64. Michael Walzer, *Spheres of Justice. A Defense of Pluralism and Equality* (New York: Basic Books, 1983), p. 31.
65. David Miller, 'Nationalism', in John Dryzek, Bonnie Honig and Anne Phillips (eds), *The Oxford Handbook of Political Theory* (Oxford: Oxford University Press, 2008), pp. 529–30. For the same line of reasoning, see also Jeff McMahan, 'The limits of national partiality', in Robert McKim and Jeff McMahan (eds), *The Morality of Nationalism* (New York: Oxford University Press, 1997), pp. 107–38 (p. 129).
66. Richard Dagger, 'Rights, boundaries, and the bonds of community: a qualified defense of moral parochialism', *American Political Science Review* 79 (1985), pp. 436–47 (p. 443).
67. Miller, *On Nationality*.
68. Walzer, *Spheres of Justice*, p. 28.
69. Ibid. pp. 3–30.
70. Will Kymlicka and Keith Banting, 'Immigration, multiculturalism, and the welfare state', *Ethics & International Affairs* 20, 3 (2006), pp. 281–304 (p. 283).
71. David Miller, *On Nationality*. For the critique of this reasoning, see Neil Hibbert, 'Citizenship and the welfare state: a critique of David Miller's theory of nationality', *Canadian Journal of Political Science/Revue canadienne de science politique* 41, 1 (2008), pp. 169–86.
72. Kymlicka and Banting, 'Immigration, multiculturalism, and the welfare state', p. 283.
73. Miller, 'Nationalism', pp. 529–30.
74. For an example of the strong version of the cosmopolitan argument against nationalism, see Thomas W. Pogge, 'Cosmopolitanism and sovereignty', *Ethics* 103, 1 (1992), pp. 48–75.
75. For these three arguments we follow the illustration made by Jones in Charles Jones, 'Human rights and moral cosmopolitanism', *Critical Review of International Social and Political Philosophy* 13, 1 (2010), pp. 115–35 (p. 116).
76. Martha C. Nussbaum, 'Patriotism and cosmopolitanism', in Martha C. Nussbaum (ed.), *For Love of Country* (Boston, MA: Beacon Press, 2002), pp. 3–20 (p. 4).
77. For the weaker version of cosmopolitanism, see, for example, Robert Fine, *Cosmopolitanism* (London and New York: Routledge, 2007), David Held, *Democracy and the Global Order* (Cambridge: Polity Press, 1995) and Daniel Archibugi and David Held (eds), *Cosmopolitan Democracy: An Agenda for a New World Order* (Cambridge: Polity Press, 1995).
78. Robyn Eckersley, 'From cosmopolitan nationalism to cosmopolitan democracy', *Review of International Studies* 33 (2007), pp. 675–92 (p. 676).
79. Fine, *Cosmopolitanism*, pp. xii–xiii.
80. Eckersley, 'From cosmopolitan nationalism to cosmopolitan democracy', p. 676.
81. Ibid. p. 676.
82. Iain Deas and Benito Giordano, 'Regions, city-regions, identity and institution building: contemporary experiences of the scalar turn in Italy and England', *Journal of Urban Affairs* 25, 2 (2003), pp. 225–46.
83. John Gerard Ruggie, 'International regimes, transactions, and change: embedded liberalism in the postwar economic order', *International Organization* 36, 2 (1982), pp. 379–415; Andreas Hasenclever, Peter Mayer and Volker Rittberger, 'Integrating theories of international regimes', *Review of International Studies* 26, 1 (2000), pp. 3–33.
84. Raimo Väyrynen, 'Regionalism: old and new', *International Studies Review* 5 (2003), pp. 25–51.
85. Jordi Solé Tura, 'The Spanish case: remarks on the general theories of nationalism', *International Political Science Review* 10, 3 (1989), pp. 183–9.
86. Andrew Moravcsik, *Why the European Union Strengthens the State: Domestic Politics*

and International Cooperation (Cambridge, MA: Center for European Studies, Harvard University, 1994), Working Paper Series #52; Tanja A. Boerzel, 'Does European integration really strengthen the state? The case of the Federal Republic of Germany', *Regional & Federal Studies* 7, 3 (1997), pp. 87–113; Viktoria Kaina and Ireneusz Paweł Karolewski, 'Why we should not believe every lesson Andrew Moravcsik teaches us: a response', *Politische Vierteljahresschrift* 48, 4 (2007), pp. 740–57.
87. Michael Keating, 'European integration and the nationalities question', *Politics & Society* 32, 3 (2004), pp. 367–88.

CHAPTER FOUR

Typologies of Nationalism

In the literature we can find several more or less successful attempts to classify nationalism. In the following section we systemise these attempts by introducing six criteria of classification of nationalism. We use the following meta-criteria:

- correspondence between culture and politics
- definition of the nation
- ethical assessment of nationalism
- techniques of generating nationalism
- main bearers of nationalism
- goals related to the statehood.

Accordingly, we refer to the Gellnerian typology *sui generis*, the typological distinctions between ethnic versus civic nationalism; typologies based on ontological and consequential assessments of nationalism; the distinctions between manifest versus banal nationalism; the elites' versus the citizens' nationalism; and those distinctions between state-framed and counter-state forms of nationalism.

Correspondence between culture and politics – the Gellnerian typology of nationalism

Gellner constructed a typology of nationalism-engendering and nationalism-thwarting social situations, as shown in Table 4.1.[1]

His typology rests on a theory of social conflict and is directed against Marxist propositions. According to Gellner, vertical conflicts occur when ethnic, and especially cultural, differences are visible and accentuate the differences in educational access and power, and when they inhibit the free flow of personnel across the lines of social stratification. Gellner's typology is based on two factors which – as he believed – influenced the making of modern societies. The first is power, which is understood as the capability of maintaining or enforcing the social order. This capability is concentrated in the hands of some members of society and engenders the distinction between the power-holders and the powerless rest. The second element is access to education or to a viable modern high culture (these two terms are understood as equivalent). This refers to the complex of skills, for instance literacy, elementary numeracy and a modicum of technical competence, which made people competent to occupy most ordinary positions in a modern society. According to Gellner, there are four possibilities combining the capacity of the rulers and the ruled to acquire access to education or high culture:

- only the power-holders have access to education
- both the power-holders and the rest have access to education
- only the rest (or some of them) have access to education, but the power-holders do not have such access
- neither the power-holders nor the rest have access to education.

Further, Gellner uses the term 'culture' in an anthropological sense. It stands for a distinctive style of conduct and communication within a given community. It does not mean the normative 'high culture' or great tradition, a style of conduct or communication imposed as superior, or a norm or set of rules codified by norm-giving specialists within a society. High cultures are literate ones. Access to them is access to education. The phrase 'access to a culture' means access to culture which is denied to individuals in virtue of their membership of another culture, and not in virtue of their lack of 'education'. The imposition of cultural unity or cultural duality on the four possible situations of the inequality of power combined with the different patterns of the distribution of access to education results in five non-nationalist situations and three possible options of nationalism.

Table 4.1 Gellner's typology of nationalism-inducing and nationalism-thwarting situations

	P E	~ P ~ E	
1	A	A	Early industrialism without ethnic catalyst
2	A	B	'Habsburg' nationalism
	E	E	
3	A	A	Mature homogeneous industrialism
4	A	B	Classical liberal Western nationalism
	~E	E	
5	A	A	Decembrist revolutionary, but not nationalist situation
6	A	B	Diaspora nationalism
	~E	~E	
7	A	A	Untypical pre-nationalist situation
8	A	B	Typical pre-nationalist situation

Source: Ernest Gellner, *Nations and Nationalism* (Ithaca, NY: Cornell University Press, 1983), p. 94.

Gellner's most important forms of nationalism are the classical Habsburg nationalism and the classical liberal Western nationalism. In the Habsburg form of nationalism the power-holders have access to the central high culture, whereas the powerless are deprived of education. The small intelligentsias of the powerless attempt to transform their folk cultures into a rival new high culture by means of standardisation and propaganda and consequently to give this new high culture a political roof through setting up a state of their own which would sustain and protect the newly born, or re-born, high cultures. This situation corresponds historically to the nationalisms of large parts of Eastern and Central Europe and the Balkans in the nineteenth and twentieth centuries, and especially to that of Slovakia, Slovenia, Lithuania and Latvia. The classical liberal Western nationalism is characteristic of territories in which some have power and others do not, and this difference correlates with differences of culture. However, there is no significant difference between the relevant populations as far as access to education is concerned and both are educationally well equipped to constitute a modern society. This situation corresponds historically to the unification nationalisms of nineteenth-century Italy and Germany.

The third form of nationalism is diaspora nationalism. It refers to ethnically distinctive minority groups, which previously had been superior in economic terms and had access to education (with their own high culture) but lacked political and military power. Under conditions of modernisation and nationalisation of the polities, these groups lose commercial monopoly and legal protection; however, because of their previous training and education they can usually perform better than their rivals in the new free economic competition. Since they are still politically impotent and have no communal right of self-defence, they are easily exposed to persecution, expulsion or even genocide by the majority groups. Consequently, they resort to diaspora nationalism, in which the major objective is to acquire a territory on which they can establish a state of their own. In his discussion of diaspora nationalism, Gellner makes reference to the Jews, Greeks and Armenians.

It has to be emphasised that Gellner does not regard situations as nationalist in which, whatever inequalities of power or access to education may prevail, there is no significant cultural differentiation. For instance, in Line 1 of the table, which according to Gellner corresponds to classical early industrialism, both power and educational access are concentrated in the hands of some, but the deprived are not culturally differentiated from the privileged, hence there is no reason to expect nationalist conflict. Line 3 corresponds to late industrialism, with generalised access to education and absence of cultural difference. Hence, the power-holders and the powerless share the same kind of modern education and are cultural co-nationals. As a result, no functional need of nationalism arises. With historical socioeconomic developments in mind, we can assume that these non-nationalist cases refer to Great

Britain, France, the Netherlands, Sweden or Denmark. According to Gellner, in these states culture has always had a political roof. Against the background of the exclusion of these states from the world of nationalism, we can better understand the Gellnerian concept of nationalism as a phenomenon distinctive to industrial society and closely connected to its functional needs.

Definition of the nation: ethnic versus civic nationalism

The typology of nationalism with the greatest resonance in scholarship and political discourse is the distinction based on the definition of the nation. Most scholars have used the distinction between ethnic and civic nationalism. This distinction overlaps to a great extent with the distinction between cultural and political or organic and voluntaristic forms of nationalism, and in most cases they are used synonymously. It also frequently merges with the normative distinction between liberal and illiberal nationalism, or 'good' or 'bad' nationalism. This normative aspect should be treated as a separate criterion of classification and will be discussed below.

The distinction between ethnic and civic nationalism has its precursor at the beginning of the twentieth century in Friedrich Meinecke. Meinecke distinguished between *Staatsnation* and *Kulturnation*[2] and argued that the *Staatsnation* (state-nation) focused on the idea of individual and collective self-determination and derived from the individual's free will and subjective commitment to the nation. In contrast, the *Kulturnation* (cultural nation) was founded upon seemingly objective criteria such as common language, religion, customs and history. Whereas the *Staatsnation* had to be mediated by a national state or other political form, the *Kulturnation* did not require mediation.

In a similar vein, Hans Kohn distinguished between 'Western' and 'Eastern' forms of nationalism.[3] According to Kohn, the Western type of nationalism had a civic character since it was a political occurrence following the formation of the state.[4] National consciousness developed here within the framework of already existing states. Western nationalism was also rational in the sense that the nation was seen as a free association of people living in a delimited territory. Kohn saw it as a product of the Enlightenment, as 'a demand of citizens for the right to criticize and limit governmental power'.[5] This type of nationalism emerged, for instance, in Great Britain, France and America. In contrast, the Eastern type of nationalism developed in societies which were 'at a more backward stage of political and social development'.[6] This type of nationalism emerged in Germany, Italy and large parts of Eastern Europe where the national consciousness developed late and both outside of and in opposition to the framework of existing states. Eastern nationalism was illiberal and particularist. The nation was believed to be constituted by traditional ties of kinship and status, not by 'obligations of contract'. Being a product of Romanticism, it was rather more mystical than rational as it construed the nation as an organic unity with an exceptional 'soul' which was inaccessible to foreigners:

> Its roots seemed to reach into the dark soil of primitive times and to have grown through thousands of hidden channels of unconscious development, not in the bright light of rational political ends, but in the mysterious womb of the people, deemed to be so much nearer to the forces of nature.[7]

It has to be emphasised that these geographical labels should be treated with caution since both models refer not only to Western or Eastern Europe but also to a number of similar cases in Asia and in Central and Southern America.

Kohn's conceptual distinction found its followers in prominent scholars of nationalism such as Anthony D. Smith and Liah Greenfeld. Similarly to Kohn, Smith departs from 'Western' civic-territorial and 'Eastern' ethnic-genealogical models of the nation. He claims that each model of the nation tends to produce different kind of nationalist movements.[8] Civic and territorial models of the nation tend to give rise to anti-colonial movements before independence of the nation has been achieved and integration movements after independence. Ethnic and genealogical models of the nation, on the other hand, tend to generate secessionist or diaspora movements before independence and irredentist or 'pan' movements after independence. On this basis Smith developed a typology of nationalisms around the distinction between territorial and ethnic nationalism.

Territorial nationalisms include anti-colonial nationalisms and integration nationalisms. Anti-colonial nationalisms are characteristic of pre-independence movements. They define the nation in civic and territorial terms and seek to eject foreign rulers and substitute a new state-nation for the old colonial territory. Integration nationalisms are characteristic of post-independence movements. Their concept of the nation is also civic and territorial and they seek to bring together different ethnic groups and to integrate them into a new political community, establishing a new 'territorial nation' out of the old colonial state.

Ethnic nationalisms include secession and diaspora nationalisms on the one hand and irredentist and 'pan' nationalisms on the other. Secession and diaspora nationalisms are characteristic of pre-independence movements. They define the nation in ethnic and genealogical terms and seek to secede from a larger political unit (secession nationalisms) or to secede and establish a state in a designated ethnic homeland (diaspora nationalisms) and construct a new political 'ethno-nation' in its place. Irredentist and 'pan' nationalisms are characteristic of post-independence movements. They also define the nation in ethnic and genealogical terms. They seek to expand in order to incorporate ethnic 'kinsmen' outside the present boundaries of the 'ethno-nation' and the territories these 'kinsmen' inhabit (irredentist nationalisms) or to form a much larger 'ethno-national' state through the union of ethnically similar ethno-national states ('pan' nationalisms).

Liah Greenfeld, one of the most prominent scholars of nationalism, extends Kohn's basic typological framework by adding the criterion of the meaning of popular sovereignty. Greenfeld begins with two dissimilar interpretations of popular sovereignty: non-particularistic and particularistic.[9] The non-particularistic concept of sovereignty emerged where the relevant population had been elevated to the 'people' and defined as a political elite, and as such started to exercise sovereignty. Hence, a profound structural political change took place before the idea of the nation emerged. The sovereignty of the people (its nationality) meant that some individuals, who were of the people, exercised sovereignty.

> The idea of the nation (which implied sovereignty of the people) acknowledged this experience and rationalized it. The national principle that emerged was individualistic: sovereignty of the people was the implication of the actual sovereignty of individuals: it was because these individuals (of the people) actually exercised sovereignty that they were members of a nation.[10]

According to Greenfeld, the particularistic idea of the nation as a sovereign people emerged where the relevant population had not been elevated to the 'people' because of a preceding structural political change. The idea of popular sovereignty was imported from outside and initiated the change in the political and social structure. The sovereignty of the people was an implication of the people's uniqueness; its very being a distinct people since this was the sense and connotation of the sovereign nation. The national principle was collectivistic. It was also authoritarian because it tended to assume the character of a collective individual representing a single will.[11]

These two interpretations of popular sovereignty underlie the basic types of nationalism. These are individualistic-libertarian and collectivistic-authoritarian. In addition, Greenfeld distinguishes nationalism according to membership of the nation, which may be civic or ethnic. Civic is defined as 'identical with citizenship'. Access to nationality is open and voluntaristic; it has to do with individual will, hence one can acquire or change it. Ethnic membership is a genetic characteristic. It is not based on individual will, hence it cannot be acquired or changed. Greenfeld asserts that civic nationalism can be either individualistic-libertarian or collectivistic-authoritarian. Ethnic nationalism, on the other hand, can only be collectivistic-authoritarian.

Greenfeld stresses that while in civic nationalisms 'nationality' is synonymous with political belonging, in ethnic nationalisms 'nationality' becomes a synonym of 'ethnicity', and national identity is seen as a reflection of possession of 'primordial' or inherited group characteristics such as language or customs.[12] Greenfeld demonstrates that whereas England and later the United States developed individualistic civic nationalism, collectivistic nationalism appeared first in France and Russia and later in German principalities. While French nationalism was collectivistic and yet civic, Russia and Germany developed collectivistic ethnic nationalism.[13]

Ontological and consequential ethical assessments of nationalism

In ethical terms, we can distinguish between ontological and consequential assessments of nationalism. Ontological ethical assessments have their precursor in Hans Kohn's dichotomy between

Western and Eastern varieties of nationalism and the idea of more and less benign forms of nationalism. Speaking more in normative than in analytical terms, Kohn pointed to the spirit of individual liberty and rational cosmopolitanism that informed the Western type of nationalism.[14] At the same time, he saw illiberal tendencies as inherent in the Eastern type of nationalism and argued that Eastern nationalism, especially the German variety, 'turned to self-glorification and lacked sober appreciation of moral and material forces'.[15] Hence, Kohn considered the Western type of nationalism as the more benign one because of its liberal nature. Despite many criticisms of Kohn's analytical and normative dichotomy, Kohn's distinction between liberal civic and illiberal ethnic nationalisms has remained the framework within which more contemporary ontological ethical assessments of nationalism are made. For instance, Liah Greenfeld asserts that civic forms of nationalism have a more open, voluntarist and inclusive nature than ethnic forms of nationalism and argues that only the idea of common nationality based on civic ties between citizens is automatically compatible with liberalism and democracy. Greenfeld treats the line between civic and ethnic nationalism as the line dividing good forms of nationalism from bad ones. Within the civic forms of nationalism she treats individualistic-libertarian nationalism, associated with Great Britain and the United States, as more desirable than the collectivistic-authoritarian nationalism associated with France.[16]

Critics of ontological ethical assessments based on the civic-ethnic distinction, such as Rogers Brubaker, emphasise that such 'Manichean' perspectives, which state that there are only two kinds of nations and nationalism, 'good' – civic nations and nationalisms – and 'bad' – ethnic nations and nationalisms – are highly misleading in normative terms.[17] According to Brubaker, the 'blanket normative condemnation' of ethnic nationalism is often problematic, for example in cases in which ethnocultural nationalism could gain normative sympathy for its defensive function against oppressive powers (as was the case of Poland during the time of partition or in the Baltic states under Soviet occupation).[18] On the other hand, it is problematic to praise civic nationalisms that seek to reduce or eliminate cultural heterogeneity within a state (as was the case in France after the French Revolution), although they are seen as indifferent to ethnicity in the sense of descent as such.

Consequential ethical assessments of nationalism are a result of attempts by several prominent scholars such as Yael Tamir,[19] Will Kymlicka[20] and David Miller[21] to combine the idea of nationality with the theory of liberalism. These scholars go beyond the ontological explanations in terms of the liberal or illiberal origins or nature of nationalism and focus on the mutual functional relationship between nationalism and liberalism, suggesting that nationalism without liberalism is intolerable and undesirable, whereas liberalism without the social ties provided by nationalism is incoherent and inconsistent. They put forward three main arguments to demonstrate the benevolent functions and consequences of nationalism for liberal political systems. First, they assert that national belonging plays a fundamental role in providing necessary continuity and context in individual lives. It is suggested that in the globalising modern world, life in a familiar, understandable and thus predictable national environment is a necessary precondition for making rational choices and becoming self-governing.[22] As for the aspect of continuity, Yael Tamir claims that

> the respect for continuity inherent in national membership enables individuals to place themselves in a continuum of human life and creativity, connecting them to their ancestors as well to future generations and lessening the solitude and alienation characteristic of modern life.[23]

Second, they maintain that a strong sense of national togetherness engenders mutual responsibilities and thus motivates and justifies egalitarian actions such as welfare provision. In doing so, it also promotes the liberal value of equality of chances and increases trust and support for the liberal welfare state as a just and caring community:

> The 'others' whose welfare we ought to consider are . . . those who are relevant to our associative identity. Communal solidarity creates a feeling, or an illusion, of closeness and shared fate, which is a precondition of distributive justice . . . the community-like nature of the nation-state is particularly well suited, and perhaps even necessary, to the notion of the liberal welfare state.[24]

Third, liberal nationalists allege that nationalism provides a stable social framework which is necessary for the very functioning of democratic institutions. It does so by promoting the ability of the citizens to communicate with each other through a linguistic homogeneity and behavioural similarity, and by building trust and general solidarity within and across different groups, which often have conflicting political and economic interests, as well as by setting boundaries of membership since restrictions on membership are regarded as a necessary condition for fulfilling the purposes of the community[25] and preserving the 'uniqueness' of communal life.[26] According to Tamir, 'A state that views itself as a community is justified in offering citizenship only to those committed to respect its communal values, collective history, and shared aspirations for a prosperous future.'[27]

Liberal nationalists generally claim that nationalism, in both its civic and its ethnic forms, can be reconciled with liberalism as long as it remains anchored within the framework of democratic states and shows respect for human rights and culture as well as for the elementary material needs of non-members.

Critics of this consequential ethical approach stress that public forums and widespread democratic participation as well as 'civic' traditions also provide the necessary context, motivation and justification for liberal values of individuality and equality and have more appeal as a social framework for liberalism.[28]

Manifest versus banal nationalism

Two dissimilar interpretations of the techniques of nationalist mobilisation, the presence and importance of nationalism for individuals' everyday life as well as the geographical diffusion of nationalism, underlie the distinction between manifest and banal nationalism.

A part of the scholarship emphasises that nationalism has an accidental and occasional character but with 'heavy' or extreme expressions. The point of departure for these scholars, for instance Eric Hobsbawm, is that the nation, as seen not by governments and the spokesmen and activists of nationalist (or non-nationalist) movements, but by the ordinary people who are the objects of their action and propaganda, is exceedingly difficult to discover.[29] It is argued that official ideologies of states and nationalist movements do not automatically provide us with knowledge of the 'real' feelings of the members of the nation, even those of its most loyal citizens or supporters. Besides, the proponents of the thesis of the accidental character of nationalism reject the assumption that for most people national identification excludes or is always superior to the remainder of the set of identifications which constitute their social being. Further, they strongly assert that national identification and what it is believed to imply can change and shift in time, even in the course of relatively short periods.[30]

Opponents of the thesis that nationalism is accidental and occasional and characterises peripheral nations rather than the centres of the West such as Great Britain, France or the United States have emphasised that in established Western societies also nationalism is not just an intermittent mood but an endemic condition. Nationalism is embodied and expressed not only in political projects and nationalist rhetoric but also in everyday encounters, practical categories, commonsense knowledge, cultural idioms, cognitive schemas, discursive frames and organisational routines. In this regard Michael Billig introduced the term 'banal nationalism' to cover the permanent ideological habits that enable Western nations to be reproduced.[31] These ideological habits include a permanent 'flagging', or reminding, of nationhood:

> nationhood provides a continual background for their political discourses, for cultural products, and even for the structuring of newspapers. In so many little ways, the citizenry are daily reminded of their national place in a world of nations. However, this reminding is so familiar, so continual, that it is not consciously registered as reminding. The metonymic image of banal nationalism is not a flag which is being consciously waved with fervent passion; it is the flag hanging unnoticed on the public building.[32]

Along with national flags, these reminders include coins and bank notes typically bearing national emblems, which remain unnoticed in daily financial transactions and are remembered without conscious awareness. Hence, the nation is indicated or 'flagged' on a daily basis in the lives of its citizenry;[33] this takes place in an extremely banal and, at the same time, subtle way. As argued by Billig, this subtle way of perpetuating nationhood misleads both general public opinion and political analysts in Western states as it does not usually consider domestic politics, ideological discourses and international behaviour as well as the political leaders of these states to be nationalistic.[34]

Main bearers of nationalism: elites' versus non-elites' nationalism

One of the most widespread theses in the literature on nationalism is that elites are usually responsible for popular nationalism. However, a part of the scholarship has argued against this thesis and has pointed to non-elite members of relevant populations as responsible for creating nationalism.

The group of prominent representatives of the thesis of an elitist character of nationalism includes, for instance, Ernest Gellner, who in his modernist approach stresses the decisive role of the members of the elites in the development of the 'Habsburg' type of nationalism. Those were the intellectuals who turned real folk cultures, or cultures invented by them, into new high cultures. These newly born – or re-born or invented – high cultures challenged the high cultures of the power-holders and the intellectual elites claimed a state of their own to be able to sustain and promote them.[35] In a similar vein, Eric Hobsbawm argues that nation and nationalism are constructed by political elites by means of invented traditions, which bind different strata to each other and to the power-holders.[36] Because of these invented traditions the elites are able to control the masses and to secure their own power position. Liah Greenfeld, in most of her research an opponent of Gellner's approach, also emphasises that groups lacking influence and status would not be able to disseminate the new identity within the rest of society. Greenfeld sees the social, political and cultural elites as articulators and disseminators of national identities. In England, France and Russia the aristocracy was the main bearer of nationalism, whereas the middle-class intellectuals took the lead in Germany. Their influence derived from status, power, wealth and their control of the means of communication.[37] In addition, Anthony D. Smith, in his ethnosymbolic approach, stresses the key role played by the elites in the maintenance of nationalism. According to Smith, the intellectuals, mainly historians, linguists and writers, attempt to rediscover the community's past and to elaborate, codify, systemise and reorganise into a single ethno-history the different collective memories, myths and traditions that have been passed down from generation to generation. Through these activities of the elites, the wider stratum of professionals and intelligentsia and finally all other classes of the nation are brought back to their real or presumed traditions and customs, symbols, myths and memories.[38] A special case of elitist creation of nationalism is demonstrated by Rogers Brubaker with regard to the bureaucratic practices in the former Soviet Union. Brubaker holds that the Soviet state elites, in order to modernise the country and strengthen their power position, classified people according to nationality, often creating new ethnic categories, and oriented policies towards these nationality categories. As a result people began to see themselves as being of the nationality that had been assigned to them by the authorities, and they frequently demonstrated nationalistic attitudes.[39]

We can find the counter-thesis – that elites do not create nationalism or are not always able to manipulate nationalist attitudes – throughout nearly all approaches to nationalism and often held by scholars also representing the elite creation or manipulation thesis. For instance, Karl Deutsch argued that all major elements of nationality, such as political and educational institutions, literature, territory, group loyalties, nationalistic movements and even sovereign states and customs areas, are dependent on the language factor.[40] The ability of the elites to encourage a certain nationalism by affecting means and levels of communication is limited because language as the key to nationalism is created and recreated by the masses.[41] Ernest Gellner regards nationalism as an interest-oriented response of individuals to conditions of industrial modernity. In his typology, classical liberal Western nationalism and diaspora nationalism are examples of how nationalist elites articulate justifications for nationalism and provide leadership for its political expression; however, they do not create it. Rogers Brubaker asserts with regard to the former Yugoslavia that although elite manipulation was an important factor in the unfolding of the civil war in Yugoslavia in the years 1991–5, the elite manipulation thesis is not sufficient to explain the specific conditions that encouraged large parts of the Yugoslav population to be involved in armed hostilities. Brubaker emphasises that a number of distinctive factors were maximised by the new Croatian regime's use of the symbols associated in the minds of the Serbian minority with the criminal wartime Ustasha regime.[42] These included the memories and narratives of the violence suffered during the Second World War, which were alive in familial settings despite the attempts of the central Yugoslav authorities to eliminate them, and the fear of the recurrence of that violence. The elitist character of nationalism is also rejected by a number of primordialists. Pierre Van den Berghe[43] and Edward Shils[44] stress that the fundamental genetic or cultural ties that generate nationalism or ethnic nepotism and ethnic favouritism exist between all members of society and there cannot therefore be a distinction between elitist and non-elitist nationalism. Further, recent historical analyses of nationalism, such as those by Joseph M. Whitmeyer, challenge the thesis of the elitist character of nationalism. Whitmeyer refers to numerous historical cases in which elites have promoted nationalisms that ordinary people have not adopted, in which nationalism has developed with little leadership by elites or in which ordinary people adopted a nationalist attitude before it was assumed by elites.[45] For instance, he argues that in twentieth-century Spain we can observe at once two failures of the elites to produce popular nationalism. On the one hand, there were authoritarian governments using their extraordinary powers to promote a single Spanish nationalism and to eradicate Catalonian and Basque nationalisms. However, these attempts were not successful and Catalonia and the Basque Country have exhibited a strong popular nationalism which has led to an enduring quest for autonomy or even independence. On the other hand, regional nationalisms in Catalonia and the Basque Country have not been led by prominent elites of these regions. The Catalonian middle-class elite fluctuated in its support for Catalan nationalism throughout the twentieth century and ultimately has not been able to be at its forefront. As for the Basque Country, the Basque bourgeoisie has been Castilianised and has participated in the Spanish power structure since the Middle Ages, and has not been interested in Basque nationalism. Hence, the strong regional nationalisms that have emerged and persisted in Catalonia and the Basque Country among 'ordinary' people have done so not because of, but in spite of, the loyalties and actions of relevant elites. In a similar vein, Whitmeyer does not attribute the recent Slovakian nationalism to elite creation as until the dissolution of Czechoslovakia in 1993 both Czech and Slovak elites had been promoting Czechoslovakian nationalism and not Czech and Slovak nationalisms separately. However, when 'ordinary' Slovakians were able to vote freely after 1989 they supported separatist parties and the dissolution of the single state.

Goals related to the statehood: state-framed versus counter-state nationalism

Rejecting the common typologies of nationalism as conceptually ambiguous, empirically misleading and normatively problematic, Rogers Brubaker proposes to distinguish different forms of nationalism on the basis of the goals related to statehood. Brubaker distinguishes between state-seeking nationalism and non-state-seeking nationalism. The state-seeking understanding of nationalism results from the belief that the primary aim of the national life is to seek independent statehood.[46] However, Brubaker argues that the understanding of nationalism as a state-seeking activity is incomplete since the fulfilment of nationalist demands for statehood would mean that nationalist programmes would be satisfied and would exhaust themselves in the attainment of their ends. Brubaker adds that focusing narrowly on state-seeking nationalist movements is to ignore the changing nature of nationalist aims, for instance all the aims other than, or in addition to, formal independence and nationalist politics that emerge after the reorganisation of political structures along national lines.[47]

Against this background, Brubaker considers the non-state-seeking forms of nationalism as more complete and meaningful. He emphasises that the non-state-seeking forms of nationalism flourished in the new or newly enlarged nation-states of interwar Central and Eastern Europe, and in the new nation-states of post-communist Eastern Europe. Brubaker specifies four forms of such nationalism.

The first form is the nationalising nationalism of newly independent or newly reshaped states. Nationalising nationalism involves claims made in the name of a 'core nation', defined in ethnocultural terms and distinguished from citizenship. This core nation sees the state as its property. Since, as a result of putative discrimination against the nation before it established its own state, it is conceived as being in a relatively weak demographic, economic or cultural position, it tries to use state institutions to promote 'compensatory' politics to improve its relative power.[48]

The second form is transborder homeland nationalism, directed towards ethnonational kin who live in other states. This form of nationalism claims that a state is entitled or even obliged to support the political, economic and cultural interests of its ethnonational kin in other states. This form of nationalism usually emerges in direct opposition to nationalising nationalisms.[49]

The third form of nationalism is the nationalism of national minorities. It involves the claim of minorities to be recognised as 'nations' and not merely as 'ethnies' and the assertion of collective, nationality-based rights.[50]

The fourth form is a defensive populist nationalism that attempts to protect the national economy and culture against external threats. These threats may include foreign capital, transnational organisations, immigrants or foreign cultural influences. This form of nationalism often expresses anti-Semitism, defines its political adversaries as anti-national, criticises the 'West' and idealises the national past.[51]

Notes

1. The following illustration is taken from Ernest Gellner, *Nations and Nationalism* (Ithaca, NY: Cornell University Press, 1983), pp. 88–109.
2. Friedrich Meinecke, *Cosmopolitanism and the National State* (Princeton, NJ: Princeton University Press, 1970).
3. Hans Kohn, *The Idea of Nationalism* (New York: Macmillan, 1944).
4. Ibid. p. 329.
5. Hans Kohn, 'Re-thinking recent German history', *The Review of Politics* 14, 3 (1952), pp. 325–45 (p. 327).
6. Kohn, *Idea of Nationalism*, p. 329.
7. Ibid. p. 331.
8. Anthony D. Smith, *National Identity* (London: Penguin Books, 1991), pp. 81–3.
9. Liah Greenfeld, *Nationalism. Five Roads to Modernity* (Cambridge, MA and London: Harvard University Press, 1993), p. 10.
10. Ibid. p. 11.
11. Ibid. p. 11.
12. Ibid. p. 12.
13. Ibid. p. 14.
14. Kohn, *Idea of Nationalism*, pp. 330–1.
15. Kohn, 'Re-thinking recent German history', p. 327.
16. Greenfeld, *Nationalism*, pp. 6–21.
17. See Rogers Brubaker, 'Myths and misconceptions in the study of nationalism', in John A. Hall (ed.), *The State of the Nation. Ernest Gellner and the Theory of Nationalism* (Cambridge: Cambridge University Press, 1998), pp. 272–306 (pp. 298–301) and Rogers Brubaker, 'The Manichean myth: rethinking the distinction between "civic" and "ethnic" nationalism', in Hanspeter Kriesi, Klaus Armingeon, Hannes Siegrist and Andreas Wimmer (eds), *Nation and National Identity: The European Experience in Perspective* (Zurich: Rüegger, 1999), pp. 55–71 (pp. 63–7).
18. According to Brubaker, their normative weakness corresponds to their analytical weakness. Brubaker rejects, for example, the characterisation of civic nationalism as inclusive and of ethnic nationalism as exclusive. He argues that all understandings of the nation and all forms of nationalism are simultaneously inclusive and exclusive. The same refers to the characterisation of civic nationalism as purely political and based on common citizenship and ethnic nationalism as cultural, as even the paradigmatic

cases of civic nationalism such as the United States and France also include significant cultural components.

19. Yael Tamir, *Liberal Nationalism* (Princeton, NJ: Princeton University Press, 1993).
20. See, for example, Will Kymlicka, *Multicultural Citizenship* (Oxford: Oxford University Press, 1995); see also Will Kymlicka, *Politics in the Vernacular: Nationalism, Multiculturalism and Citizenship* (New York: Oxford University Press, 2001).
21. David Miller, *Market State and Community: Theoretical Foundations of Market Socialism* (Oxford: Clarendon Press, 1989); see also David Miller, *On Nationality* (Oxford and New York: Clarendon Press, 1995).
22. Tamir, *Liberal Nationalism*, p. 84.
23. Ibid. p. 86.
24. Ibid. p. 121.
25. Ibid. p. 125.
26. Ibid. p. 127.
27. Ibid. p. 129.
28. See, for instance, Albert W. Dzur, 'Nationalism, liberalism, and democracy', *Political Research Quarterly* 55, 1 (2002), pp. 191–211.
29. Eric Hobsbawm, *Nations and Nationalism Since 1780. Programme, Myth, Reality* (Cambridge, New York and Melbourne: Cambridge University Press, 1990), p. 10.
30. Ibid. p. 11.
31. Michael Billig, *Banal Nationalism* (London: Sage, 1995), p. 6.
32. Ibid. p. 8.
33. Ibid. p. 6.
34. Ibid. pp. 6–8.
35. Gellner, *Nations and Nationalism*, p. 97.
36. Hobsbawm, *Nations and Nationalism Since 1780*.
37. Greenfeld, *Nationalism*, p. 22.
38. Anthony D. Smith, *Nations and Nationalism in a Global Era* (Cambridge: Polity Press 1995), p. 65.
39. Rogers Brubaker, *Nationalism Reframed: Nationhood and the National Question in the New Europe* (Cambridge: Cambridge University Press, 1996).
40. Karl W. Deutsch, 'The trend of European nationalism – the language aspect', *American Political Science Review* 36, 3 (1942), pp. 533–41 (p. 533).
41. Karl W. Deutsch, *Nationalism and Social Communication: An Inquiry into the Foundations of Nationality* (Cambridge, MA: MIT Press, 1966).
42. Brubaker, 'Myths and misconceptions', p. 291.
43. Pierre L. Van den Berghe, *The Ethnic Phenomenon* (New York: Elsevier, 1981).
44. Edward Shils, 'Primordial, personal, sacred and civil ties: some particular observations on the relationships of sociological research and theory', *British Journal of Sociology* 8, 2 (1957), pp. 130–45 (pp. 134–8).
45. Joseph M. Whitmeyer, 'Elites and popular nationalism', *British Journal of Sociology* 53, 3 (2002), pp. 321–41.
46. Brubaker, 'Myths and misconceptions', pp. 272–306 (p. 276).
47. Ibid. p. 276.
48. Ibid. p. 277.
49. Ibid. p. 277.
50. Ibid. p. 277.
51. Ibid. pp. 277–8.

CHAPTER FIVE

Four Levels of Nationalism

As was made apparent in Chapters 3 and 4, the research on nationalism is rich in concepts, approaches, typologies and foci, with scholars describing several different phenomena and objects as nationalism or nationalist. Despite this multiplicity, most scholars regard nationalism as a one-dimensional or one-level phenomenon. This deficit leads to confusion regarding how the empiric dimension of nationalism may be examined in more complex situations with several regional, national or supranational actors acting at different levels and in different political and social structures. For instance, using the existing approaches or theories we are barely able to develop a more complex and wide-ranging explanation of what to define as nationalism and nationalist actors with regard to nationalist developments in contemporary European states or to the relationship between nationalism and European integration. Or, rather, we are unable to do so if we resort to using single approaches or theories, which cover only some aspects of nationalism.

In the following chapter we suggest examining nationalism at several levels. We regard these levels of analysis as heuristics that allow nationalism to be observed from differentiating analytical angles. To our examination of levels we apply the rather abstract concept developed by Abraham Edel for whom it

> involves the idea of some continuity of the new with the old,
> a maturing causal process which constitutes the emerging,

afield of novel or distinctive qualities with some order of its own (hence an element of discontinuity with the past), some degree of alteration in the total scene and its modes of operation because of the presence of the new. Methodologically, a new level requires new descriptive concepts and, many scholars believe, new empirical laws, independent of those of the old level.[1]

This definition allows for treating the levels as relatively open categories with their own concepts and laws and not necessarily as an interlocking system in which hierarchy plays a relevant role and levels can exist only when a system fails to fully divide into subsystems.[2] Further, we suggest that levels can exist for themselves without influencing or interacting with other levels. However, we do not exclude the possibility that as they are open categories, levels might well interact with other levels. Further, we argue that we cannot blindly generalise findings across levels of analysis. Findings at one level of analysis do not generalise neatly and exactly to other levels of analysis except under very restricted circumstances. Just because a relation holds at the lower level does not mean that it will also hold at higher levels. Relationships that hold at one level of analysis may be stronger or weaker at a different level of analysis, or may even reverse direction.[3]

Accordingly, we propose to deal with nationalism at four levels: first, at the level of the individual; second, at the level of societal or political discourse; third, at the governmental level; and fourth, at the level of international relations.[4] We argue that our level heuristics do not require any hierarchy between the four levels of analysis. Further, we are not primarily interested in exploring linkages between the levels of analysis, as is frequently the case with researchers in international relations or, more recently, in the field of European integration theory.[5] However, since we treat levels as heuristic constructs which are thus permeable, and we believe that it is difficult to determine the exact line of demarcation between the levels of nationalism, we do not exclude interaction or interdependence between them. For instance, nationalist attitudes of citizens can be nurtured by certain government policies, while at the same time popular nationalist sentiments can cause nationalist policies of the government or nationalist policies of governments may influence the polarity of the international system. Further, we argue that findings from one level of nationalism are seldom transferable to other levels, as each level of analysis functions according to its own logic. For instance, the discovery that the degree of citizens' nationalism is closely related to the current economic performance of the state in question may not generalise to governmental level, as a putative nationalist policy of the government is largely influenced by more (or at least different) factors than individuals' attitudes.

In sum, we suggest exploring levels of nationalism not necessarily as parts of a bigger whole, as at every level we can analyse specific aspects of this phenomenon. Consequently, the image of nationalism as a multi-level phenomenon does not imply that we must constantly analyse it in its entire complexity. However, we also argue that nationalism can be scrutinised as a complex, multi-level phenomenon covering all four levels and that these levels might interact with one another.[6] The choice of focus is the privilege of the observer who can decide which levels to concentrate on, be it all four levels or merely one.

Finally, by treating nationalism as a complex, multi-level phenomenon we do not view it as a 'complete' phenomenon, as the notion of completeness denotes a methodological finality. Complete phenomena are not subject to change and thus remain methodologically self-sufficient.

In the following section we introduce the four levels of nationalism, which together constitute our analytical framework for demonstrating this multi-level phenomenon in selected European states in Chapter 6 and with regard to European integration in Chapter 7.

The micro level of nationalism

The micro level of analysis refers to the nationalism of individuals. It is mainly a domain of quantitative research which provides us with insights on auto-categorisations and xeno-categorisations in terms of national distinction as well as individuals' expressions of interests and emotions related to national attachment. It thus focuses mainly on the psychology of nationalism.

Analysing nationalism at the micro level we can, in conceptual terms, distinguish between individuals' nationalist and nationalistic attitudes. Nationalist attitudes can be defined as expressions of feelings of national identity and a commitment to the interests of a particular nation without negative connotations towards other

nations. In cases in which the attachment to the nation is characterised by support for the questioning and criticism of current group
practices that are intended to result in positive change, we may also
speak of constructive nationalism, or patriotism.[7] Most scholars
believe that we can expect a 'healthy' patriotic sentiment among
individuals to be related to the high self-esteem and the wellbeing
of those individuals and consequently patriotism being a means
of reducing international conflicts or belligerence.[8] In contrast,
nationalistic attitudes can be seen as expressions of a devotion to
the interests or ideas of a particular nation, including unquestion-
ing positive evaluation, staunch allegiance and intolerance of criticism as well as the pursuit of national interests and ideas even to
the detriment of other nations. In this case we may also refer to
blind nationalism or blind patriotism.[9]

The meso level of nationalism

Here we refer to Robert Merton's notion of meso-level analysis.[10]
Accordingly, the meso level functions as a 'theoretical field in which
the structural mechanisms and the interactions between macro and
micro levels might be observed'[11] but – in our understanding –
might also be absent. Hence, the meso level of nationalism is an
intermediary level between the nationalism of individuals and that
of central government or, in other words, between the individual
and the state.

Nationalism at the meso level can be described as a discursive
commitment of non-governmental actors to national interests,
be it the welfare of the nation or national security, or to national
ideas such as the notion of a particular identity or cultural grandness of the nation. Often, these national interests or ideas take the
form of specific mega-narratives of national identity and can differ
from state to state. Generally, the referential framework is constructed on the basis of the three nationalist principles, that is, the
principle of popular sovereignty; the principle of the uniqueness of
the people; and the principle of fundamental equality among all
strata in the community.[12] Of course, the national narratives are
exposed to permanent changes in the contemporary political and
societal discourse as discourses are not stable or fixed and are not
safe from exposition to and penetration by elements alien to them.
However, discourses usually maintain their essential core, as the

variety of meanings would otherwise make any of the meanings impossible. That is why, according to Laclau and Mouffe,[13] we can always observe some nodal points that stabilise the meaning of signifiers and have a certain degree of rigidity. The mega-narratives of national identity can be seen as such nodal points.

The meso level can be considered as a part of society or of politics, or, more likely, a mixture of the two. Relevant actors at this level are political and societal groups, for instance representatives of political life (political parties and other political organisations), economic and social interest groups and trade unions, and representatives of cultural and religious institutions. The meso level includes various meanings of narratives referring to national interests and ideas, their construction and reconstruction, and conflicts between contending visions of these narratives, as they are defined and perpetuated by different political and societal groups.[14]

Nationalism at the meso level might be an instrument to gain control of central power in a state, as is often the case with political parties. Alternatively, it might remain merely an expression of particular ideas without (directly) claiming control of central government, frequently occurring with discourses made by representatives of religious or cultural institutions. Accordingly, the two most common forms of nationalist discourse at the meso level are instrumental and ideological discourse.[15] Instrumental nationalist discourse is associated with a general instrumentalist understanding of politics as dominated by the pragmatic, self-interested pursuit of material resources and political advantage. It mostly addresses and tries to remove the relative political or socio-economic deprivation. In ethnically divided societies, instrumental nationalist discourses are sustained or strengthened by patron–client relations that pervade social structure and political culture. Instrumental nationalist discourse might highlight, for example, that ethnic conflicts occur when competing societal groups mobilise their political support along the lines of language, religion or race.[16] The ideological nationalist discourse tries to mitigate social heterogeneity by constructing a confrontation between the 'Us' and the significant 'Other'. By doing so, it often promotes feelings of fear and distrust and engenders collectivist prejudicial stereotyping of the 'Other'. In other words, whereas instrumental nationalist discourse is a reflection of interest, ideological nationalist discourse finds its fulfilment in the pursuit of moral certainty or superiority.

Of course, nationalist discourses are seldom homogeneous at the societal level. In many cases, we can discern a series of nationalist discourses conveying different meanings and ethical assessments. Frequently, nationalist discourses are subject to fragmentation, as competing groups attempt to push through with their vision of nation and national interests and identity.[17]

The macro level of nationalism

Political action of national governments usually has two main goals to which the macro level of nationalism refers. This level includes, first, governmental strategies of maintaining and strengthening the state, as the most important goal of national governments is, in nearly all cases, the survival of their states. This goal results from the immanent interest of the institution of the state in self-maintenance[18] and the elimination of functional differentiation between the state units in international politics, or, in other words, their original need to survive. Hence, every national government is expected to protect and strengthen the institution of the 'state' it represents and administrates. This goal becomes particularly important in states with ethnic minorities, in federal multi-ethnic states and in states with severe socioeconomic cleavages between regions with different ethnic settings, hence in states whose political existence or territorial integrity may possibly be endangered by separatist tendencies. Possible forms of governmental responses and, at the same time, expressions of nationalism include, for instance, practices of enforcing cultural homogeneity[19] and, more likely in democratic states, the politics of identity-building through an extensive use of national symbols, myths and the ceremonies of national liturgy,[20] or the emphasis on 'significant Others' threatening the national security or wealth with the aim of stimulating citizens' loyalty, solidarity and sacrifice. Other state-strengthening polices include the socioeconomic integration of regions inhabited by ethnic minorities,[21] or even the policy of reducing gaps in socioeconomic development between different parts of the country.[22]

Second, the macro level of nationalism includes the strategies of the legitimisation of political action related to the 'pure' governmental dimension of politics, hence the interest of governments in the maintenance of their domestic power position. The maintenance of domestic power in modern democratic states depends primarily on the satisfaction of the socioeconomic interests of society. The central concern of the government of democratic states is therefore to guarantee the continuous supply of the collective socioeconomic goods for which the state is responsible in a national system. These goods include, for instance, macroeconomic stability, social security and socioeconomic equality. For this purpose governments attempt to promote economic growth, the maintenance of or an increase in the employment rate, new tax sources and a balance between conflicting social interests. In addition, governments must satisfy the interest of the public regarding internal security.

As in democratic systems every political action must be legitimised before the voters and in non-democratic systems important decisions must be explained before the relevant groups supporting the power-holders, the choice of discursive arguments is fundamental in being able to define whether or not we are dealing with nationalism. Here, we assume that nationalism at the macro level is the legitimisation of the policies of governmental actors through their discursive commitment to national interests, be it the welfare of the nation, national security or national ideas such as the idea of a particular identity or cultural grandness of the nation.

The supranational level of nationalism

Nationalism at the domestic level, be it the micro level, meso level or macro level, frequently influences the international environment of the nation-state. However, the level at which we can examine this influence is not another level of nationalism, since, speaking in theoretical and methodological terms, there cannot be any nationalism beyond the nation-state. We can only speak of the effects of nationalism at the supranational level, hence beyond the levels of micro, meso and macro nationalism.

This supranational level of the effects of nationalism might include, first, the consequences for the structure of the international system. In neo-realist understanding, to which we refer in the following section, the structure of the international system is determined by its polarity and anarchy. Polarity may be defined as the number of poles of power, that is, the number of great powers in the system. It determines the possibility of the use of relative power resources by single actors.[23] Anarchy is the ordering principle of the system. The international system is anarchic in the sense that there is no authority above states capable of regulating their interactions and potential conflicts. In most cases, states must interact with other states on their own, rather than being determined by a 'world government' – a higher-control entity. Because states exist in anarchy, self-help is necessarily the principle of their action. As pointed out by Waltz, in order to realise their interests states cannot rely on other states; they must instead rely on the means they can generate and the arrangements they can make for themselves.[24]

As to the consequences of nationalism for polarity, changes in polarity can take place through, for example, war, a rise in economic capabilities and/or military spending by some actors and an implosion of a great power, with nationalism possibly being a significant factor in all these situations. Nationalistic attitudes of citizens (micro nationalism), strong discursive appeals to pursue national interests and ideas (meso nationalism) or governmental policies justified by means of national interest and ideas can lead to interstate conflicts and wars, as several historical events demonstrate, among them the most prominent case of Germany under Hitler conducting a war which resulted in the systemic change from multipolarity to bipolarity. The same might refer to economic growth or, even more plausibly, an increase in military spending caused by meso-nationalist discourses claiming a prominent role of the nation in international politics and the respective governmental policies. A systemically relevant implosion of states can also be a consequence of nationalism. This situation refers especially to great multinational powers with domestic ethnic conflicts, which in a more or less violent way contribute to a collapse of central state institutions, as was the case with the former Soviet Union.

As far as the consequences of nationalism for anarchy are concerned, we might think of a situation in which the nationalism of a great power promotes a decrease in or even an elimination of anarchy if this great power, acting under the conditions of unipolarity, establishes hegemony in the whole system. This will remain rather a hypothetical situation, as empirical examples show that throughout world history no great power has been able to control the entire system, with the possible exception of pre-modern and regionally delimited systems. More frequently, nationalism will belong to factors leading to a stabilisation of or an increase in anarchy. For instance, in the scenario in which a single great power with nationalist motives chooses a policy of isolationism, the result

– from the systemic perspective – could only be the more anarchic character of international politics. Under conditions of multipolarity, in which several more or less equal powers will try to safeguard their national sovereignty and freedom of action against external control mechanisms, anarchy will increase.[25] Under conditions of bipolarity nationalism seems to be of limited importance, as because of the structurally determined check between the two great powers, the nationalism of any great power can have a very limited effect on the level of anarchy.[26]

The supranational level of the effects of nationalism might include, second, consequences for the processes of regional integration, which often lead to the emergence of regional subsystems. Nationalism might be a catalyst for integration when relevant actors at the meso level and macro level consider it to be advantageous for their states or compatible with their fundamental beliefs and values. Nationalism might also function as a barrier to European integration if ordinary citizens at the micro level and relevant actors at the two other levels expect more losses than gains from this process, be it in economic terms or in terms of relative power position.[27] Whereas structural changes in the international system may be mainly caused by the nationalism of great powers, in regional subsystems even nationalism in smaller states can have significant effects on the political and economic processes.[28]

It has to be emphasised that at the supranational level we are not dealing with the two-sided relationship of nationalism and international politics. We are instead only examining how domestic politics (micro, meso and macro nationalism) influence international politics (the so-called second image in international relations). We do not examine the impact of international politics on the domestic level of nationalism (second image reversed).[29] This impact is examined as external factors at the micro, meso and macro levels.

Notes

1. Abraham Edel, 'The concept of levels in social theory', in Llewellyn Gross (ed.), *Symposium on Social Theory* (Evanston, IL: Row, Peterson, 1959), p. 167.
2. The hierarchical understanding of levels is present, for instance, in Herbert Simon's level concept: 'By a *hierarchic system*, or hierarchy, I mean a system that is composed of interrelated subsystems, each of the latter being, in turn, hierarchic in structure until we reach some level of elementary subsystems.' See Herbert A. Simon, 'The architecture of complexity', *Proceedings of the American Philosophical Society* 106 (1962), pp. 467–82 (p. 468); Herbert A. Simon, 'The organization of complex systems', in

Howard H. Pattee (ed.), *Hierarchy Theory: The Challenge of Complex Systems* (New York: George Braziller, 1973).

3. Katherine J. Klein and Steve W. J. Kozlowski, 'From micro to meso: critical steps in conceptualizing and conducting multilevel research', *Organizational Research Methods* 3, 3 (2000), pp. 211–36 (p. 213).

4. The notion of levels of analysis has been applied to different sub-disciplines of political science, mainly in international relations. See David. J. Singer, 'The levels-of-analysis problem in international relations', *World Politics* 14, 1 (1961), pp. 77–92; Kenneth N. Waltz, *Man, the State and War: A Theoretical Analysis* (New York: Columbia University Press, 1959): Yuri A. Yurdusev, 'Levels of analysis and units of analysis: a case for distinction', *Millennium: Journal of International Studies* 22, 1 (1993), pp. 77–88.

5. See, for example, Gabriel A. Almond, 'The international-national connection', *British Journal of Political Science* 19, 2 (1989), pp. 237–59; Alexander Wend, 'Levels of analysis vs. agents and structures: Part III', *Review of International Studies* 18, 2 (1992), pp. 181–5; Peter Gourevitch, 'The second image reversed: the international sources of domestic politics', *International Organization* 32, 4 (1978), pp. 881–912.

6. See James Lee Ray, 'Integrating levels of analysis in world politics', *Journal of Theoretical Politics* 13, 4 (2010), pp. 355–88.

7. Robert T. Schatz, Ervin Staub and Howard Lavine, 'On the varieties of national attachment: Blind versus constructive patriotism', *Political Psychology* 20, 1 (1999), pp. 151–74.

8. Rick Kosterman and Seymour Feshbach, 'Toward a measure of patriotic and nationalistic attitudes', *Political Psychology* 10, 2 (1989), pp. 257–74.

9. Schatz, Staub and Lavine, 'On the varieties of national attachment'.

10. Robert Merton, *Social Theory and Social Structure* (New York: Free Press, 1968).

11. See also Leena Haanpaa, 'Structures and mechanisms in sustainable consumption research', *International Journal of Environment and Sustainable Development* 6, 1 (2007), pp. 53–66.

12. See also the three nationalist principles referred to by Greenfeld in Liah Greenfeld, *Nationalism. Five Roads to Modernity* (Cambridge, MA and London: Harvard University Press, 1993), pp. 8–11.

13. Ernesto Laclau and Chantal Mouffe, *Hegemony and Socialist Strategy: Towards a Radical Democratic Politics* (London: Verso, 2nd edn, 2001).

14. Alain Finlayson, 'Ideology, discourse and nationalism', *Journal of Political Ideologies* 3, 1 (1998), pp. 99–118.

15. For the distinction between an instrumental nationalism and an ideological nationalism, see, for instance, David Brown, 'Why independence? The instrumental and ideological dimensions of nationalism', *International Journal of Comparative Sociology* 45, 3/4 (2004), pp. 277–96.

16. In this sense, nationalist discourse in favour of ethnic autonomy or dominance can be seen as bargaining demands for access to state patronage.

17. For instance, in Italy there have been strongly competing notions of the Christian and laical bases of Italian national identity. They dominated the political and societal discourses of the Italian nation-state, even though their relative importance has decreased in recent decades. In the case of Turkey, Tanil Bora points to a fragmentation of nationalist discourse, as he distinguishes 'Kemalist' nationalism, 'left-wing' nationalism, idealist nationalism, 'radical nationalism' and even a 'neo-nationalism'. See Tanil Bora, 'Nationalist discourses in Turkey', *South Atlantic Quarterly* 102, 2/3 (2003), pp. 433–51.

18. See Claus Offe, *Strukturprobleme des kapitalistischen Staates. Aufsätze zur politischen Soziologie* (Frankfurt am Main: Suhrkamp Verlag, 1972). For this argument see also Bruce E. Moon, 'The state in foreign and domestic policy', in Laura Neack and Jeanne Hey (eds), *Foreign Policy Analysis. Continuity and Change in its Second Generation* (Englewood Cliffs, NJ: Prentice-Hall, 1995), pp. 187–200 (p. 191).

19. Here, there exists a long list of historical examples in Europe. We might think of

the policies of Magyarisation pursued by the Hungarian governments in the period between 1867 and 1918 towards the Slovak, Romanian and Serbian minorities; the Polonisation policies towards the Ukrainian minority in Poland in the 1930s; the policies of Romanisation pursued by communist Romanian governments towards the Hungarian minority; or the Castilianisation efforts of Spanish governments in Catalonia and the Basque country until 1975.

20. One prominent example of this is the commemorations of Belgian National Day on 21 July. This commemorates the oath of the first King of Belgium on 21 July 1831 and has been used in recent decades by Belgian governments and the Royal House as an instrument to underplay the increasing conflicts between Flanders and Wallonia.

21. An example of this policy is the financial aid of the central Italian government for the region of South Tyrol in Northern Italy inhabited by a German-speaking majority which demonstrated separatist tendencies for decades after it had been incorporated into the Italian state in 1918.

22. It relates to ethnically homogeneous states with a weak sense of national belonging. Italy is again a good example here, as the reduction of the huge socioeconomic differences between the north and the south of the country has traditionally been a major concern of Italian central governments fearing negative consequences of these differences for the unity of the Italian state.

23. Kenneth N. Waltz, *Theory of International Politics* (Reading, MA: Addison-Wesley, 1979), pp. 134–7.

24. Ibid. p. 125.

25. Speaking in more general terms, nationalism of powerful states in the international system has traditionally tried to undermine national sovereignty of weaker states, which is a cornerstone of the ideology of nationalism and a founding principle of international law. For instance, Krasner argues that national sovereignty as a legal principle underpinning international relations has never been effective. By discussing an entire spectrum of subjects ranging from human rights to international investments, Krasner shows that international law based on sovereignty failed on many occasions to protect the weaker states from the nationalist behaviour of powerful states. See Stephen Krasner, *Sovereignty: Organized Hypocrisy* (Princeton, NJ: Princeton University Press, 1999).

26. In bipolar systems, the level of anarchy generally remains stable since, even though both great powers can reduce the level of anarchy within the group of states that they control, they can hardly protect their allies from all dangers coming from the rival alliance.

27. See, for instance, Ireneusz Paweł Karolewski and Andrzej Marcin Suszycki, *Nationalism and European Integration. The Need for New Theoretical and Empirical Insights* (New York and London: Continuum, 2007).

28. Most prominent examples are nationalist attitudes in small states such as Denmark and Ireland which led to the rejection of the Maastricht Treaty in a referendum in Denmark in 1992 and of the Lisbon Treaty in a referendum in Ireland in 2008.

29. Gourevitch, 'The second image reversed', pp. 881–912.

CHAPTER SIX

Nationalism in Europe in Practice

In this chapter we will sketch the development of nationalism in some selected countries in Europe. The goal is to illustrate the diversity of nationalism in Europe and to use our analytical categorisation of the macro, meso and micro levels of analysis as well as of the supranational level. We demonstrate the more recent trends of nationalism in selected European countries such as Belgium, Bulgaria, Great Britain, Germany, Italy, Latvia, Poland and Sweden. The description of the intricacies of nationalism in these countries does not raise any claim of completeness. Its goal is to offer an overview as an illustration, rather than a systematic analysis. Therefore, we have decided not to cover every issue linked to nationalism in these countries but instead have selected specific ones, either the most controversial or the most interesting.

These cases have been selected according to the criterion of 'isolated variety', which allows for a reconciliation of two methodological goals. First, we intended to reduce the complexity of the field of inquiry through selected case studies, as it is impossible to include every country in Europe in an interpretative study. Second, the goal of the selected case studies is not to exhibit the central tendency as in a large sample of cases, but rather to preserve the variety of the cases using the 'method of difference', where one examines cases with differing general characteristics.

Belgium

Since 1970 Belgium has been transformed from a unitary state into a federal state with a strong position of both regions and communities. In addition to the federal parliament, there are regional parliaments and communitarian councils. The Flemish, Walloon and Brussels Capital regions each have their own legislatures. Besides, there are councils governing the Flemish, French and German linguistic communities. The division of powers between the federal and the regional levels is extremely complex, with some policy areas devolved completely, some partially to the regions and the core issues of foreign and defence, as well as judiciary policies remaining in the hand of the federal government.[1] The main political conflicts in Belgium in the recent decades have reflected the ethnic divisions between the Flemish and the francophone Walloon population. Fragmentation of the political parties along ethnic lines, the demise of national (federal) parties and the demise of power competition between government and opposition at the nationwide level are the results of these conflicts.

Against the background of this reduced central governmental dimension, the case of Belgium is particularly interesting because of its meso level of nationalism in which we can observe a strong Flemish discourse in favour of a further disempowerment of the federal institutions and the creation of an independent Flemish state. The most prominent representative of this discourse is the right-wing political movement Vlaams Belang (Flemish Interest),[2] which until 2004 went under the name Vlaams Blok, in relative terms the most successful political party in Flanders in the last three decades. Vlaams Belang continually states that Flanders and Wallonia are 'two completely different countries'.[3] The party presents a solidaristic view of society based on ethnicity: membership of the nation is based on blood, or Flemish descent, not language (a strategy by which the party can claim that the French speakers of Brussels, if descended from Flemings, are actually Flemish), and cannot be acquired through birth in Flanders or by naturalisation. Vlaams Belang distinguishes between the 'ethnically committed' and the 'non-ethnically committed' Flemish people. The former are the elite, with 'higher moral values such as a perception of responsibility, self-sacrifice, social justice, solidarity and tolerance'; the latter, the masses, need to be shown the 'right national path'.[4]

The contemporary nationalist discourse of Vlaams Belang is based on two main narratives. The wealth narrative portrays Flanders as one of the most prosperous regions in Europe with a high gross domestic product per capita (producing approximately 75 per cent of the Belgian gross domestic product) and with an effective innovative, internationally oriented economy (accounting for more than 80 per cent of Belgian exports). The narrative of the oppressed people depicts the Flemings as people deprived of the possibility to take full advantage of their economic activity and social order as well as discriminated against in cultural terms. In this regard, the discourse identifies three main problems. The first is the 'unjust' principle of welfare redistribution on which the Belgian state is based. It results in the 'compulsory and opaque' transfer of billions of euros from Flanders to Wallonia and the loss of a significant part of the Flemish gross domestic product. Vlaams Belang calls this transfer the world's biggest contribution to another community, and, at the same time, one which remains unfruitful as neither the federal government nor the Walloon politicians are capable of dealing with these resources in an efficient and effective way. Generally, the Belgian state is accused of holding back an even more prosperous Flemish economic development. The second problem is linked to the first. As the Walloons have a privileged socioeconomic position in Belgium, so they are also advantaged in sociocultural and linguistic terms. The discourse emphasises that the French language is dominant at the federal level, that the linguistic rights of the Flemish citizens are constantly violated and that the French-dominated political and judicial establishment torpedoes any real equality between the two languages. The third problem is immigration to Belgium. Vlaams Belang warns that, despite the official efforts of the Belgian federal government to reduce immigration, the stream of legal and illegal immigrants as well as asylum seekers is increasing and makes the Flemish people feel alienated from their 'home' as most immigrants' knowledge of Flemish is insufficient. In particular, immigrants from Islamic countries are depicted as not able to adapt to the Western lifestyle and Western values such as equality of men and women, freedom of speech and the separation of church and state, and their children are deemed to be 'behind from the start'. In addition, the discourse points to a massive overrepresentation of immigrants and Belgian citizens of foreign origin in crime statistics and accuses immigrants of endangering the security of Flemish cities and municipalities through crime, vandalism and illegal dumping, even if Vlaams Belang has slightly softened its general xenophobia in recent years. The Belgian state is regarded as neither able nor willing to combat foreigners' criminality as successive Belgian governments have 'invariably waved aside the truth about immigrant crime'.[5] According to Vlaams Belang, the same refers to risks of fanatical Islamism. The party considers Belgium, because of its inadequate legislation and a government that refuses to deport fundamentalist imams, as one of the operating bases of Islamic fundamentalism. Hence, the discourse constructs two 'significant Others', on the one hand the Belgian state symbolised by the francophone federal government and on the other hand the immigrants. Both of them are threatening, not inspiring.

Against this background, and as the 'only solution', the discourse of Vlaams Belang calls for Flemish independence. It refers to the 'universal' and 'moral' right of self-determination of the Flemings and argues that the Belgian state should be dissolved in a 'democratic' and 'peaceful' way into Wallonia and 'the Flemish Republic'. As an immediate measure, it wants to drastically reduce immigration from outside the European Union. Further, it claims that immigrants already living in Belgium should lose the municipal right to vote, Belgian citizenship should only be granted to fully assimilated immigrants and multiple citizenship should be abolished. New immigrants in Flanders, if any, should be forced to adapt to Flemish culture, values and the 'important traditional principles of the European civilization', such as the separation of church and state, democracy, freedom of speech and the equality of men and women. Immigrants refusing, neglecting or disputing these principles should be deported to their countries of origin. As far as European integration is concerned, Vlaams Belang rejects a European federal state. Instead, it pleads for a confederate Europe and argues that the EU should not become a 'larger version of Belgium'.[6] Vlaams Belang is also the only party in Belgium that firmly opposes the accession of Turkey to the European Union.

Since 2006 this nationalist discourse of Vlaams Belang has been accompanied and challenged by the discourse of its new competitor, the neo-liberal populist Lijst Dedecker (LDD), a new party which has profited from the particular Flemish electoral opportunity structure – the ideological gap between the mainstream parties, which had converged in the centre, and Vlaams Belang on the radical right – and the populist appeal of its charismatic leader

Jean-Marie Dedecker to gain representation in the Belgian parliament in 2007, with a significant number of votes from earlier supporters of Vlaams Belang.[7] The ideology of LDD can be described as populist since the party considers society as separated into two homogeneous and antagonistic groups – 'the pure people' versus 'the corrupt elite'. The LDD is critical of the Belgian political elite, as can be seen in its denunciation of the Belgian 'particracy', which is said to function by means of compromises between party leaders without the citizens having any influence. The people, on the other hand, are seen as a homogeneous group. For instance, the party declaration mentions that it pursues a 'policy of common sense' and that it represents all the Flemish people.[8] The populist ideology of LDD is attached to a neo-liberal ideology, which refers to classical liberal values such as individualism, (negative) freedom, a minimal state and the free market. LDD argues that the individual should be left unrestrained and that the government should only provide the most essential services. The LDD manifesto associates the federal Belgian government with a burdensome bureaucracy, over-regulation, inefficiency, abuse of social insurance and financial transfers from Flanders to Wallonia. Solutions are to be found in a smaller government, privatisation, a flat tax and limited unemployment benefits. Hence, LDD combines a populist ideology – as it denounces the consensual politics in Belgium – with a neo-liberal approach to politics in general and socioeconomic matters in particular.[9] The party claims a 'maximum of Flanders within a minimum of Belgium'.[10] Consequently, even though Flemish independence is not directly addressed, it constitutes another medium-term challenge to the unity of the Belgian state.

The nationalist discourse of Vlaams Belang has led all other political parties to create a 'cordon sanitaire' around Vlaams Belang in order to prevent the party from taking part in government at any political level. However, the political establishment has not been able to develop a coherent discursive response to Vlaams Belang. Rather, it was societal groups such as the organisation 0110 that developed a discourse *sui generis* to counter the nationalist discourse of Vlaams Belang. On 1 October 2006, in four Belgian cities a large number of Belgium's most popular artists from many different genres held a series of concerts 'for tolerance, against racism, against extremism, and against gratuitous violence'.[11] The goal of the 0110 concerts was to question the claim made by Vlaams Belang on the signifier 'people' and 'popular culture' (as opposed to elitist Belgian culture) and to turn popular culture against Vlaams Belang. The 0110 organisation stated that it did not want to become involved in party politics; it presented the concerts as a cultural event with political relevance. The 0110 event was organised by artists and their managers without the support of the political and societal actors that are usually involved in anti-racist events, such as labour unions, non-governmental organisations and the peace movement. This distance from institutionalised politics made the appeal of 0110 broader and, at the same time, more difficult for Vlaams Belang to disarm the initiative with the populist argument that 0110 constituted an attack on this party organised by the Belgian political establishment.[12] The 0110 manifesto stated that 'Flanders deserves better than the extreme-right'[13] and that it aimed to show a 'tolerant face' of Antwerp (one of the strongholds of Vlaams Belang).[14] Without referring directly to Belgian unity, the 0110 discourse (re)constructed the picture of a tolerant Flanders as a part of the 'complexity of life'.[15] Since, as demonstrated below, the nationalist multicultural discourse at the macro level made for state-preserving purposes also appealed to the complex cultural and political system of the federal state without any direct reference to 'Belgium', the discourse of the 0110 organisation can also be interpreted as an indirect Belgian nationalist discourse.

The macro level of nationalism is represented in its state-preserving form. To cope with the Flemish separatist demands, the Belgian central government and the Belgian Royal House have practised a multicultural nationalist discourse. This discourse attempts to relegitimise or reconstruct the nation as a community that allows different cultural and ethnic groups to live together in harmony. It constantly defines the Belgian nation in terms of its constituent cultural segments, that is, the Flemish-speaking, French-speaking and German-speaking communities. At the same time, the multicultural nationalist discourse avoids defining the Belgian nation in political or economic terms. The definition in cultural-linguistic rather than economic or political terms allows, on the one hand, for acknowledging the existence of significant differences between the constituent parts of Belgium, whose inhabitants have a different language and different sensibilities.[16] On the other hand, it also allows for reducing the reasons for the differences between the Flemings and the Walloons to their different languages. In this way, the nationalist multicultural discourse suggests that these differences are not insurmountable, as by learning the language of the other community, citizens can better understand its worldview or even adopt its identity. Consequently, the discourse encourages the Belgians to become acquainted with the other communities' cultures by learning their language.[17] Hence, the discourse uses the notion of multilingualism to downplay the tensions which result from a multicultural understanding of the nation. The right of each community to fully experience and develop its own cultural identity is counterbalanced by the notion that the citizens should acquire a second identity by acquiring the language of the other and in this way become 'genuine' Belgians.[18] It has to be stressed that the nationalist multicultural discourse limits the application of the notion of linguistic multiculturalism to the relationship between the constituent regions and communities of Belgium. It does not extend the multicultural perspective to foreigners and immigrants who are expected to adapt to the multilingualism of the Belgian cultural communities.[19] A particularity in the European comparison, though one that seems to be reasonable in the face of the nationalist claims in Flanders, is that the words 'nation' or 'national' are seldom used in this governmental nationalist discourse. Belgium is generally referred to in a very neutral way as 'our country', and even the words 'Belgium' and 'Belgian' are used infrequently and mostly in a purely functional way, for instance to refer to the Belgian peacekeeping forces abroad.[20]

Further, a recurring narrative in the discourse of the Belgian monarch is the portrayal of Belgium as a model for other countries and for the European Union. Belgian federalism is often described as a means to achieve intercultural harmony. Belgium is depicted as a successful demonstration that population groups with different cultures can cooperate harmoniously within a federal system. In this sense, the discourse speaks of an international 'vocation of the country'.[21] In sum, the multicultural nationalist discourse with the construction of the multicultural Belgian nation is a subtle governmental instrument of defending the unity of the Belgian state in the face of the separatist demands of Vlaams Belang.

Bulgaria

Bulgaria presents a further interesting case of nationalism. Dating back to the 1960s Bulgarian communist elites (in a similar way to their Romanian counterparts) espoused a high degree of national-ism under the circumstances of one-part monopoly, and against the official internationalism of communist ideology. This type of nationalism showed remarkable continuation even after the break-down of the Soviet Union and became an essential aspect of the newly established independent Bulgarian state.

With regard to the macro level of nationalism, in 1984 Bulgaria's communist elites started the so-called 'Rebirth Process', which was a campaign of forced assimilation regarding the country's Turkish minority of around 850,000 people. This led to a mass exodus of roughly 300,000 people to Turkey in 1989. In addition, the nation-alist ideology of the Bulgarian communist party had stimulated historical claims on territories belonging to Bulgaria's neighbours. For instance, Bulgaria was engaged in a prolonged dispute with the former Yugoslavia concerning the history and national belonging of the People's Republic of Macedonia, which Bulgaria viewed as part of the Bulgarian nation.[22] Both aspects of Bulgarian national-ism continued throughout the 1990s and are still apparent in the present day.

As an example, the Turkish minority in Bulgaria is currently considered a demographic and political threat. After reports of 'voting tourism' by Bulgarian Turks living in Turkey, the Bulgarian parliament passed a measure restricting voting in the 2007 elections for the European Parliament to those who had lived in the country for three months prior to the elections, which amounted to refusing voting rights to migrant Bulgarian Turks. In this context, Turkish membership is seen as a major problem for Bulgaria. It is feared that Turks will flood the Bulgarian labour market and strengthen the Turkish minority at the expense of ethnic Bulgarians. As a result, public support for Turkish membership is rather low, even though the Bulgarian public supports further enlargement of the EU.[23]

Bulgaria's present-day stance towards Macedonia resembles to some degree a type of homeland nationalism, even though it does not support a minority within another state (as is the case in Hungary and its support for the Hungarian minority in Romania) but regards the entire Macedonian population as part of the Bulgarian national community. As a homeland nation Bulgaria assumes the position of a protector of Macedonia, not only showing explicit interest in Macedonia's domestic and foreign politics but also behaving as if it wanted to defend the Macedonian population from its 'local political elites'.[24]

For instance, as a result of its homeland nationalism Bulgaria unilaterally recognised Macedonia after the breakdown of Yugoslavia. On several occasions Bulgaria supported Macedonia militarily. In particular, during the Albanian-Macedonian conflict Bulgaria delivered to Macedonia military equipment such as tanks, cannons and munitions. This armed conflict began when the ethnic Albanian National Liberation Army attacked the security forces in Macedonia at the beginning of January 2001. Bulgaria justified the Macedonian position in the conflict, as according to its doctrine of Macedonians being part of the Bulgarian national community Albanians were threatening the Bulgarian nation.[25] Interestingly enough, Bulgaria recognises Macedonia as a state, but not as a nation. Recognition of a Macedonian nation would imply surrendering a part of the Bulgarian national identity.[26] This tension in Bulgarian nationalism between recognition of the Macedonian state and non-recognition of the nation sometimes leads to a seemingly incoherent foreign policy towards Macedonia.

The Bulgarian government has, for example, tacitly supported Greece in its dispute with Macedonia regarding the 'name issue', which escalated in the Greek veto of Macedonia's accession to NATO at the Bucharest Summit in April 2008. A further example is the effort of the Macedonian government to confirm a date for opening EU membership negotiations in 2008, which were blocked by Greece again. Further, in this case, Bulgaria did not argue in favour of Macedonia.

At the meso level of nationalism, we can identify in Bulgaria, for instance, the party of the Movement for Rights and Freedoms (MRF). Even though ethnic parties are illegal under Bulgarian law, the party is dominated by Turkish Bulgarians. The MRF has been part of governments both of the left and of the right and is therefore a relevant political actor. It controls the votes of the Turkish minority and thus often holds the key to construct and disband governments. The party is rather controversial in the eyes of ethnic Bulgarians who view it as an agent of Turkey's influence in Bulgaria. In the worst-case scenario, Bulgaria would become 'cypriotised' with the influence of the MRF from within and could even be annexed by Turkey. The result would be a Bulgarian version of the Turkish Federal Republic of Cyprus.[27]

At the same meso level, we can also identify a specific narrative of Bulgarian nationalism represented by the ATAKA (Attack) party. ATAKA articulates specific tendencies of non-democratic and exclusionary ideology, underpinned by offensive language against minority groups. Its mobilisation strategy rests on the language of ethnic nationalism, emphasising the exclusive uniqueness of the Bulgarian nation, degraded by various 'others'. As a result, ATAKA's representatives describe it as the only party to represent the real Bulgarian national interest and the only one able to return Bulgaria to the Bulgarians.[28]

In the ATAKA's nationalist ideology foreigners and minorities threaten Bulgaria's glorious nation, which not only established the first-ever nation-state but also originated from the oldest culture in Europe, afterwards civilising large parts of Europe. This type of retrograde discursive is directed against minority groups, as 'nation' is equated to 'pure Bulgarian ethnicity' being under attack from ethnically inferior minority groups. At the same time, ATAKA's ethnobiological nationalism is associated with an anti-democratic and anti-systemic character, since it questions the validity of the post-communist transition in Bulgaria. The strongly collectivistic form of ATAKA's nationalism contradicts the accentuation of individual freedom in democracies, in particular regarding civil society. In ATAKA's ideology there is no place for civil society and pluralism in the Bulgarian nation. With this anti-systemic rhetoric ATAKA was successful in convincing many Bulgarians of the corruptive effects of the transition process on the Bulgarian nation.[29]

At the same time, ATAKA's nationalism is directed against the European Union, which is also defined as a foreign or 'other' institutional entity. The true European culture is, according to ATAKA, to be found in Bulgaria, which is the last bastion of 'European civilisation' guarding the EU from Asia. In this sense, Bulgaria has always been in Europe, even though the five centuries of 'foreign' Ottoman rule represented an act of 'kidnapping' of Bulgarians from their natural development. But even in this process the 'inherent Bulgarian "Europeanness"' remained untarnished. As a result, the EU should acknowledge Bulgaria's rightful place as one of its own.[30]

In sum, Bulgarian nationalism shows at the macro level clear-cut continuity lines from the communist past. On the one hand, it represents a specific homeland nationalism vis-à-vis Macedonia and homogenising nationalism regarding the Turkish minority. In addition, at the meso level we can identify a Turkish ethnic party, which due to its participation in the government was able to mitigate discriminating anti-minority legislation. Also, at the same level there is ATAKA, which follows a retrograde nationalism of nineteenth-century provenance espousing ideas of a 'pure' Bulgarian nation.

Germany

Germany is a complex case with many facets of nationalism, in particular given the history of the country. We will start with supranational nationalism, which is concerned with the effects of nationalism on the supranational level of politics.

A good example of the effects of German nationalism at the supranational level is the German politics in the Convention on the Future of Europe of 2003, in particular concerning the issue of a new decision-making system. Shortly before the draft of the Treaty on European Constitution had been concluded, the Convention Presidency introduced new regulations on the decision-making system, which was to replace the system agreed upon in Nice in 2000. The double-majority system was strongly supported by Germany, with the argument that it would make the decision-making process more efficient by reducing the number of states able to form a blocking minority. A more efficient decision-making system, it was argued, would be essential in the EU of twenty-five and more member countries. As a result, the double-majority system has been interpreted as a public good that ensures the proper functioning of an enlarged EU. Countries that rejected the new decision-making system were accused, especially by Germany and France, of being nationalist or not civilised enough to understand the values of the community. German political elites attempted to ridicule the Polish and Spanish rejection and also focused on a shaming strategy, pointing to the lack of experience among the new members of the European club.[31]

At the same time, the German government casually ignored the fact that the new decision-making system would give large countries, such as its own, much more power than had been intended by the Nice Treaty. According to an analysis by the Vienna Institute of Higher Studies, the new system would move the balance of power (on the scale between equality and fairness) from 40 points (slightly in favour of small countries) to 80 points (largely in favour of large countries). The new system would take the population of the countries more strongly into account, favouring Germany as the largest country in particular.[32]

This suggests that Germany carried out a nationalist strategy of its power enhancement under the veil of common European interest. The result was a radical change in power relations in the EU in favour of Germany, which is situated at the supranational level of nationalism effects. Shaming and ridiculing strategies such as soft power were easy to apply since these focused on Poland and other non-compliant countries, which were about to become EU members. Their behaviour could be delegitimised, since these countries did not have any credibility with regard to having a strong commitment to Europe compared to the founding members such as Italy or the integration motor countries of France and Germany.[33]

The double majority was consistent with the preferences of the large member states of the EU, particularly Germany, to modify power relations in the EU in their favour.[34] Even before the Nice Treaty, Germany had voiced quite aggressively its critique of the EU decision-making system in order to make it more population-adjusted. It was frequently argued that one vote made by a Luxembourg citizen had the power of 80,000 German votes, making the system undemocratic. While Germany wanted to modify the decision-making system of the EU after the Nice Treaty, the Convention was deemed much more democratic and endowed with higher legitimacy than intergovernmental conferences. Therefore the Convention provided a welcome opportunity to deliver the appropriate legitimacy to the power accumulation by the large member states.[35]

Since the European Convention on the Future of Europe was linked to the constitutionalisation of the EU, it not only promised to change the power relations within the EU, but also to 'freeze' them. Constitutions can congeal the hegemonic positions of certain political actors and can legitimise radical shifts of power relations, as they offer political actors a one-time opportunity to achieve a dominant position. By the same token, the European constitution-making offered a unique opportunity for change and for the freezing of new power relations, as well as for delivering legitimating strategies by claiming its democratic legitimacy through deliberation in the European Convention.[36] Even though the Constitutional Treaty in its original form was not adopted as a result of French and Dutch referenda, the Reform Treaty/Lisbon

Treaty retained its substance. Giscard d'Estaing argued that 'in the Treaty of Lisbon, the tools are largely the same. Only the order in which they are arranged in the tool-box has been changed.' In addition, references to the constitution had been removed 'above all to head off any threat of referenda by avoiding any form of constitutional vocabulary'.[37]

In brief, the German policy of maximising its national power in the decision-making system of the EU was successfully carried out between 2003 and 2007. Germany was capable (in alliance with France) of pushing through with a radical enhancement of its power in foreign policy. In this sense, we can speak of the effects of German nationalism at the supranational level. These politics of power enhancement also apply to the German goal of receiving a permanent seat in the UN Security Council. Since German reunification in 1990, German governments regardless of their ideological orientation have sought to push forward with a comprehensive reform of the UN Security Council to become a permanent member of the Security Council itself. In this way, Germany would increase its international standing and global influence in order to match its national ambition. The main justification of this narrative is that Germany is ready to assume more global responsibility or to act in accordance with the common good. The German campaign to be granted a permanent seat is expected to receive a further boost with the decision of the UN General Assembly in October 2010 to select Germany as one of five new non-permanent members of the Security Council. Berlin has already begun lobbying for sweeping changes to the make-up of the UN Security Council. On 12 October 2010 German Foreign Minister Guido Westerwelle called the UN decision a significant vote of confidence and pledged to 'do everything possible to justify the confidence shown in us by the United Nations'. He went on: 'The world knows that it can count on Germany. We are now faced with the responsibility to establish peace, security and development around the globe.'[38]

At the meso level of nationalism in Germany we can identify the *Leitkultur* (dominant culture) debate as a marker of German nationalism. In the last ten years, there has been a revival of a public discourse on German national identity, which has increasingly focused on the large foreign population in Germany territory, consisting mainly of the Turkish Muslim minority. In particular, representatives of the Christian Democratic Union (CDU) and its Bavarian sister party the Christian Social Union (CSU) were active and visible in this debate. The CSU politician Edmund Stoiber expressed his fears that German society would lose its identity because of 'over-foreignisation' and the then parliamentary leader of the CDU Friedrich Merz coined the term *Leitkultur*. The notion suggests that there is a clear-cut spectrum of German cultural values and mores to which foreigners living in Germany have to subscribe. The *Leitkultur* debate was triggered by the decision of the CDU and the CSU to use the issue of migration in the election campaign for the Landtag in Hessen in 1999. While the centre-left government acknowledged that national homogeneity is a fiction in Germany, it introduced new migration laws and reformed citizenship regulation bound radically by the *ius sanguinis*.[39] The conservative opposition of the CDU and the CSU accused the government of jeopardising German identity, in particular by allowing double citizenship, which was by and large prohibited in Germany until then. What followed was the *Leitkultur* debate about the necessity of German predominant culture as a prerequisite for the successful integration of foreigners. This was part of the conservative attempt to re-establish a national German homogeneity against the trend of multiculturalism. In the Landtag elections in 1999, the CDU under Roland Koch began collecting signatures to show resistance in the population to the plans of the federal government to make dual citizenship easier for foreigners to obtain and to legalise it. Probably as a result of this campaign the conservatives won the regional elections in Hessen. This ethnoculturalist view of the German nation with sharp exclusivity rejecting multicultural elements sometimes assumed 'xenophobic' overtones. During the campaign for the 2000 Landtag election in North Rhine-Westphalia (NRW) the CDU front-runner for the office of prime minister of NRW Jürgen Rüttgers used repeatedly and broadly the slogan 'Children instead of Indians', which pointed to the necessity of more children to be born to ethnic Germans and their support by the German government to become properly educated for the IT labour market. It was a critique of the centre-left federal government, which was planning to facilitate the immigration law by introducing the so-called 'green card' for IT specialists (the main aim being to attract guest workers from India, known for its highly skilled IT professionals) in order to satisfy the growing demand of the German IT labour market.

In 2000 Friedrich Merz of the CDU announced that there must be a 'policy on foreigners', in particular regarding their integration into German society. The CSU questioned whether the ruling centre-left government was fit to run the country, as it was jeopardising the 'German cultural identity' by defining the immigration criteria carelessly.[40] One of the biggest proponents of the ethnic-cultural understanding of German citizenship has been the CDU politician Jörg Schönbohm, at that time Minister of the Interior in Brandenburg. Schönbohm argued that in Germany there are incompatible parallel societies of immigrants and Germans. However, this could result in the demographic death of the German nation, unless the minorities can be assimilated. In this sense, 'immigrants have to aspire to German culture, which has developed since Otto the Great, wholeheartedly, and not just because of the personal benefits [to migrants] of immigration'.[41]

The debate on the assimilation of migrants into the German nation experienced a new peak in 2010, when Thilo Sarrazin, a member of the board of the Bundesbank and the former minister of finance in Berlin of the SPD, published a book entitled *Deutschland schafft sich ab (Germany Abolishes Itself)*. Sarrazin caused a heated debate, as he not only expressed his concern that immigrants do not integrate easily in Germany, but also argued that they undermine German identity. Sarrazin claimed that Germany is becoming less intelligent as a result of migration, since Muslim immigrants are intellectually less capable than other immigrant groups, a fact that is rooted in their culture of Islam. Even though Sarrazin was heavily criticised and pressurised into resigning from the Bundesbank board, a study by the Friedrich Ebert Foundation argues that many Germans from the 'middle of society' regardless of their political orientation share Sarrazin's sentiment.[42] In addition, a number of German senior politicians supported Sarrazin, such as the former chancellor Helmut Schmidt, who told the *Bild-Zeitung* on 23 November 2010 that:

Sarrazin is correct regarding the willingness and ability of many Muslims to integrate: when one grows up in an environment that is completely different from Europe, with entirely different norms of behaviour concerning fathers, and women, and with a different code of honour, they will have difficulty fitting into German society ... I'm very pessimistic if we allow Turkey to join the European Union. Then millions of Muslims will gain entry to all of Europe and will flood our labour market and social systems. We might as well just include Algeria, Morocco, Lebanon and Syria. And then their conflicts, like that between the Kurds and the Turks, would occur in our cities. That would be a terrible development! [translated by the authors]

At the meso level of nationalism we can additionally identify the *problématique* of German victimhood nationalism.[43] The Federal Republic of Germany was deeply influenced by collective memories of the Nazi period and the Holocaust. In this narrative Germans had to come to terms with their horrifying past. These Holocaust-focused memory trends also continued after German reunification.[44] However, since 1999, marked by the relocation of the German capital from Bonn to Berlin and German military participation in the NATO bombings of Serbia, we have been able to witness a rise of new memory dynamics. The new trend highlights more strongly German suffering during the Nazi era and makes it an official part of the mainstream politics of commemoration.[45]

The rhetoric of victimisation was in the early Federal Republic already part of the politics of commemoration, but rather on the fringe of German conservative politics. The annual meetings of the regional organisations of expellees from the former Eastern territories were dedicated to mourn the lost homeland (*Heimat*) in the German East, and monuments were raised in memory of those who died in the *Heimat*.[46] The *Heimat* nationalists were for a long time against the official recognition of the Oder-Neisse border with Poland, even during the negotiations of German reunification, as this would legitimise the loss of the German territories. Furthermore, representatives of the expellees' organisations questioned the Eastern enlargement of the EU, mainly with regard to Poland and the Czech Republic, accusing them of not being willing to come to terms with their shameful past act of expelling the Germans after the Second World War. *Heimat* nationalism was until 1989 the main vehicle for the German politics of victimisation. Interestingly, it uses a self-perpetuating mechanism of the inherited status of being an expellee. In other words, the children and the grandchildren of the expellees are also recognised as such. In a sense, *Heimat* nationalism duplicates the membership mechanism of an ethnic German nation, based on *ius sangunis*.[47]

In addition, the legacy of falling bombs on cities in Germany during the Second World War also became part of victimisation politics in the early Republic of Germany. The extent of the destruction was documented with care and monuments were raised to commemorate the German victims of the bombings.[48] The German losses were also the subject of annual ceremonies such as in 1952, when the president of the West German parliament, Hermann Ehlers, dedicating a memorial to the victims of the bombing of Hamburg, declared: 'All regions of Germany have their share of the wounds that the air war inflicted on the property and blood of our entire nation.' Afterwards, Dresden too (long before German reunification) was integrated into the series of commemorative events in the Federal Republic.[49]

Both trends of the German victimhood nationalism (*Heimat* nationalism and the commemoration of bomb raid victims) have since 1999 become more visible in the public discourse and acquired a stronger degree of victimhood in the mainstream nationalist narrative. In a speech given in 2002, the president of the Federation of German Expellees (BdV) spoke of the pain of leaving one's homeland and how this pain lasts forever. Further, the destruction of German cities is increasingly often put on an equal footing with the destructive history of Hiroshima and Nagasaki.[50]

Daniel Levy and Natal Sznaider argue that in 1999 Germany underwent a change in its interpretation of the Holocaust. Paradoxically, it was not the conservative right, which was hitherto preoccupied with the politics of the German victimhood, but the leftist Foreign Minister Josef Fischer of the Green party who in the German Kosovo policy emphasised that Germany treats the expulsion of the Albanians from Serbian Kosovo as a form of genocide.[51] The German military participated in air raids on Serbia, and the German government justified this with the slogan 'No more Auschwitz!', thus universalising the Holocaust.[52] In addition, Kosovo Albanians were depicted in the public discourse as refugees, while Serbs were compared to Nazis, becoming both expellers and perpetrators. Levy and Sznaider argue that this allowed for a moral comparison of Kosovo refugees to Jews as victims of genocide, but also to Germans as victims of expulsion from their homeland. This created an underlying equalisation of suffering and victimhood, which allowed the Germans to join the universal community of victims of ethnic cleansing. In addition, in the German public memories of the Wehrmacht war crimes in the Balkans were replaced with a humanitarian image of the Bundeswehr.[53]

A further example of the shift of victimhood nationalism into the centre of the public discourse was the 2006 exhibition in Berlin entitled 'Flight and Expulsion in Twentieth-Century Europe', which, according to the BdV, stressed the universality of suffering of the German expelled. In order to highlight the universal character of these expulsions, the BdV introduced the notion of the 'century of expulsions', which underscored genocidal events predating the Holocaust, including the 1915 Armenian genocide. As a consequence, the singularity of the Holocaust was watered down and expulsions in cases of ethnic cleansing are put on an equal footing with genocide.

Within the same trend of victimhood nationalism becoming a phenomenon of the mainstream, the BdV has successfully lobbied since 2008 to establish a Centre Against Expulsion in Berlin. The project gained the support of the conservative-liberal government and was established with federal funding. For some observers, the Centre Against Expulsion project shows that the German victimhood nationalism is in the process of replacing the German memory of guilt as witnesses of the Holocaust are becoming scarce and a new generation of Germans is susceptible to new politics of victimhood. While the topic of expulsion gains only limited attention in the broad German public sphere, it is believed that German conservatives together with the BdV view the Centre as a vehicle to strengthen victimhood nationalism by using memories of expulsion.

Samuel Salzborn says that the BdV lobbied for a Centre Against Expulsions to be built in Berlin, in 'historical and spatial proximity' to the Holocaust memorial.[54] This underscores the fact that the goal of establishing this geographical proximity reflects the nationalist politics of generating a discursive proximity between the expulsion of the Germans and the Holocaust. Moreover, the location of the Centre Against Expulsions in the reunified nation's capital under the tutelage of the federal government renders the expellees the representatives of a national tragedy.[55] As a result, victim status is ascribed to the entire German nation, whereby historically and thus morally Germans acquire a similar status to that of the murdered Jews. In the words of the BdV president: 'Principally, the topics of Jews and expellees are complementary. This inhuman racism in both cases should be the topic of our Centre' [translated by the authors].[56] For Salzborn, it is not only an ill-conceived interpretation of history but also a reflection of the shift in German victimhood nationalism. It is visible in the disproportionate funding, as the Centre Against Expulsions is expected to cost an estimated 82 million euros, while the Holocaust memorial will cost around 25.5 million euros.[57]

To summarise, German nationalism can be explored with regard to its politics of power enhancement in the international system, to the issue of dominant culture in respect of the 'endangered' German national identity as well as to the new dynamic in the victimhood nationalism.

Great Britain

It is not easy to identify British nationalism, given the multinational character of Great Britain.[58] Instead, we should discern English, Scottish and Welsh nationalisms.

At a macro level of English nationalism we can point to the eurosceptical tendencies of English political elites, since political resistance to European integration laid the foundations for contemporary English nationalism.[59] Until 1997 both the Labour party and the Conservatives were at odds with Europe, despite the British accession to the EEC. However, euroscepticism experienced a surge under the Thatcher government, which added an anti-European twist to the nascent English nationalism and is still today a relevant feature of English conservatism.[60] Against this background, English nationalism was directed against the threat to British and English sovereignty represented by European integration, and as a result of this Britain has remained at odds with the practice of European integration.[61] In this context, England has led a struggle for British independence in the EU, as Welsh and Scottish nationalisms have not merged with the British view on Europe.

Britain joined the EC in 1973 and its membership was affirmed by the positive vote in the 1975 popular referendum. Shortly afterwards the Labour government complained that its financial contribution was excessively high in relation to what it was receiving from the EC. James Callaghan first expressed the demand for a rebate before he left office in 1979 and Margaret Thatcher pursued this further. The successful conclusion of the issue of the British rebate in 1984 meant that Britain would never pay what it was obliged to by becoming a member of the EEC. Consequently, other states (much poorer ones than Britain) had to make up the difference.

After 1979 a growing resistance to further deepening British political and monetary integration into Europe became a feature of English nationalism.[62] In addition, during the late 1980s German reunification contributed further to a surge in eurosceptical trends in British foreign policy. In particular, Margaret Thatcher was suspicious of containing postwar Germany within the framework of Europe. According to Thatcher European integration did not contribute to solving 'the German problem' but instead worsened it. A strong Germany in a strong Europe was the worst-case scenario for Britain.[63] The issue of Germany growing stronger in Europe and the European Community having increasingly more impact strengthened the tendency within the Conservative party to view the Germany-dominated EC as a threat to Britain's sovereignty. This position became particularly visible when the political project of the European Union was being negotiated at Maastricht. The British Prime Minister John Major was confronted with a large and strident eurosceptical bloc in the Conservative party.[64] Consequently, the British government was against a deepening of the European Community but in favour of the further enlargement of its members, in order to dilute the concentrated influence of Germany in the EU.

The issue of European integration continued to be challenged by the Conservative party between 1992 and 1997. On the one hand, the Conservatives described their opposition to the EU as the 'last-ditch stand for British nationhood against galloping statist Euro-federalism'. As a result, John Major had serious difficulty getting the Maastricht Treaty passed in the House of Commons, as the Treaty marked for the Conservatives a Rubicon on the way to Euro-federalism.[65] This nationalist discourse used a language reminiscent of that describing the wartime menace to Britain from Nazi Germany. Before the Intergovernmental Conference in 1996 Bill Cash and Iain Duncan Smith of the Conservative party accused German Chancellor Helmut Kohl of supporting the introduction of 'a system of authoritarian and bureaucratic European government which would extinguish the opportunity to disagree'.[66] This type of annihilation of liberty was attempted by Germany between 1939 and 1945. The historically based German threat might reappear in Europe if the German hegemonic position is not checked, and could result in the destabilisation of Europe into the next millennium.[67] In accordance with such statements, until 1997 the representatives of the British government described most Anglo-European tensions as conflicts that could be seen as a continuation of history from wartime. Germany was not the only reference to war in the English conservative nationalism.

This held particularly true for the so-called 'Beef War', when economic tensions between Britain and France grew to the point of provoking an all-out trade war between the two countries. The EU imposed a ban on British beef in 1996 because of an alleged link between eating BSE-infected meat from Great Britain and a new variant of the deadly human brain-wasting disorder Creutzfeldt-Jakob disease. A serious tension between Britain and France arose when the French government announced that it would reject the European Commission's decision to lift a ban on British beef. The British press reacted with denunciations of the French people dating back to the battle of Agincourt in 1415 and including nationalist references to France's defeat at the hands of Nazi Germany in the Second World War.

Such debates about and in the European Union in the 1990s deepened the association made between the British nation, the historical past and the defence of sovereignty. Currently, the new potential for tension revolves around the issue of the new EU budget and the proposals by the British prime minister to reduce structural funds. Britain has allegedly offered to reduce the overall EU budget with the resources it does not utilise itself (structural funds), while the country's dearly held budget rebate would survive unscathed.[68]

At the micro level of British nationalism there is a highly relevant study by Enric Martínez-Herrera on national feelings in Britain and the tenets of liberal nationalism in Scotland and England.[69] Herrera tests empirically the effects of national identity (feelings of belonging) on political confidence and communitarian solidarity. One of the most significant arguments of liberal nationalism is the conviction that national identification helps maintain individuals' political confidence as well as their solidarity tendencies, for instance their support for the welfare state. Herrera differentiates between the liberal nationalism espousing high solidarity towards and trust in compatriots and the community in general and the illiberal nationalism combining uncritical national pride and reluctance to allow 'other countries' to influence domestic politics in any way. Although liberal nationalists are in favour of sharing a sense of belonging, they do not accept mistrust towards cultural minorities, foreigners or other countries while being uncritical towards their own 'nation'.[70]

The empirical findings presented by Herrera show little evidence to support the expected effects of liberal nationalism but they exhibit diverse patterns between England and Scotland. Support for the British political community only has a significant positive impact on political confidence in Scotland.[71] Interestingly enough, it is British illiberal nationalism that has an impact on political confidence, but only in England. Concerning support for solidarity in the form of welfare schemes, the effects both of support for the political community and of illiberal nationalism are either irrelevant or negative.[72] Individuals showing a greater reluctance towards any influence of other countries in British politics and espousing an uncritical British pride tend to be the least supportive of welfarism.

Herrera shows that in England support for the political community does not correlate with political confidence, which is contrary to what might be expected of liberal nationalism. In England political confidence tends to increase with illiberal British nationalist attitudes. Only in Scotland does the support for the political community yield a statistically significant effect. In other words, the liberal-nationalist argument works in Scotland, but it is irrelevant with regard to England, where rather illiberal nationalist feelings show effects.

At the meso level of nationalism, we can differentiate Scottish and Welsh minority nationalisms in Britain. For Michael Keating Scottish nationalism can be viewed as a nation-building project recognising the limitations of the nation-state formula, rather than traditional state-seeking nationalism. Scotland is therefore engaged in 'stateless nation-building'.[73] In Scotland, the Scottish National Party (SNP) represents a specific nationalism, in particular that concerning the EU. The SNP has accepted membership of the European Union and is more strongly committed to it than either of the two main British parties. However, it supports an intergovernmental EU with Scotland among the states. On the other hand, since the 1980s there has been a revalorisation of Scottish culture vis-à-vis English culture in which it has been recognised as a European culture in its own right and a way of representing Scotland's position in the EU and in the world.[74] In this sense, Scotland wants to be a nation among equals without surrendering its place in Great Britain.

Since the establishment of the SNP, there have been two main lines of tension within the party.[75] First, there is a conflict between 'fundamentalists' and 'gradualists' who disagree on how to achieve independence for Scotland. Second, 'Traditionalists' are in dispute with 'Socialists'. While the former are preoccupied with independence and want to remain ideologically neutral, the latter tend to a left-of-centre position. The SNP went through a number of ideology and independence debates in the 1970s and 1980s, as a result of which it became a European social democratic party and decided to apply a gradualist strategy to gain independence.[76]

In the process, the SNP has developed a positive perception of the EU. The strategy of gradual independence from Britain is to be accompanied by placing an independent Scotland firmly in the context of EU membership, under the slogan of 'Independence in Europe'. The core of this strategy is to ensure that more Scots will vote for the SNP and for gradual independence when they see Europe as a counterweight to London.[77] In this sense, the SNP appears almost EU-friendly as compared with the euroscepticism of the English Conservatives.

Welsh nationalism differs both from Scottish and from English nationalism. The Welsh nationalist party Plaid Cymru was established in 1925. Initially a pressure group lobbying for the promotion of the Welsh language and culture, it developed from the 1960s a farther-reaching political programme targeting bilingualism and self-government for Wales.[78] Ideologically, Plaid Cymru combines substate nationalist goals with a sort of a decentralised socialism, based on the principle of redistribution. In addition, pacifist and environmentalist ideas are fundamental to the Welsh nationalists.[79] However, the form of nationalism represented by Plaid Cymru was for a long time 'nationalism light' without radical calls for independence. Not only has Wales never been an independent state, but it was also integrated and assimilated within Great Britain.[80] Against this background, Welsh nationalists supported a moderate version of self-government. Saunders Lewis, the first president of Plaid Cymru, argued in favour of 'freedom', rather than 'independence', as the former could be realised for the Welsh nation without creating an independent Welsh state. In this sense, the party became more concerned with the cultural preservation of Wales, rather than with traditional political sovereignty. Further, the methods of Plaid Cymru subscribed to non-violent, internationalist and decentralist nationalism, which rejected nineteenth-century state-seeking nationalism and avoided the terms 'state', 'sovereignty' and 'independence'. Instead, the party sought to achieve full national status for Wales in the context of the European Union and as a full member of the UN. As a consequence, Plaid Cymru regarded Wales for a long time as a 'small European nation' and rejected independent statehood with the argument that it was outdated within the European context, in which states lose their traditional meaning and nations find alternative forms of self-government.[81]

However, there has recently been a growing tendency within Welsh nationalism to shift its 'nationalism light' towards more policies of independence. Since 1999 there have been an increasing number of calls for more traditional nationalism, which would go hand in hand with the extension of the political powers of the Welsh Assembly. It seems that Welsh nationalists are dissatisfied with the current state of devolution and that a change of mood towards greater radicalisation is under way. This radicalisation of Plaid Cymru's political position became apparent in September 2003, when at a party conference the delegates decided that the new political aim of the party was Welsh independence within the European Union, in which Wales would play a progressive and radical role.[82] Marcus Hoppe argues that there are at least two reasons for this radicalisation. First, the party decided on a strategy to stress its distinctiveness as the only party defending Welsh interests. With the existing Welsh Assembly and other political parties supporting devolution, Plaid Cymru had to find a new identity as a different force in Welsh politics. Second, the party seemingly adapts to the political reality of the EU, where states remain the key players in the political process, while the idea of a 'Europe of the Regions' did not materialise.[83]

In summary, British nationalism assumes various faces, in particular regarding the issue of European integration. While English nationalism retains an anti-European core, which is often associated with historical anti-German and anti-French warlike overtones, Welsh nationalism appears to be almost pro-Europe. The latter has regarded Europe as an opportunity structure and for some time even a post-nationalist organisation, in which Welsh 'freedom' could be realised. The case of Scottish nationalism is different. The SNP did not surrender the traditional nationalist notions of independence and sovereignty, but adapted to European integration while seeking an intergovernmental EU with Scotland as an equal nation.

Italy

Italy is an interesting case study for research on nationalism in contemporary Europe for at least two reasons. First, since the beginning of the 1990s we can observe, at the meso level, a conflict between the nationalist discourse made by the separatist political movement Lega Nord[84] and the nationalist discourse made by the political elites of the state. This conflict emerged as Lega Nord called the unity of the Italian state into question and appropriated or modified some of the national narratives. As a reaction to the political discourse made by Lega Nord, an overwhelming part of the political elites has practised a modified nationalist discourse including the narratives connected with European integration. Second, these developments at the meso level have been accompanied at the macro level by governmental nationalism aiming to achieve not only the maintenance of the domestic power position but also the consolidation of the unitary state.[85]

The conflict at the meso level between the nationalist discourse of Lega Nord and that of the majority of Italian political and societal elites is still a conflict between two discourses of Italian nationalism. Although Lega Nord calls for a disempowerment of the central authorities in Italy and a long-term separation of the North from the rest of the country, its discourse can be seen as a modification of Italian nationalism since it amends and usurps three main narratives of the Italian national identity in order to justify the separatist claims.[86] These narratives include, first, the narrative of belonging to the West, which depicts Italy as a prominent member of the Western cultural community and one of the bastions of Western European civilisation.[87] The second narrative is that of *Risorgimento* ('Resurgence'), a narrative of national unity dating from the unification period which portrays Italy as a nation born out of a strong popular will to fight against any intervention by foreign governments. This narrative has tended to obscure the fact that the Southern Italian regions were forced into a North Italian nation-building project which was unwilling to include them on equal terms.[88] It has also tended to downplay the enormous socioeconomic and sociocultural differences between the Italian regions.[89] The third narrative is that of openness and tolerance, constructing the Italians as a specific society placing a particularly high value on personal and political freedom and a model for liberal attitudes to different lifestyles and cultures.[90] Intertwined with this narrative is the widely accepted myth of Italians as good or nice people (*italiani brava gente*),[91] which has made public discourse in postwar Italy resistant to a sincere examination of conscience regarding its responsibility for aggressive or criminal behaviour towards other nations.[92] These three narratives have shaped the Italian national identity and Italian nationalism.

At the meso level of nationalism we can observe a contestation or reformulation of these narratives by Lega Nord. First, Lega Nord challenged the narrative of national unity (the *Risorgimento* narrative). The unification of the country in 1861 was presented as a historical artificiality and a mistake because of the 'obvious impossibility to unite the North and the South'.[93] It accused the central government of conducting unjust redistribution policies favouring the 'corrupt' and 'economically and socially incapable' South to the disadvantage of the 'productive' and 'effective' Northern regions.[94] Ignoring the fact that the unification of the country was largely a result of the political forces coming from Northern Italy, Lega Nord argued that the claims to national self-determination have not yet been realised in the North and presented the North as colonised and enslaved by the South.[95] Consequently, it called the very existence of the Italian nation into question and claimed that the socioeconomic differences between the North and the South made the maintenance of the Italian state impossible.[96] The fact that Lega Nord itself three times – in 1994, between 2001 and 2006, and after the elections of 2008 – formed part of the Italian government was presented as a necessary step to transforming Italy into a federal state (since the end of the 1990s, the party has replaced its calls for independence for the 'North' by this more moderate demand) and the path of 'Padanian' nation-building.[97]

The discourse of Lega Nord also challenged two other Italian national narratives. The narrative of Italy's belonging to the West was reinterpreted in the sense that the North, because of its culture, was seen as a part of Western civilisation. In contrast, the Southern regions of Italy were excluded from Western civilisation and often referred to as a part of 'Africa'. Lega Nord thus limited the application of the narrative of the West to Northern Italy.[98] The self-understanding of Italians as open and tolerant people was criticised by Lega Nord. Openness and tolerance towards other people and cultures was depicted as a disadvantage because of the increasing numbers of immigrants coming to Italy.[99] The meaning of the *brava gente* myth was also reinterpreted and used as a metaphor both for Italians' naivety towards immigrants' alleged abuse of the Italian welfare system financed by the taxes raised in the North and for their lack of willingness to act against immigrants committing crimes in Italy.[100] Hence, according to the reconstructed narrative, the good and honest people living in Northern Italy were exploited not only by Southern Italians but also by millions of immigrants.[101] Consequently, the discourse of Lega Nord implied two demands. Lega Nord demanded a reduction in the numbers of immigrants and, domestically, the party representatives confined the notion of 'citizens' within the boundaries of 'Padanian' political communities, excluding Italians from the South from the privilege of being referred to as 'citizens'.[102] In sum, the political discourse made by Lega Nord countered the efforts of a broad majority of the Italian political spectrum to maintain a national solidaristic public culture with its obligations to provide assistance for economic and social welfare in the South.[103] Consequently, it seriously challenged the cohesion of the referential framework of the Italian national identity.[104]

As a response to the discourse of Lega Nord, the majority of the political elites made an instrumental nationalist discourse emphasising the need for the unity of the state. They tried, for instance, to enlarge the national referential framework by introducing new supranational narratives linked to the process of European integration. Here, the narrative, which portrayed Europe as a new homeland of all the Italians and the united Italian state as an indispensable part of a united European Union, was used to explain decisions regarding important issues of monetary, economic and foreign policy, such as the adoption of the common European currency and the support of the European constitutional treaty, all of these decisions being strongly opposed by Lega Nord. In this context, at the meso level, we can speak of the emergence of new forms of Italian nationalism, in particular Euronationalism.[105] Besides, against the background of mass immigration from Albania in 1997, the nationalist discourse of the political elites portrayed the negative phenomena associated with the illegal arrival of Albanians as a threat to the whole country and the elimination of these threats as a common nationwide task.[106] With the increasing numbers of immigrants from North Africa, Albania and Romania, the political elites modified the national narrative of *Risorgimento* insofar as immigrants replaced the foreign powers as the new (threatening) 'significant Other'.[107] In the old narrative, foreign powers threatened the political unity of the Italian state; now the reference to immigrants was used to strengthen the unity of all Italians threatened by the discourse of Lega Nord.[108]

At the macro level, a prominent example of governmental Italian nationalism is the policy towards mass immigration from North Africa, Albania and Romania. In this policy field the different governmental goals of welfare, internal security and the unity of the state have been justified by a strong discursive commitment to the national interest and ideas. For instance, in 1997 the flood of several thousand Albanian refugees led to the declaration of a state of emergency by the left-wing Prodi government over the whole Italian state territory and not just over the affected Southern parts of the country.[109] In the same exaggerated way, the centre-left government generated a sense of a national emergency after the public had been alarmed by several crimes committed by Romanian immigrants in 2007.[110] Prime Minister Prodi described 'the psychological and social impact' of the presence of the large numbers of Romanians in Italy as 'incredible'[111] and the Italian government undertook extensive measures at the national, bilateral and European levels to reduce the arrivals of Romanian immigrants to Italy.[112] The state-cementing aim of this nationalist discourse becomes clear when considering the fact that the Northern regions were statistically affected by the negative aspects of immigration to a much greater extent than the Southern regions, and Lega Nord continually argued that the central state authorities were incapable of actions securing law and order in the Northern regions.[113] Further, the governmental dimension of nationalism has been evident in Italian foreign policy during the long debate on the reform of the Security Council of the United Nations in the recent two decades. Italy has been one of the most active participants in this debate and first advocated the addition to the five permanent members of the present Council of new non-permanent seats, to be taken, for rotating terms, by the top contributors to UN activities, including Italy, moving later to a new proposal that would provide a stronger role for regional groups in the Security Council.[114] However, the openly declared objective of all Italian governments since 1994 has not been a reform of the Security Council – quite the contrary; since the Italian government was aware of the minimal chances of Italy becoming a permanent member of the Security Council, Italy could easily accept the continuation of the existing distribution of power in the international system.[115] The main goal has constantly been the prevention of the enlargement of the Security Council to include Germany.[116] A permanent seat for Germany has always been viewed as a degradation of Italy, since Italy in this event would be the only one of the four 'major European powers' without a permanent seat on the Security Council. The firm opposition of the Italian governments to this 'humiliation' of the country can be explained not only by the fear of negative consequences for the relative power position of Italy in the international system but also by the domestic context.[117] The more the separatist Lega Nord questioned the unity of the Italian state and downsized the international significance of Italy, the stronger the Italian governments and the opposition leaders emphasised the narrative of Italy as an important European power which should be treated on equal terms with Germany, and the more strongly the prevention of a disadvantageous reform was declared to be a 'national task'.[118]

Another striking example of Italian nationalism at the macro level was the unsuccessful quest made by the Prodi and Berlusconi governments for participation in the 5 + 1 group negotiating over Iran's nuclear programme (this group included the five permanent members of the UN Security Council and Germany).[119] We can also find nationalist motives for foreign policy action at the European level, as, for instance, during the negotiations on the Constitutional Treaty of the European Union and the Treaty of Lisbon, the Italian government strongly backed the introduction of the controversial double-majority system for qualified majority voting in the Council of the European Union. It did so because it saw the new distribution of power as advantageous for the pursuit of Italian national interests.[120] In 2010, the Italian government vetoed the proposal made by the European Commission to use only English, French or German for the future patent set-up in the European Union, although the majority of EU member states supported the proposal. The Italian government argued that the trilingual regime for the patent set-up gave an unfair advantage to French and German competitors.[121] To break the deadlock caused by Italy (and Spain) a number of member states asked the European Commission to start an 'enhanced cooperation' using the trilingual regime.[122] Another example of nationalism at the macro level was demonstrated by the Italian head of state Giorgio Napolitano when in 2007 he repeatedly referred to the national myth of Italians as 'good' people (*italiani brava gente*) and described the displacement of Italians from Istria and Dalmatia after the Second World War as ethnic cleansing and the expelled Italians as innocent war victims.[123] As a response, the Croatian president Stjepan Mesić accused the Italian president of supporting racism, historical revisionism and political revanchism.[124]

At the supranational level, we might think of two significant consequences of Italian nationalism. As far as the structure of the international system is concerned, Italian governments have blocked reforms of the Security Council of the United Nations and thus prevented a change of the polarity or, in other words, the formal integration of Germany (and three other candidate states: Japan, Brazil and India) into the club of great powers. In the European context, the Italian government's strong nationalist attitude has prevented a reduction of the number of Italian seats in the European Parliament. During the negotiations on the Treaty of Lisbon in October 2007 the proposed redistribution of seats in the European Parliament saw a reduction of Italian parliament members from seventy-eight to seventy-two and the loss of parity with France (seventy-four seats) and Great Britain (seventy-three seats). The Italian government threatened to block the whole treaty unless Italy obtained an additional seat to be on a par with France and Great Britain even though both France and Great Britain have more inhabitants than Italy.[125] In addition, governmental calculations in terms of the Italian national interest led to strong Italian support for the double-majority voting rule in the Council of the European Union and consequently to the change of power distribution in the European Union from 2014 with the emerging system of four major powers, Italy being one of them.

Latvia

Latvia is an especially interesting case for the exploration of nationalism. With the collapse of the Soviet Union and the subsequent independence of Latvia in 1991, a minority group of ethnic Latvians in the Soviet Union became a majority and a majority group of ethnic Russians in the Latvian Soviet Socialist Republic became a minority in the newly established independent Latvian state. These geopolitical changes had a great impact on the Latvian rediscovery of its national identity and its ensuing ethnopolitics of nationalism.

At the macro level of nationalism we can point to the ethnopolitics of the Latvian governments regarding the Russian-speaking minority. Shortly after 1991 the new nationalist elites of Latvia promoted ethnopolitics of nationalism, based on 'voluntary' repatriation of minorities.[126] As a result, tens of thousands of members of the Russian-speaking minority were denied citizenship, and even more members of the minority were confronted with difficult legal, bureaucratic and linguistic obstacles to Latvian citizenship. However, citizenship is critical in newly democratising states, as non-citizens are excluded from political, civic and social rights. For instance, they are not allowed to establish political parties, run for political office or vote in national and local elections. In addition, their rights to free movement, employment and ownership are limited. The scale of forced migration from Latvia in the 1990s is estimated at around 168,000 people.[127] Even though the majority of Russian-speaking residents stayed in Latvia, legal regulations aimed at their fragmentation divided them into three major categories: citizens, permanent residents and temporary residents. The latter two categories equalled statelessness, unless they were granted citizenship of Russia, which only encouraged collective distrust towards them. The ethnopolitics of Latvian nationalism peaked in 2004, when during the elections to the European Parliament in June 2004 hundreds of thousands of Russian-speaking residents were disenfranchised, while foreigners from other EU countries were allowed to vote. While the nationalist governments in Latvia proposed radical plans to exclude minorities from Latvian politics and society, eventually a moderate plan was adopted which focused on social integration rather than exclusion.

At the micro level of analysis we can point to the changes in perceptions of threat between the majority and the Russian-speaking minority in Latvia. Shortly after independence in 1991 the expectation of Latvian citizens was that a great number of Russians in the Baltic states thought of themselves as Baltic Russians, which not only called into question their attachment to the newly established state but also led to the perception of them them as a threat to Latvian sovereignty and security. However, recent data suggests that a large majority of Russians in Latvia think of themselves as Russian-Latvians or Latvian-Russians, which suggests that there has been a growth of multiple identities within the minorities.[128] As a consequence, one can even speak of 'conglomerate identities', shared among groups, and a growing convergence between the majority and minority groups in Latvia. While this convergence is partly the result of changes to the migration policy, this process of social integration has also influenced how Latvians perceive the Russian-speaking minority.[129] The perception of threat from the minority is declining and people's attitudes are becoming more moderate and thus less nationalistic.

At the meso level of Latvian nationalism we can identify the 'invention' of the Latvian nation in the discourse of intellectuals and ethnopolitical parties after 1991. The process of 'inventing' Latvians from the peasant population of Russia's periphery was based on a set of ideas that combined Russian and German nationalist ideologies and applied them to the local cultural context. In the process, the local culture was transformed into national symbols such as folk songs, national myths, language and national history.[130] Characteristic of the Latvian nationalist discourse was a combination of nature and nation which rested on the German notion of *Heimat*. For instance, during the late 1980s, Latvia's independence movement was boosted by a public protest that was able to stop the construction of a hydroelectric dam on the Daugava river.[131] This 'eco-nationalism' linked threats to nature with threats to the nation and was an expression of the national understanding of Latvianness. As Katarina Schwartz suggests, the Daugava river became a catalyst for resistance because of its significance for the Latvian ethnoscape. As an integral part of Latvian national mythology, the river's symbolic meaning made it easy to mobilise Latvians to defend their ethnoscape, whereby the proximity to nature became essential in the construction of Latvia's restored national identity.[132]

With regard to the nationalist party landscape, two strong nationalist forces struggled over the meaning of Latvian nationhood in the 1990s: the pro-Latvian nationalist force For Fatherland and Freedom (Tēvzemei un Brīvībai – TB), which in 1997 merged with the Latvian National Independence Movement (Latvijas Nacionālās Neatkarības Kustība – LNNK), versus the pro-Russian nationalist People's Harmony Party (Tautas Saskaņas Partija – TSP). The TB supported the blood principle in definition of citizenship and discriminatory language legislation.[133] While it was willing to participate in the coalition governments, the pro-Russian nationalists from the TSP remained opposed. This ethnonationalist dichotomy was still present in 2006, as pro-Latvians versus pro-Russians structured ethnopolitics at the meso level. The TB/LNNK party kept ethnic nationalist principles at the heart of its programme. For the party citizenship was a contract between Latvian identity and the individual, rather than an agreement between the state and an individual. TB/LNNK continued to state that 'the protection of Latvians' interests is our most important task' and insisted that Latvian should be the only language of instruction in minority schools.[134] Equally, the ethnonationalist narrative was a feature of the pro-Russian coalition PCTVL. This party built on the TSP's parliamentary faction and took over its ideology. PCTVL promoted the notion of Latvia as a divided society of two ethnic enclaves and criticised policies of social integration. PCTVL's programme concentrated on the issues of citizenship, protection of Russian as the second official language and preserving state-funded education in Russian. Interestingly, PCTVL argued against the presence of Latvian soldiers in Iraq in tune with Russian foreign policy and demanded negotiations about decreasing Latvia's financial and military engagement with NATO.[135]

To summarise, Latvia's nationalism has been evolving since 1991 and has mainly centred around minority issues. It involves both the minority nationalism of the Russian-speaking parts of the Latvian society and the majority nationalism of the titular nation. This type of nationalism resembles to some extent the nation-building processes after the breakdown of other empires that spawned new nation-states with strong minorities such as Hungary and Slovakia. However, Latvian nationalism appears to be different from nationalisms of Central Europe as regards the perception of the Russian-speaking minority as an ongoing threat to Latvia's sovereign national politics. In contrast, the Hungarian transborder nationalism has sought to reunite all Hungarians in the context of the European Union and therefore supported Romania's access to the EU.

Poland

Poland belongs to states with particularly strong narratives of national identity around which Polish nationalism emerges. This referential narrative framework of national identity includes three mega-narratives. First, it contains the self-understanding of being a Catholic country and one of the fortresses of Christianity in Europe. The second mega-narrative portrays Poland as a specific nation placing a particularly high value on the values of freedom and solidarity both at the domestic and the international level. Referring to the historical oppression suffered by Poland from Germany and Russia, this narrative even implies activism in this regard as it presents Poland as an honest and moral player. The third mega-narrative is linked to the second and constructs Poland as a country threatened by powerful neighbours like Germany and Russia and exposed to the disloyalty of allied great powers.[136] This narrative implies the moral superiority of Poland over its oppressors. In this context, the Polish notion of significant Others includes both Germany and Russia, with Germany being both a threatening and an inspiring significant Other and Russia being only a threatening one.[137] Here, a threat does not necessarily mean a military threat. Against the background of the fact that Poland has been anchored in the most important institutions of the West, such as the European Union and NATO, the worst-case scenarios are almost entirely absent in the dominant Polish discourse. However, the German economic and financial preponderance and the supply of energy resources from Russia are constant areas of Polish concern. These three mega-narratives are not the only referential points of discursive commitments of political or societal actors; however, even in cases of the actors' more abstract appeals to 'national interests' or 'national values', the three mega-narratives remain the framework of interpretation of what 'national interests' or 'national values' might be. Of course, even if these narratives are exposed to permanent changes in the contemporary political and societal discourse, we still can observe some nodal points made by them.

For instance, at the meso level, a majority of political parties and societal actors including the Catholic church refer to the narrative of Catholic Poland to legitimise the prominent power position, which the mighty Polish Catholic church acquired in Polish politics after 1989. This position goes beyond its official definition as cooperation between state and church. The church has become an important political actor to an extent hardly comparable to any other European state. This position guarantees the church significant financial privileges and a strong influence on legislation in all issues related to morality and sexuality such as abortion, the use of contraceptives and same-sex marriage. In addition, representatives of the church usually participate in most national commemorations and celebrations as constituents of the nation. In political and societal discourse, the terms 'Poland' and 'the church' often merge with each other, and the terms 'Pole' and 'Catholic' are difficult to decouple. Whereas right-wing and centre parties concordantly accept the influence of the church, left-wing parties have been critical of this influence but have avoided open conflicts with the church. Besides, the narrative of the Catholic nation is used to legitimise a firm opposition to the liberal Western philosophy of life and legal practices with respect to gender parity and equality, abortion, sexuality and the rights of homosexuals. The claims of proponents of liberal practices in this regard are described as being at odds with 'Polish traditions and habits' and rejected.

Similar nationalist trends can be found at the macro level. In 2007, then Polish Prime Minister Jarosław Kaczyński expressed his concerns that the anti-discrimination provisions of the Charter of Fundamental Rights attached to the Treaty of Lisbon could become a way to push through more liberal rules on same-sex marriages in the country.[138] Prime Minister Kaczyński also rejected the criticism expressed in April 2007 by the EU Parliament of a ban on 'homosexual propaganda' introduced in Polish schools by his government, saying, that it was 'not in society's interests to increase the number of gay people'.[139] In 2008, then Polish head of state Lech Kaczyński warned in a television address against the dangers of adopting the EU Treaty of Lisbon and its Charter of Fundamental Rights. He said that the Charter, because it had no clear definition of marriage as a union between a man and a woman, might leave signatory nations open to attacks on the institution by the homosexual lobby.[140]

As far as the narrative of a nation committed to freedom and solidarity is concerned, it is used by political actors to legitimise actions in foreign policy in favour of the freedom of selected other nations. For instance, at the meso level, it was possible to observe broad support for the separatist claims of the Chechen people against Russia and a condemnation of the brutal military action of the federal Russian government in Chechnya. The most symbolic example of this support at the meso level was the decision of the authorities of Warsaw in March 2005 to rename one of the capital's roundabouts after Dzokhar Dudayev, the first president of Chechnya, killed by Russian troops in 1996. This decision led to harsh protests about the Russian government.[141] Of course, this moral commitment is rather selective and determined by one's own history of suffering at the hands of Russia, as, to take one example, similar expressions of support for the Kosovars in the late 1990s were absent. At the macro level this narrative implied, for instance, a strong condemnation by the then Polish foreign minister Adam Rotfeld[142] of the killing of the Chechen president Aslan Maschadov as well as strong support for the Polish government and then Polish president Lech Kaczyński for Georgia during the war between Russia and Georgia in August 2008. This support culminated in a visit by the Polish president in Tbilisi at a moment when Russian invasion troops were approaching the Georgian capital and in his unprecedented declarations of solidarity with Georgia in the face of 'Russian aggression'. Addressing the applauding crowds gathered at a rally in Tbilisi, Kaczyński stated: 'We are here to take up the fight. For the first time in years our eastern neighbours show their true face that we have known for hundreds of years . . . They think other nations should be subordinated to them. We say no! That country is Russia . . .' The Polish president accused Russia of still believing that 'the era of the empire was coming back' and that 'domination was a characteristic of the region'. He explained that many nations had been familiar with the Russian domination that 'had brought disaster upon all of Europe'.[143]

We can also observe nationalism as discursive commitments to the third mega-narrative of Poland as a country still threatened by its powerful neighbours. At the meso level, one of the most striking recent examples was the revelations made by Lech Kaczyński's campaign team on the eve of the presidential election's decisive second round in October 2005 that the grandfather of Kaczyński's rival Donald Tusk had served in the German Wehrmacht during the final months of the Second World War.[144] Kaczyński's campaign chief accused Tusk of concealing the fact that his family was a part of the German culture and suggested that the German past of Tusk's family might help to account for his pro-German sympathies and that the candidate for the highest state office should have a transparent family background.[145] According to some observers, these revelations might have been the main reason for Tusk's electoral defeat.[146] The still-dominant discursive understanding of Germany as a threatening significant Other, or Poland's historical oppressor, has also led, both at meso and macro level, to a firm rejection of the more recent German discourse on the consequences of the Second World War. The growing tendency in the political and cultural discourse in Germany to consider the Germans as victims of the Second World War, and not solely as perpetrators, as well as the decision to locate a centre commemorating German victims of expulsions from Poland and Czechoslovakia in Berlin resulted in unusual tensions in bilateral relations at a time when both governments asserted that relations between Germany and Poland should resemble those between Germany and France. An overwhelming majority of Polish societal actors stresses the genocidal character of the German occupation in Poland and the enormous material losses of Poland including the loss of Polish eastern territories, as well as the forced resettlement of millions of Poles from the former eastern territories. At the same time, it considers the expulsion of the Germans from the former German eastern territories as a result of the decisions of Great Powers at the Yalta and Potsdam conferences and rejects any Polish responsibility for the expulsion of the Germans.[147] The German politics of memorising the German victims thus are perceived as an attempt to 'rewrite' history and erase the memory of German crimes committed on the Poles and to draw Poland into the responsibility it denies on the basis of its most stable national narratives.[148] Hence, it is apparent that the Polish rejection of the recent German discourse can be interpreted as a need to defend its self-understanding as a victim and thus a morally superior nation. We can also see the conflicts between Poland and Germany in the framework of the European Union as a result of this negative perception of Germany. Such were – at the macro level – the reactions of Polish governments during discussions on the EU Constitutional Treaty in 2003–4 and on the Treaty of Lisbon in 2007 to the Germany-driven plans to replace the voting rules established by the Treaty of Nice which gave Poland almost the same number of votes as Germany despite Germany having double the population (twenty-seven votes for Poland and twenty-nine for Germany) by the double-majority system. This would make Germany, with its high demographic potential, the most powerful EU member state and reduce by over the half the relative voting power of Poland against Germany. The Polish government saw the new voting system, which transformed the size of the population into relative voting power, as a historical injustice in the face of the fact that Poland had lost one-third of its population as a consequence of the Second World War started by Germany. A striking expression of this position was the claim made by then Polish Prime Minister Jarosław Kaczyński during the treaty negotiations in June 2007 that Poland should be given more voting power in the EU to compensate for the millions of Poles killed by the Germans in the Second World War. With a spectacular lack of diplomacy, Kaczyński declared that he was only

> demanding one thing – that we get back what was taken from us . . . If Poland had not had to live through the years of 1939–45, Poland would be today looking at the demographics of a country of 66 million.[149]

The same extent of nationalism resulting from the narrative of oppressed Polish people can also be observed, at both the meso and the macro level with regard to Russia. This narrative implies, first, the pursuit of claims on the Russian political authorities and judiciary to classify the Katyn Forest massacre on several thousand Polish officers and members of the intelligentsia in 1940 ordered by Stalin and other high representatives of the Soviet Union[150] as a war crime and an act of genocide, and thus to go beyond the mere acknowledgment of the fact that Soviet authorities were responsible. The Russian refusal to accept the Polish position is regarded as an insurmountable obstacle in relations between Poland and Russia. As stated by then Polish Prime Minister Donald Tusk on the occasion of the seventieth anniversary of the massacre in April 2010, 'memory and truth about Katyn constitute the basis for Polish-Russian reconciliation'. Tusk asserted that the truth about Katyn had become the grounding myth of independent Poland after 1989 and that all Poles were 'one big Katyn family'.[151] Second, this narrative implies the pursuit of strategic alliance with the United States, regarded as the only power able to guarantee Polish security and to balance the increasing Russian influence in Eastern Europe. The most important decision in this context was the agreement on the US missile defence complex in Poland signed in Warsaw in August 2008 shortly after the war between Russia and Georgia. The Polish government decided to take this step even though Russian officials threatened that Poland 'was making itself a target by agreeing to host the anti-missile system' and that the Polish decision 'could not go unpunished'.[152] Polish president Lech Kaczyński openly argued in this regard that he was a proponent of the agreement with the United States on the missile shield in Poland not because he believed that Iran would launch a nuclear attack but because the American missile shield deepened the interest of the United States in Central and Eastern Europe and that it was in the interests of his country to have the closest possible relations with the United States at a time when Russia was showing its 'imperial face'.[153]

At the supranational level, we might consider two consequences of Polish nationalism. First, Polish insistence on maintaining strong transatlantic relations within NATO and its bilateral cooperation with the United States in security issues strengthens the power political presence of the United States in Europe, even against that of other big European states such as France and Germany. Consequently, the relative power of France and Germany is more balanced. Second, in the context of European integration, in 2007 during the negotiations on the Lisbon Treaty Poland achieved a prolongation of the voting system of the Nice Treaty until 2017. Hence, until 2017 there still will be parity between the four largest member states (Germany, France, Great Britain and Italy) and between the two medium-sized states (Poland and Spain) with small differences between the two groups. Although after 2017 the distribution of power in the EU will change because the double-majority system will be applied, Poland still achieved the introduction of the additional 'Joanina mechanism', permitting a continuation of negotiations in cases in which the envisaged blocking minority has not been mustered.[154] As a result, medium-sized states such as Poland and Spain will still be able to delay disadvantageous decisions, making the system of power distribution within the EU more multipolar.

Sweden

Sweden is a state with particularly strong narratives of national identity.[155] Whereas in the case of several other European states, nationalist political actors at the meso or macro level refer to national interests or ideas that often remain unspecified and contextual, Swedish nationalism can be identified at both the meso and the macro level by strong discursive commitments to a set of clear narratives of national identity. This referential narrative framework of national identity includes the narratives of welfare, democracy, neutrality and modernity as well as a sense of belonging to the *Norden* ('the North').[156] All these narratives are emphasised equally and in the political discourse they merge with one another. Swedish national identity is linked to a democratic neutral Nordic welfare state with a modern character. In addition, the dominant discourse uses the terms 'state' and 'nation' almost synonymously.[157] In the following we will exemplify expressions of Swedish nationalism as discursive commitments to these narratives at both the meso and the macro level in selected domestic and EU-related issues.

With regard to the meso level, one of the most important issues of Swedish politics in the last decade has been the possible Swedish participation in the third stage of the Economic and Monetary Union (EMU). This issue was highly controversial and Swedish citizens rejected EMU membership in the national referendum in September 2003. During the debate, which took place before the referendum, political and societal proponents and opponents of the EMU referred to national interests in order to legitimise their positions. Proponents stressed the expected positive effects of the EMU for Swedish national welfare. Membership of the EMU was presented as possibly leading to lower interest rates and a lower consumer price level as well as beneficial for economic growth, employment rates, retail competition, the global competitiveness of the Swedish economy and the long-term financing of the generous Swedish public pension system.[158] Generally, EMU membership was supported because of the expected advantages for social cohesion in Sweden and non-membership was seen as a threat to Swedish welfare.[159]

Opponents of the EMU, on the other hand, maintained a linguistic border line between the 'hostile' EU and the 'threatened' Swedish national values and interests. They referred, first, to the national narratives of welfare to justify their rejection of the EMU. They maintained that effective solutions to the fundamental problems of national economic growth and unemployment could be found only on a national basis and not on an EU basis because as the economic structures of the member states differed from each other, national monetary policies also had to differ from each other.[160] The same interest rate for all member states would undermine Swedish economic growth and increase unemployment and inflation rates.[161] Besides, the EMU would lead to a harmonisation of social policies of the member states, which would threaten social cohesion in Sweden.[162] For instance, Per Gahrton, one of the leaders of the Green party and a member of the European Parliament, argued that the EMU would lead to a strengthening of economic neo-liberalism and have detrimental consequences for the utilitarian Swedish welfare state.[163] In a similar vein, Jonas Sjöstedt, member of the European Parliament and one of the leaders of the Left party, emphasised that only continued control of the Swedish nation-state over its currency would allow national welfare in Sweden to be secured.[164]

Second, referring to the national narrative of transparent democracy, and assigning a complete moral agency and political authority to the Swedish people, the nationalist anti-EMU discourse depicted the EMU as not compatible with the fundamental principles of the specific – and therefore ideal – Swedish democracy. It pointed out that the EMU project would damage the specific Swedish principle of transparency because since Sweden had first been an EU member important decisions affecting the country had been taken 'behind closed doors' in Brussels without any real political debate or popular support in Sweden.[165] The EMU would even cause a comprehensive de-democratisation of Swedish society by strengthening the tendencies of elitism and centralisation as well as gender inequality, thus endangering the 'modern' character of Swedish society.[166] According to some representatives of this discourse, the EMU would even mean an end to democracy in Sweden[167] and a danger for the Swedish right to national self-determination. The EMU was accused of being a political elites' adventure through which the EU was in the process of being transformed into a 'European super-state'. This 'super-state' would be subordinate to the power of the European Central Bank and would increasingly assume the decision-making powers of the individual member states.[168]

Third, representatives of the nationalist anti-EMU discourse like the Green party and the Left party appealed to the national self-image of being a country placing a particularly high value on independence in foreign and defence affairs and 'human' immigration policies as well as on tolerance, non-discrimination and global solidarity.[169] Both parties warned that the political effects of the EMU would deprive Sweden of the rest of its 'traditional' neutrality policy and freedom of action at the global level and that they would put an end to Sweden's generous policy of Third World aid and asylum. Besides, through the EMU, Sweden would be involved in a policy of creating barriers against the less developed parts of the world and in 'unjust' trade policies.[170] In general, instead of joining the EMU, the medium-term goal of the country should be withdrawal from the EU.[171] In this context, the nationalist discourse also claimed that relations among the EU member states

were determined by their relative power position measured in economic and demographic terms as smaller EU member states like
Sweden and Denmark had often been forced to follow the decisions
made by Germany and France.[172] It was claimed that the deeper
the integration, the better big and powerful member states could
realise their interests compared to smaller states like Sweden[173] and
that projects like the EMU would damage the principles of equality
between the member states and thus also Sweden's position within
the EU even more.[174]

We can observe another example of nationalism at the meso
level in the debate on the new law on citizenship in the years
2000–1 as the second-largest Swedish party, the Moderate party,
opposed the introduction of full legal acceptance of dual or multiple citizenship with party representatives referring exclusively to
narratives of the Swedish national community and solidarity. They
accused the proponents of dual citizenship of devaluing Swedish
citizenship and argued that in a time of increasing internalisation
and integration, national belonging should remain indivisible and
the status and substance of citizenship should be strengthened.[175]
Party representatives even declared that recognition of dual citizenship violated the fundaments of the Swedish nation-state.[176] The
Liberal party also made a nationalist discourse with regard to the
new law. It clearly stated that it advocated the introduction of dual
citizenship not in order to privilege immigrants in Sweden but as
a tool for reducing the negative consequences of the naturalisation
of ethnic Swedes abroad, which under the old law automatically
resulted in the loss of Swedish citizenship.[177] In addition, after the
new citizenship law had come into force in 2001, the Liberal party
started a campaign for obligatory tests in Swedish for all immigrants wanting to be naturalised in Sweden and turned immigrants'
knowledge of the Swedish language and Swedish 'values' into one
of its most important issues in the parliamentary elections in 2002
and 2006.[178]

Another example of nationalism at the meso level might sur-
prise but defining nationalism as a legitimisation of political
action by means of a discursive commitment to the narratives of
national identity makes it possible to regard as nationalist even
those actions of political actors that call the position of important nation-state institutions into question. Such was the case in
the debate on the separation of the Lutheran church, which had
belonged to the constitutive institutions and identifying symbols of

the Swedish nation-state for almost 500 years, from the Swedish state. Under the law which was approved by the Swedish parliament in 1995 and which came into force on 1 January 2000, the Church of Sweden became a separate legal entity and was no longer an organ of the government. It also lost its special financial status.[179] All the main political parties in Sweden supported the separation process of the Lutheran church and the Swedish state. They resorted to using strong narratives of Swedish national identity to legitimise their decision. They argued that the removal of the special status from the former state church was made necessary by the 'modern', 'democratic', 'tolerant' and 'inclusive' character of Swedish society. Another argument for the separation was that the state would perform legally binding services, in particular those connected with the welfare system, in a more effective way than the church.[180] Therefore, against the background of these arguments, the discourse in favour of separation can be seen as a reweighing of constitutive elements of the 'national archaeology' rather than as an expression of a post-national attitude.[181]

We can find a striking example of nationalism at the macro level in the debate on free movement of the labour force from new EU member states. Under transitional agreements between the EU and new member states, the old member states were allowed to limit movements of the labour force from the new member states for a period of up to seven years after the enlargement on 1 May 2004. The Swedish Social Democratic government announced that it would make use of the transitional period. The government tried to legitimise this protectionist policy towards the new EU member states by a commitment to the narrative of national welfare but it did not balk at arguing in a xenophobic way.[182] It claimed that free labour migration from these states would lead to disturbances on the Swedish labour market and 'wage dumping'.[183] Prime Minister Persson even pictured an 'invasion' of poor Eastern European 'social tourists', who would exploit the Swedish welfare system once they were let into Sweden.[184]

Notes

1. For the specificities of the Belgian federal system, see, for example, Wilfried Swenden and Maarten Theo Jans, '"Will it stay or will it go?" Federalism and the sustainability of Belgium', *West European Politics* 29, 5 (2006), pp. 877–94.
2. Vlaams Belang is the successor to Vlaams Blok. The name was changed on 14

November 2004 as a response to the earlier decision of the Belgian Court of Cassation which had found Vlaams Blok to be in violation of the law against racism. The decision of the court forced Vlaams Blok to disband and re-establish itself on a legally acceptable agenda in order to keep receiving state subsidies as a political party. Jan Erk, 'From Vlaams Blok to Vlaams Belang: the Belgian far-right renames itself', *West European Politics* 28, 3 (2005), pp. 493–502 (p. 493).

3. Unless otherwise indicated, the following illustration of the nationalist discourse of Vlaams Belang is based on the party programme. See www.vlaamsbelang.org/57/2/ (accessed on 16 December 2010).

4. Janet Laible, '"Back to the Future" with Vlaams Belang? Flemish Nationalism as a modernizing project in a post-modern European Union', in Ireneusz Paweł Karolewski and Andrzej Marcin Suszycki (eds), *Multiplicity of Nationalism in Contemporary Europe* (Boulder, CO: Rowman & Littlefield, 2009), pp. 135–50 (p. 143).

5. For this aspect, see also Nick Schuermans and Filip De Maesschalck, 'Fear of crime as a political weapon: explaining the rise of extreme right politics in the Flemish countryside', *Social & Cultural Geography* 11, 3 (2010), pp. 247–62.

6. For the relationship between Flemish nationalism and European integration, see Marijke Breuning, 'Flemish ethnopolitical parties in an integrating Europe', in Ireneusz Paweł Karolewski and Andrzej Marcin Suszycki (eds), *Nationalism and European Integration* (New York and London: Continuum, 2007), pp. 101–16.

7. For this, see Teun Pauwels, 'Explaining the success of neo-liberal populist parties: The case of Lijst Dedecker in Belgium', *Political Studies* 58, 5 (2010), pp. 1,009–29.

8. Ibid. p. 1,012.

9. Ibid. p. 1,012.

10. See the party programme at www.lijstdedecker.com/nl/federaal-verkiezings programma-2010-1818.htm (accessed on 19 December 2010).

11. Benjamin De Cleen and Nico Carpentier, 'Contesting the populist claim on "the people" through popular culture: the 0110 concerts versus the Vlaams Belang', *Social Semiotics* 20, 2 (2010), pp. 175–96.

12. Ibid. p. 186.

13. Ibid. p. 186.

14. Ibid. p. 187.

15. Ibid. p. 186.

16. Bart Maddens and Kristine Vanden Berghe, 'The identity politics of multicultural nationalism: a comparison between the regular public addresses of the Belgian and the Spanish monarchs (1990–2000)', *European Journal of Political Research* 42 (2003), pp. 601–27 (p. 609).

17. Ibid. p. 609.

18. Ibid. p. 610.

19. Ibid. pp. 610–11.

20. Ibid. p. 606.

21. Ibid. p. 611.

22. Dimitar Bechev, 'From policy-takers to policy-makers? Observations on Bulgarian and Romanian foreign policy before and after EU accession', *Perspectives on European Politics and Society* 10, 2 (2009), pp. 210–24.

23. Ronald H. Linden, 'The burden of belonging: Romanian and Bulgarian foreign policy in the new era', *Journal of Balkan and Near Eastern Studies* 11, 3 (2009), p. 285.

24. Victor Roudometof, 'Nationalism and identity politics in the Balkans: Greece and the Macedonian question', *Journal of Modern Greek Studies* 14 (1996), pp. 253–301.

25. Milena Mahon, 'The Macedonian question in Bulgaria', *Nations and Nationalism* 4, 3 (1998), pp. 389–407.

26. Anton Kojouharav, 'Bulgarian "Macedonian" nationalism: a conceptual overview', *OJPCR: The Online Journal of Peace and Conflict Resolution* 6, 1 (2004), pp. 282–95 (p. 288).

27. Ronald H. Linden, 'Balkanizing security: Romania, Bulgaria, and the burdens of alliance', *The National Council for Euroasian and East European Research*, available

at www.ucis.pitt.edu/nceeer/2008_822-07g_Linden.pdf (accessed on 14 February 2011); Peter Stamatov, 'The making of a "bad" public: ethnonational mobilization in post-communist Bulgaria', *Theory and Society* 29, 4 (2000), pp. 549–72.

28. Emilian Kavalski, 'The grass was always greener in the past: re-nationalizing Bulgaria's return to Europe', in Karolewski and Suszycki (eds), *Multiplicity of Nationalism*, pp. 213–37.

29. Ibid. p. 224.

30. Ibid. p. 227.

31. Ireneusz Paweł Karolewski, 'Pathologies of deliberation in the European Union', *European Law Journal* 17, 1 (2011). pp. 66–79.

32. Berhard Felderer, Iain Paterson and Peter Silraszky, *Draft Constitution: The Double Majority Implies a Massive Transfer of Power to the Large Member States – Is this Intended?* (Vienna: Institute of Advanced Studies, 2003).

33. See Ben Crum, 'Politics and power in the European Convention', *Politics* 24, 1 (2004), pp. 1–11.

34. See Paul Magnette and Kalypso Nicolaïdis, 'The European Convention: bargaining in the shadow of rhetoric', *West European Politics* 27, 3 (2004), pp. 381–404.

35. George Tsebelis and Sven-Oliver Proksch, 'The art of political manipulation in the European Convention', *Journal of Common Market Studies* 45, 1 (2007), pp. 157–86.

36. Ireneusz Paweł Karolewski, 'Constitutionalization of the European Union as a response to the Eastern enlargement: functions versus power', *Journal of Communist Studies and Transition Politics* 23, 4 (2007), pp. 501–24.

37. 'EU Treaty is a constitution, says Giscard d'Estaing', *The Independent*, 14 January 2008.

38. *Frankfurter Allgemeine Zeitung*, 12 October 2010.

39. Randall Hansen and Jobst Koehler, 'Issue definition, political discourse and the politics of nationality reform in France and Germany', *European Journal of Political Research* 44 (2005), pp. 623–44.

40. See Harald Bauder and Jan Semmelroggen, 'Immigration and imagination of nationhood in the German Parliament', *Nationalism and Ethnic Politics* 15, 1 (2009), pp. 1–26.

41. Hartwig Pautz, 'The politics of identity in Germany: the Leitkultur debate', *Race and Class* 46, 4 (2005), pp. 39–52 (p. 44).

42. Oliver Decker, Marliese Weißmann, Johannes Kiess, Elmar Brähler, *Die Mitte in der Krise: Rechtsextreme Einstellungen in Deutschland 2010* (Berlin: Friedrich Ebert Stiftung, 2010).

43. For the term, see Jie-Huyn Lim, 'Victimhood nationalism and history of reconciliation in East Asia', *History Compass* 8, 1 (2010), pp. 1–10.

44. See Dan Michman (ed.), *Remembering the Holocaust in Germany, 1945–2000: German Strategies and Jewish Responses* (New York: Peter Lang, 2002).

45. Eric Langenbacher, 'Changing memory regimes in contemporary Germany?', *German Politics and Society* 67, 21 (2) (2003), pp. 46–68; Bill Niven, *Facing the Nazi Past: United Germany and the Legacy of the Third Reich* (London: Routledge, 2002).

46. See Celia Applegate, 'Heimat and the varieties of regional history', *Central European History* 33, 1 (2000), pp. 109–15.

47. See Gilad Margalit, 'On ethnic essence and the notion of German victimization: Martin Walser and Asta Scheib's Armer Nanosh and the Jew within the Gypsy', *German Politics and Society* 64, 20 (3) (2002), pp. 15–39.

48. See Gilad Margalit, 'Dresden and Hamburg – official memory and commemoration of the victims of Allied air raids in the two Germanies', in Helmut Schmitz (ed.), *A Nation of Victims? Representations of German Wartime Suffering from 1945 to the Present* (Amsterdam and New York: Editions Rodopi BV, 2007), pp. 125–40.

49. Robert G. Moeller, 'Germans as victims? Thoughts on a post-Cold War history of World War II's legacies', *History and Memory* 17, 1/2 (2005), pp. 147–94.

50. See Gilad Margalit, *Guilt, Suffering and Memory: On German Commemoration of the German Victims of WWII* (Bloomington, IN: University of Indiana Press, 2010);

Bill Niven, 'War memorials at the intersection of politics, culture and memory', *Journal of War and Culture Studies* 1, 1 (2008), pp. 39–45.

51. Daniel Levy and Natan Sznaider, 'Memories of universal victimhood: the case of ethnic German expellees', *German Politics and Society* 75, 23 (2) (2005), pp. 1–27.

52. *Newsweek*, 19 April 1999.

53. Levy and Sznaider, 'Memories of universal victimhood', pp. 1–27 (p. 6).

54. Samuel Salzborn, 'The German myth of a victim nation: (re-)presenting Germans as victims in the new debate on their flight and expulsion from Eastern Europe', in Schmitz (ed.), *A Nation of Victims?* pp. 87–104.

55. Ibid. p. 91; see also Bill Niven (ed.), *Germans as Victims: Remembering the Past in Contemporary Germany* (London: Palgrave Macmillan, 2006).

56. *Die Welt*, 29 May 2000.

57. Salzborn, 'The German myth of a victim nation', pp. 87–104.

58. See Arthur Aughey, 'Anxiety and injustice: the anatomy of contemporary English nationalism', *Nations and Nationalism* 16, 3 (2010), pp. 506–24; Krishan Kumar, 'Negotiating English identity: Englishness, Britishness and the future of the United Kingdom', *Nations and Nationalism* 16, 3 (2010), pp. 469–87.

59. See Anthony D. Smith, 'Set in the silver: English nationalism identity and European integration', *Nations and Nationalism* 12, 3 (2006), pp. 433–52.

60. David Baker, Andrew Gamble and David Seawright, 'Sovereign nations and global markets: modern British Conservatism and hyperglobalism', *British Journal of Politics and International Relations* 4, 3 (2002), pp. 399–428.

61. Ben Wellings, 'Losing the peace: Euroscepticism and the foundations of contemporary English nationalism', *Nation and Nationalism* 16, 3 (2010), pp. 488–505; Helen Wallace, 'At odds with Europe', *Political Studies* XLV (1997), pp. 677–88.

62. Ibid. p. 496.

63. Margaret Thatcher, *The Downing Street Years* (London: HarperCollins, 1995), p. 791; Menno Spiering, 'British Euroscepticism', *European Studies* 20 (2004), pp. 127–49.

64. Michael J. Baun, 'The Maastricht Treaty as high politics: Germany, France, and European integration', *Political Science Quarterly* 110, 4 (1995–6), pp. 605–24 (p. 610).

65. David Baker, 'Britain and Europe: The argument continues', *Parliamentary Affairs* 54 (2001), pp. 276–88.

66. Bill Cash and Iain Duncan Smith, *A Response to Chancellor Kohl. A European Germany or a German Europe?* (London: The European Foundation, 1996), p. 39.

67. Wellings, 'Losing the peace', p. 497.

68. *Financial Times*, 16 December 2010.

69. Enric Martínez-Herrera, 'The unbearable lightness of British "Liberal Nationalism"', in Karolewski and Suszycki (eds), *Multiplicity of Nationalism*, pp. 31–55.

70. Ibid. p. 39.

71. Ibid. p. 48.

72. Ibid. p. 39.

73. See Michael Keating, 'Stateless nation-building: Quebec, Catalonia and Scotland in the changing state system', *Nations and Nationalism* 3, 4 (1997), pp. 689–717.

74. Ibid. p. 703; Jack Brand, James Mitchell and Paula Surridge, 'Social constituency and ideological profile: Scottish Nationalism in the 1990s', *Political Studies* XLII (1994), pp. 616–29.

75. Marcus Hoppe, 'The Europeanization of nationalist parties? Evidence from Scotland, Wales, and Padania', in Karolewski and Suszycki (eds), *Nationalism and European Integration*, pp. 66–81.

76. Ibid. p. 74; B. A. Farbey, C. R. Mitchell and K. Webb, 'Change and stability in the ideology of Scottish nationalism', *International Political Science Review* 1, 3 (1980), pp. 404–24.

77. Paolo Dardanelli, 'Ideology and rationality: the Europeanisation of the Scottish National Party', *Österreichische Zeitschrift für Politikwissenschaft* 32, 3 (3) (2003),

pp. 271–84; David McCrone and Lindsay Paterson, 'The conundrum of Scottish independence', *Scottish Affairs* 40 (2002), pp. 54–75.

78. Marcus Hoppe, 'The Europeanization of nationalist parties? Evidence from Scotland, Wales, and Padania', in Karolewski and Suszycki (eds), *Nationalism and European Integration*, p. 71.

79. Richard Wyn Jones and Roger Scully, 'Devolution and electoral politics in Scotland and Wales', *Publius: The Journal of Federalism* 36, 1 (2006), pp. 115–34.

80. Laura McAllister, 'The new politics in Wales: Rhetoric or reality?', *Parliamentary Affairs* 53 (2000), pp. 591–604.

81. Hoppe, 'The Europeanization of nationalist parties?', p. 72.

82. Laura McAllister, 'The perils of community as a construct for the political ideology of Welsh nationalism', *Government and Opposition* 33, 4 (1998), pp. 497–517; Hoppe, 'The Europeanization of nationalist parties?', p. 72.

83. Ibid. p. 73.

84. La Lega Nord per l'indipendenza della Padania (the Northern League for the independence of Padania) was founded in 1991 as a federation of regional parties from North Italian regions such as Lega Lombarda and Liga Veneta. The Lega Lombarda and the Liga Veneta have continued to act as regional and local sections of the 'federal party'.

85. For recent developments in Italian nationalism see also Andrzej Marcin Suszycki, 'Nationalism in Italy', in Karolewski and Suszycki (eds), *Multiplicity of Nationalism*, pp. 175–91.

86. For this aspect see also Benito Giordano, 'A Place Called Padania?', *European Urban and Regional Studies* 6, 3 (1999), pp. 215–30.

87. See also Enrica Di Ciommo, *I confini dell' identita. Teorie e modelli di nazione in Italia* (Roma-Bari: Editori Laterza, 2005), pp. 157–61.

88. Pasquale Verdicchio, *Bound by Distance. Rethinking Nationalism through the Italian Diaspora* (Madison, NJ: Fairleigh Dickinson University Press, 1997), p. 22.

89. Suszyaki, 'Nationalism in Italy', p. 177.

90. Ibid. p. 177.

91. For this aspect see Angelo Del Boca, *Italiani, brava gente? Un mito duro a morire* (Vicenza: Neri Pozza Editore, 2005). For the myth of Italians as *brava gente* see also Filippo Focardi, *L'immagine del cattivo tedesco e il mito del bravo italiano* (Padova: Edizioni Rinoceronte, 2005).

92. Suszycki, 'Nationalism in Italy', p. 177. See also Filippo Focardi and Lutz Klinkhammer, 'The question of Fascist Italy's war crimes: the construction of a self-acquitting myth (1943–1948)', *Journal of Modern Italian Studies* 9, 3 (2004), pp. 330–48 (p. 344).

93. Suszycki, 'Nationalism in Italy', p. 177.

94. See, for example, the statements by the representatives of the Lega Nord in Camera dei Deputati, *Atti Parlamentari, Discussioni, Seduta del 7 Ottobre 1997*, pp. 36–9; Senato della Repubblica, *429 e 430 Resoconto sommario, 21 Luglio 1998*, pp. 34–5; see also Daniele Albertazzi, '"Back to our roots" or self-confessed manipulation? The uses of the past in the Lega Nord's positing of Padania', *National Identities* 8, 1 (2006), pp. 21–39.

95. Suszycki, 'Nationalism in Italy', p. 178.

96. See the representatives of the Lega Nord in Camera dei Deputati, *Atti Parlamentari, Discussioni, Seduta del 7 Ottobre 1997*, pp. 36–9; Senato della Repubblica, *429 e 430 Resoconto sommario, 21 Luglio 1998*, pp. 34–5.

97. For an analysis of the political discourse of Lega Nord see Isabelle Fremeaux and Daniele Albertazzi, 'Discursive strategies around "community" in political propaganda: The case of Lega Nord', *National Identities* 4, 2 (2002), pp. 145–60.

98. Suszycki, 'Nationalism in Italy', p. 178. See, for example, the statements made by Giovanni Fava, one of the leaders of the Lega Nord, in Camera dei Deputati, *Atti Parlamentari, Resoconto stenografico dell'Assemblea, Seduta n. 183 del 4/7/2007*, pp. 18–19.

99. For the dimensions and problems of immigration in Italy, see Antonio Golini (ed.), *L'immigrazione straniera: indicatori e misure di integrazione* (Bologna: Il Mulino, 2005) and Giovanna Zincone, 'The making of policies: Immigration and immigrants in Italy', *Journal of Ethnic and Migration Studies* 32 (2006), pp. 347–75.

100. Suszycki, 'Nationalism in Italy', p. 178. For example, see the statement by Roberto Calderoli, one of the leaders of the Lega Nord and vice president of the Italian Senate in 'Cinque anni per la cittadinanza italiana. Si del governo al ddl di Amato', *La Repubblica*, 4 August 2006. See also the statement made by Roberto Cota, Lega Nord's member of the Italian Deputy Chamber in Camera dei Deputati, *Atti Parlamentari, Resoconto stenografico dell'Assemblea, Seduta n. 187 dell'11/7/2007*, p. 65.

101. 'Su immigrazione ed economia e rissa nella maggioranza', *La Repubblica*, 23 October 2003.

102. Suszycki, 'Nationalism in Italy', p. 178.

103. Ibid. p. 179.

104. Ibid. p. 179.

105. Ibid. p. 181.

106. See the statement made by Valdo Spini, Chairman of the Defense Committee of the Chamber of Deputies, in Camera dei Deputati, *Atti Parlamentari, Discussioni, Seduta del 9 Aprile 1997*, p. 14,670.

107. Suszycki, 'Nationalism in Italy', p. 183.

108. See, for example, Roberto Zuccolini, 'Napolitano: severita sui clandestini', *Corriere della Sera*, 23 July 1998.

109. For more on this issue see Andrzej Marcin Suszycki, *Italienische Osteuropapolitik 1989–2000* (Münster, Hamburg and London: LIT Verlag, 2003), pp. 230–55.

110. Suszycki, 'Nationalism in Italy', p. 183. For this see also Dino Martirano, 'Allarme invasione dalla Romania', *Corriere della Sera*, 22 January 2007. Prime Minister Prodi described the case of an infamous murder committed by a Romanian immigrant on an Italian woman in November 2007 as an injury to all Italians; see 'Veltroni e Rutelli stiano ziti', *Corriere della Sera*, 2 November 2007.

111. Ian Fisher, 'Romanian premier tries to calm Italy after a killing', *New York Times*, 8 November 2007.

112. Fiorenza Sarzanini, 'I romeni espulsi sono 177', *Corriere della Sera*, 18 November 2007.

113. Suszycki, 'Nationalism in Italy', p. 183.

114. Ferdinando Salleo and Nicoletta Pirozzi, 'Italy and the United Nations Security Council', *The International Spectator* 43, 2 (2008), pp. 95–111 (pp. 100–4).

115. Suszycki, 'Nationalism in Italy', p. 179. See also Suszycki, *Italienische Osteuropapolitik*.

116. See also ibid. p. 106.

117. For the domestic context of Italian foreign policy, see also Maurizio Carbone, 'The domestic foundation of Italy's foreign and development policy', *West European Politics* 30, 4 (2007), pp. 903–23.

118. Suszycki, 'Nationalism in Italy', p. 182. For example, see the statement made by the Speaker of the Parliament Pier Ferdinando Casini in 'Riforma ONU un impegno nazionale', *Corriere della Sera*, 12 August 2004. For a broad consensus in this respect between the government led by Berlusconi and the opposition, see, for example, Riccardo Bruno, 'Napolitano: riforma Onu, Casini ha ragione', *Corriere della Sera*, 13 August 2004.

119. The Italian claim was openly opposed by Germany. See Maurizio Carbone, 'Italy in the European Union, between Prodi and Berlusconi', *The International Spectator* 44, 3 (2009), pp. 97–115 (p. 101).

120. Even though Prime Minister Prodi tried to stress that 'European interests' were at stake. See Maurizio Caprara, 'Prodi: "Molti hanno perso lo spirito europeo"', *Corriere della Sera*, 24 June 2007.

121. 'Lo scontro sulla "Lingua di Dante", Brevetto unico, l'Italia mette il veto "No all'Europa senza competitività"', *La Stampa*, 8 October 2010.

122. Ivo Caizzi, 'Brevetto europeo, lo scontro va a Strasburgo', *Corriere della Sera*, 11 December 2010.

123. Marzio Breda, 'Napolitano: sulle foibe una congiura del silenzio', *Corriere della Sera*, 11 February 2007.

124. Mara Gergolet, 'Foibe, la Croazia contro Napolitano: un discorso razzista e revanscista', *Corriere della Sera*, 13 February 2007.

125. Ivo Caizzi, 'D'Alema: inaccettabile la riduzione dei seggi', *Corriere della Sera*, 16 October 2007.

126. Rogers Brubaker, 'Citizenship struggles in Soviet successor states', *International Migration Review* 26, 2 (1992), pp. 269–91.

127. James Hughes, 'Exit in deeply divided societies: regimes of discrimination in Estonia and Latvia and the potential for Russophone migration', *Journal of Common Market Studies* 43, 4 (2005), pp. 739–62.

128. David J. Galbreath, 'From nationalism to nation-building: Latvian politics and minority policy', *Nationalities Papers* 34, 4 (2006), pp. 383–406.

129. Ibid. p. 398.

130. Ieva Zake, 'Inventing culture and nation: intellectuals and early Latvian nationalism', unpublished manuscript (Department of Sociology, University of Massachusetts, 2004).

131. Katrina Z. S. Schwartz, 'The occupation of beauty: Imagining nature and nation in Latvia', *East European Politics and Societies* 21, 2 (2007), pp. 259–93.

132. Ibid. p. 283.

133. Ieva Zake, 'Nationalism and statism in Latvia: The past and current trends', in Karolewski and Suszycki (eds), *Multiplicity of Nationalism*, pp. 195–212.

134. Ibid. p. 203.

135. Ibid. p. 204.

136. For an illustration of the origins and the evolution of Polish nationalism, see Brian Porter, *When Nationalism Began to Hate. Imagining Modern Politics in Nineteenth-Century Poland* (New York and Oxford: Oxford University Press, 2000); see also Andrzej Walicki, 'Traditions of Polish nationalism in comparative perspective', *Dialogue and Universalism* 11, 4 (2001), pp. 5–50, and Andrzej Walicki, 'The troubling legacy of Roman Dmowski', *East European Politics & Societies* 14, 1 (2000), pp. 12–46. For nationalism in Polish foreign policy, see George Sanford, 'Overcoming the burden of history in Polish foreign policy', *Journal of Communist Studies and Transition Politics* 19, 3 (2003), pp. 178–203.

137. For the role of Russia in the Polish nationalism, see Tomasz Zarycki, 'Uses of Russia: the role of Russia in the modern Polish national identity', *East European Politics and Societies* 18, 4 (2004), pp. 595–627.

138. Kaczyński declared: 'We want to avoid seeing this argument being used for pressing on us in morality and tradition-related issues; or forcing us for example to introduce homosexual marriages in Poland including the right of such couples to adopt children'. See Lucia Kubosova, 'Poland predicts lively Portuguese finale on new EU treaty', euobserver.com, 2 July 2007 at: http://euobserver.com/9/24403 (accessed on 18 December 2010).

139. www.guardian.co.uk/world/2007/apr/27/gayrights.poland (accessed on 18 December 2010).

140. Kaczyński said: 'An article of the charter . . . may go against the universally accepted moral order in Poland and force our country to introduce an institution in conflict with the moral convictions of the decided majority of our country.' See 'Polish President warns EU could force "gay marriage" on the country', *Christian Telegraph*, 20 March 2008 at: www.christiantelegraph.com/issue1230.html (accessed on 19 December 2010).

141. See 'Sesja Rady Warszawy: Będzie rondo Dudajewa', *Rzeczpospolita*, 18 March 2005. As a response to the Dudayev roundabout in Warsaw, Moscow officials threatened to rename the street in which the Polish embassy in Moscow is situated after the Russian general Muraviov who had brutally suppressed the Polish

national uprising in 1863. See 'Wieszatel za Dudajewa', *Gazeta Wyborcza*, 25 March 2005.

142. See 'Czeczenia: Warszawa krytykuje, Moskwa zdumiona', *Gazeta Wyborcza*, 3 March 2005.
143. Cited in thenews.pl, 'Kaczyński in Tbilisi: we are here to take up the fight', at www.freerepublic.com/focus/news/2061279/posts (accessed on 17 December 2010).
144. Aleksandra Majda and Piotr Śmiłowicz, 'Tusk zmaga się z historią', *Rzeczpospolita*, 15 October 2005.
145. See the interview with Jacek Kurski, 'Komuna poparła Tuska', *Angora* 42 (2005).
146. Adam Szostkiewicz, 'The Polish autumn', 25 October 2005 at www.opendemocracy.net/democracy-protest/ironic_2963.jsp (accessed on 16 December 2010).
147. For this aspect see also Paweł Lutomski, 'The debate about a center against expulsions: an unexpected crisis in German–Polish relations?', *German Studies Review* 27, 3 (2004), pp. 449–68.
148. For this opinion, see, for example, Marek A. Cichocki and Dariusz Gawin, 'Nowa przeszłość Niemiec', *Rzeczpospolita*, 4 November 2006.
149. 'We'd have more power in EU if Germans hadn't "reduced our population" in WWII, says Polish PM', *Evening Standard*, 21 June 2007.
150. For the Katyn massacre see George Sanford, *Katyn and the Soviet Massacre of 1940: Truth, Justice and Memory* (New York: Routledge, 2005).
151. 'Tusk: Ofiary Katynia czekają, by przemoc i kłamstwo zmienić w pojednanie', *Gazeta Wyborcza*, 7 April 2010 at wiadomosci.gazeta.pl/Wiadomosci/1,80708,7741000,Tusk__Ofiary_Katynia_czekaja__by_przemoc_i_klamstwo.html (accessed on 18 December 2010).
152. Cited in Thom Shanker and Nicholas Kulish, 'Russia lashes out on missile deal', *New York Times*, 15 August 2008.
153. Andrew Nagorski, 'Lech Kaczynski: how the West got Georgia wrong', *Newsweek*, 27 September 2008.
154. www.msz.gov.pl/Signing,of,the,Lisbon,Treaty,13685.html (accessed on 19 December 2010).
155. For this, see, for example, Andrzej Marcin Suszycki, 'Nationalism in Sweden and the EU membership', in Karolewski and Suszycki (eds), *Nationalism and European Integration*, pp. 85–100 (pp. 87–9).
156. Suszycki, 'Nationalism in Sweden and the EU membership', p. 87.
157. Ibid. p. 87.
158. See, for instance, Bo Lundgren, 'Sverige växer med euro', *Svenska Dagbladet*, 21 December 2002; Ulf Adelsohn, Carl Bildt and Bo Lundgren, 'Var inte rädd för EMU', *Svenska Dagbladet*, 5 August 2003; see also the official position of the Moderate party: 'Moderaterna, Ja till svenskt inflytande', 26 August 2003 at www.moderat.se.fcctemp\jatillsvenskt.doc/AM/2003 (accessed on 15 July 2004); for the arguments made by Swedish Prime Minister Persson, see 'Göran Persson öppnar för nya samtal med LO', *Svenska Dagbladet*, 25 June 2003.
159. Sveriges Riksdag, *Snabbprotokoll, 2002/03:113, Onsdagen den 28.05.2003*, at www.riksdagen.se.
160. Suszycki, 'Nationalism in Sweden and the EU membership', p. 92. See also Birgitta Swedenborg, 'EMU orar mig starkt', *Svenska Dagbladet*, 29 December 2002.
161. Suszycki, 'Nationalism in Sweden and the EU membership', p. 92.
162. For example, Sture Eskilsson, the executive vice president of the Confederation of Swedish Employers (SAF) and a key figure in the 1994 Swedish 'Yes to EU' campaign, argued that the monetary policy should not be independent from the political will and that it should remain a domain of the Swedish nation-state, particularly of the Bank of Sweden which was more politically steered than the European Central Bank. See Sture Eskilsson, 'Ja till EMU blir ett adjö till demokratin', *Dagens Industri*, 7 May 2003.
163. Suszycki, 'Nationalism in Sweden and the EU membership', p. 93. See also Per Gahrton, *Med euron mot EU-staten* (Stockholm: Carlsson Bokförlag, 2003), p. 65.

164. Jonas Sjöstedt, 'Euron bygger superstaten', *Svenska Dagbladet*, 1 December 2002.

165. Suszycki, 'Nationalism in Sweden and the EU membership', p. 93.

166. Ibid. p. 93. See also Anna Rosenberg and Anders Orrenius, 'EMU leder till ökad centralstyrning', *Riksdag och Departement*, 7 August 2003.

167. Eskilsson, 'Ja till EMU blir ett adjö'. Even Carl Tham, Swedish ambassador to Germany, former education minister and one of the most eminent Swedish politicians, stated before the Swedish euro referendum that the EMU would limit Swedish democracy for ever. 'EMU begränsar demokratin för evigt', *Dagens Nyheter*, 25 June 2003.

168. Suszycki, 'Nationalism in Sweden and the EU membership', p. 92. See also Sture Eskilsson, 'Med EMU hamnar ännu fler beslut längre bort', *Dagens Industri*, 31 May 2003.

169. Suszycki, 'Nationalism in Sweden and the EU membership', p. 93

170. Ibid. p. 93.

171. See Sveriges Riksdag, *Snabbprotokoll, 2003/04:109, Onsdagen den 5.05.2004*, at www.riksdagen.se; and see Miljöpartiet, at www.mp.se, Vänsterpartiet at www.vansterpartiet.se/csmedia/xyz/000024305.pdf

172. Suszycki, 'Nationalism in Sweden and the EU membership', p. 92.

173. See, for example, Eskilsson, 'Med EMU hamnar ännu fler beslut längre bort'.

174. Torsten Sverenius, *Krona eller Euro? Experternas argument för och emot EMU* (Stockholm: Fischer & Co., 2003), p. 66.

175. Suszycki, 'Nationalism in Sweden and the EU membership', p. 96.

176. See, for example, the statement by Gustav von Essen, a moderate member of parliament in Sveriges Riksdag, *Snabbprotokoll 2000/01:70, Onsdagen den 21.02.2001* at www.riksdagen.se

177. See Ana Maria Narti in: Sveriges Riksdag, *Snabbprotokoll 2000/01:70, Onsdagen den 21.02.2001* at www.riksdagen.se

178. See the statement by Lars Leijonborg, leader of the Liberal party, Sveriges Riksdag, *Snabbprotokoll 2002/03:122, Fredagen den 13.06.2003* at www.riksdagen.se; for this argument see also 'Folkpartiet vill öppna Sverige för arbetskratsinvandring', *Dagens Nyheter*, 3 August 2002; 'Skarp kritik mot fp:s integrationsplaner', *Dagens Nyheter*, 5 August 2002; see also 'Fp tar fram gammalt krav om språktest för invandrare', *Svenska Dagbladet*, 28 June 2006.

179. Under the new law bishops were no longer appointed by government officials, the church could no longer automatically receive tax money and children of church members no longer automatically became members of the church. After 2000, the Church of Sweden was member-supported by a church fee.

180. Sveriges Riksdag, 'Motion 1998/99: K16'; 'Motion 1998/99: K12'; 'Motion 1998/99: K18'; 'Motion 2000/01: L404'; 'Motion 2003/04: K363' at www.riksdagen.se

181. Andrzej Marcin Suszycki, 'Contextual and Nordic: the case of Swedish nationalism', in Andrzej Marcin Suszycki and Ireneusz Paweł Karolewski (eds), *Nation and Nationalism: Political and Historical Studies* (Wrocław: Oficyna Wydawnicza ATUT, 2007), pp. 89–100 (pp. 99–100).

182. Ibid. p. 92.

183. Sveriges Riksdag, *Snabbprotokoll 2003/04:67, Onsdagen den 11.02.2004*, at www.riksdagen.se

184. 'Perssons EU-linje får kritik', *Svenska Dagbladet*, 7 February 2004 and 'Persson varnar för lönedumpning', *Svenska Dagbladet*, 19 March 2004; see also 'Immigration from Central Europe', *The Economist*, 5 February 2004.

CHAPTER SEVEN

Nationalism between Regionalism and European Integration

In this chapter, we explore the relationship between governmental nationalism, regionalism and European integration, which pertain to the different levels of analysis of nationalism discussed in Chapter 5. This linkage has been largely neglected in the mainstream research on nationalism but has gained some attention in the fields of political science and international relations.[1]

The point of departure for our exploration is the broadly discussed thesis on the supposed erosion of nation-states, stemming from the disintegration of the hitherto overlapping cultural and political spheres of the nation and the state. As a result, the disintegrated nation-state becomes culturally challenged (the nation ceases to be the main point of reference for collective identity-building) and the state loses its ability to solve collective problems (because of globalisation processes). This thesis reverses the Gellnerian understanding of nationalism, in which the principle of integration between culture and political authority is crucial for the modern concept of the nation-state. The wearing down of the nation is expected to result from new processes of collective identity-building, mainly at the regional and supranational levels. As a result, a new complexity arises, since new identities do not simply replace national identity or make nationalism redundant. This new complexity places research on nationalism between the macro level of national government, the meso level and the supranational level of nationalism.

Whereas nationalism on the macro level refers to the policy of central government to justify its actions as promoting national identity, welfare of the nation or national security, the meso level of nationalism is an intermediary level between the nationalism of individuals and that of central government. Both levels relate to the issue of how far central government and the actors at the meso level are able to stimulate the identification of individuals with the national community (the micro level). In addition, the supranational level of nationalism pertains to the consequences of nationalism for the structure of the international system. In this sense, European integration belongs to the supranational level of nationalism, since it is to be considered as a product of nation-states. However, when we consider the practices of the EU to generate European collective identity (European nationalism), it remains at the macro level of nationalism of the EU. Moreover, it can be viewed as an external environment for both the meso level and the macro level of nationalism, as European integration can be conceptualised as a catalyst for new nationalism as well as a factor weakening the nation-state and promoting regionalist tendencies.

Nationalism at the macro level versus nationalism at the meso level

In this section we deal with the semantic triangle of regionalism (the meso level), central government nationalism (the macro level) and European integration (the supranational level).[2]

In recent years scholarly interest in regionalism has been on the increase.[3] Numerous authors have been using their own definitions of regionalism, regions and regionalisation, which has generated great conceptual variety in the field.[4] As a result, we can see on the one hand a conceptual development similar to the case of the nation and nationalism. On the other hand, the concept of regionalism has become semantically intertwined with nationalism and placed in the context of the EU.[5] While scholarly debate on regionalism oscillates between nationalism and European integration, regionalism is becoming increasingly regarded as regional nationalism, that is nationalism at the meso level. As a consequence, the perspective of regional nationalism suffers from the same fallacies as research on nationalism at the macro level. First, we can observe a tendency of ontologising collective phenomena, of which regional nationalism seems to be an example. Second, approaches to regional nationalism tend to mimic the characteristics of the nation (such as territory, integrated economy and political power, which are all present in Anthony D. Smith's definition of a nation, discussed earlier in this book) in the analysis of regions and regionalism. In this sense regions are treated as partial nations, or nations on a smaller scale.

In the next section, we will first discuss the concept of the region and illustrate the problems of ontologisation and mimicry, similar to some conceptions of the nation. Second, we will explore the notion of regional identity as the semantic core of regionalism and thus central to the understanding of regionalism. Afterwards we will juxtapose regionalism (or regional nationalism) and central government nationalism. We will propose a typology of regional identities, which should make possible a further distinction between regionalism/regional nationalism and central government nationalism. The final section will elaborate on the notion of regional identity against the background of the growing heterogeneity and multitude of identities in the European Union.

Is there a regional nation?

The convention is to regard regions in an ontologising manner similar to nations, as if they actually and materially existed. Regions are given characteristics of agency, in particular the capacity for intentional action. However, this view ignores the fact that regions are imagined constructs, in a similar way to nations. The alleged agency of regions is linked to three types of feature, which are territorial-ascriptive, functional and politico-administrative in nature. It is apparent that those features are drawn from the context of the nation-state and present a nation-like vocabulary.

If we bear in mind Anthony D. Smith's definition of nation, then the nation equals a human population sharing a historic territory, common myths and memories, a mass or public culture, a single economy and common rights and duties for all members.[6] Since many characteristics of nations are often applied to regions, we face a methodological mimicry implying that regions should be regarded as partial nation-states, or as nations-states on a smaller scale. The three features mentioned above lead us to the three basic 'imagined criteria' of regions. First, regions are regarded as areas that can be delineated according to the similarity of certain topographical characteristics distinguishing them from their environment.[7] The imagined nature of the region becomes obvious if we understand that the demarcation of regions directly depends on the criterion we select for our analysis. The selected template of analysis leads to a discovery of geographically similar clusters, interpreted as regions, which means that almost every territory can be depicted as a region.[8] The condensed similarity of topographic features is believed to reflect the boundaries of regions as existing individual entities, which in turn underlines the belief in their agency, that is their ability to act intentionally.

Second, regions are also conceived of as specific patterns of functional relations and interactions. Also in this case, the selection of a given function is arbitrary, as the indicators for the density of regional interactions are selected and evaluated according to the choice of function. For instance, if economic interdependence is viewed as a relevant characteristic of regionalism, it leads consequently to a perspective defining regions as resulting from economic processes.[9]

Third, the region is conceived of as an area of political and administrative activity, whereby it is delineated as an entity differing in size from the nation-state but constructed in a similar manner.[10] The region is expected to fulfil political tasks and to be interested in its own self-determination, at least to a certain degree (frequently being autonomist, rather than secessionist). In addition, the criterion of the cultural peculiarity of regions overlaps with the difference between the self and the other, sometimes even in the more extreme form of friend–foe differentiation, which strongly resembles the concept of a nation as bounded community. As a result of the differentiation between the in-group and the out-group (very similar to the 'Othering' of nations), the construct of a region allows for identity-building and a mobilisation of the in-group against the out-group.

All three imagined criteria of regions share the same characteristics of ontologising regions as collective phenomena with condensed similarity, high density of interactions and cultural peculiarity. They imply that regions imitate features of nation-states on a smaller scale. On one hand, for example, regionalism becomes a catchword for different types of collective phenomena beneath the nation-state, rendering it a 'smaller' nationalism. On the other hand, it implies that regions mimic nation-states, mostly in the context of the national loss of problem-solving capacities, whereby regions are expected to be a functional equivalent for nations.

In order to understand what regions are, we should juxtapose the concept with nations. Regions can be associated with political demands that conflict with those of their national governments, or on a durable political orientation not represented in the national government, or even on an ethnic or cultural cleavage. Thus, regionalist actors can espouse an ideology that may be in conflict with the national government but that does not necessarily strive for their own state, as is the case with nationalist actors. In addition, nations have much higher entry and exit barriers than regions, since regions are more open to the social mobility and political participation of 'aliens'. We suggest that we could de-ontologise regions by applying the concept of regional identity, just as we approach the concept of a nation by exploring national identity. The ontologisation of regions arises from ascribing agency to regions, ignoring the fact that regional actors, rather than regions, integrate or make decisions.

Regional identity: between the micro level and the meso level of analysis

Some scholars of regionalism have contested the concept of regional identity as elusive.[11] In the mainstream social sciences there seems to be a consensus on the individualist approach to collective identity, even though some authors ascribe it to collectivities, rather than to individuals.[12] The individualist approach to collective identity differs from rational choice or instrumental rationality on different perspectives on nations, discussed in Chapter 1, as the latter argues solely on the basis of cost-benefit calculation. The main feature of the individualist approach is, however, that it treats collective identity as a characteristic of individuals, rather than of groups, since the latter do not exhibit any group consciousness. The motives for such collective identity are secondary. In this context, regional identity is a type of collective identity which can be measured using the individual feeling or perception of belonging to a certain group (the micro level of analysis). Even though groups often refer to territorial boundaries, as is often the case of nations, in the micro perspective it is counterproductive to exogenously define them, as the very individuals in question endogenously construct the specific dimensions of identity. In this way, this perspective escapes the ontologisation of collectives, since their identity is constructed by the actions of their members. Against this backdrop, collective identity (including regional and national identities) can be characterised by the individuals' feeling of belonging among themselves (the horizontal dimension) and presupposes a self-recognition of individuals as group members (the vertical dimension). This perception of belonging influences the actions of individuals, as they would behave differently if they were not group members. Therefore, collective identity is expected to be associated with 'moral resources', mainly loyalty and solidarity towards other members of the same collectivity.

In general, collective identity is a feature of communities. Small-scale communities develop their social cohesion as a result of face-to-face communication among its members. This direct communication among the members of the group is expected to limit potential transgressions of loyalty and solidarity such as free riding by imposing norms of legitimate behaviour. However, communities growing in size and anonymity become increasingly less immune to transgressions of loyalty and solidarity. Hence, members of large-scale communities require an abstract collective identity, based on shared imagination of commonness, reflected in Benedict Anderson's concept of 'imagined community'. While the individual feeling of belonging to a collectivity is a micro-level occurrence, the very construction of collective identity by elites of regional collectivities and other subnational groups should be viewed as a phenomenon on the meso level.

In the case of nations, the abstract collective identity is constructed by, among other things, institutionalised myths of common origin as well as common history and values, whereas individuals with regional identity relate primarily to the territory as an 'integral amalgamate' of topographical, social and economic images. As mentioned above, this amalgamate is constructed and intersubjectively recognised with reference to collective narratives. Such narratives relate, for instance, to the native characteristics of the region's inhabitants. There has been, particularly in Germany since the 1980s, a political revival of the narrative of the *Heimat* (native country), based on the claim that every individual has a native identity and therefore possesses rights associated with his or her place of birth. This has resulted in the sometimes controversial policy of promoting *Heimat* culture and *Heimat* regional identity.

Against this backdrop of the concept of regional identity, a region can be regarded as a perceived phenomenon pertaining to a community membership, located between the nation, which is an abstract community, and the local community, which offers a framework for face-to-face communication. Consequently, the inhabitants of regions are supplied with a sufficiently large, but more easily comprehensible, semantic framework, allowing for the interpretation of their individual experiences in the collective context, thus rendering regional identity semi-abstract. This projection surface can stimulate regional collective identity by providing the opportunity to disassociate oneself from other regional groups/regions through a generation of boundaries. In this context, the territory of a region remains a relevant reference for regional identity (although it is subject to arbitrary definition) and thus carries implications for regionalism as ideology or policy.

Regional identity can have several implications. First, on the basis of regional identity elites can mobilise individuals for active regionalism based on the regional narrative. The regional ideology, addressing individual feelings of belonging but situated on the meso level, conveys an image of the region as an independent (collective) actor, as if the regions were willing to defend their position regarding other regions, or realise their interests vis-à-vis the central government. In this sense, regional identity can be used as a source for political regionalist mobilisation.

Second, the strength of regional identity depends on a plethora of specific as well as contingent factors. In this sense, regional identity often lacks institutionalised mechanisms for its promotion, such as an educational system acting as a transmission belt of identity, which is provided by the nation-state regarding national identity. Still, there are certain exceptions, including strongly federally organised countries such as the Federal Republic of Germany or the existence of a strong regional party that is able to mobilise against the central government.

Third, regional narratives are less frequently associated with specific characteristics such as a common and exclusive language or an integrated and exclusive legal system, as is the case with nations. As the vernacular and legal character of identity is on average more common to nations than regions, it also leads to different relations to loyalty and solidarity in these two types of collective identity.[13] In consequence, regions can be linked with collective identity, which differs from the collective identity of national as well as of local communities.

In short, the difference between national and regional identity is based on two criteria: the type of community and the moral resources expected from the individuals. As mentioned above, regions are semi-abstract communities, since they are not based entirely on face-to-face communication. Nevertheless, they can function as reducers of cognitive complexity, frequently in a more effective manner than nations. As regards moral resources, regions encourage solidarity rather than loyalty. As a result of territorial mobility, regional elites have fewer instruments than nation-states with which to establish loyalty. Since mobility within nations is higher than that between them, individuals dissatisfied with regional development or the quality of their life may choose to leave the region but stay within the nation.[14] They have stronger incentives for doing so, since the labour market is likely to be integrated nationally. This Gellnerian argument overlaps with research suggesting that when options for individual mobility exist, as a result of open or permeable boundaries, people are more likely to abandon their group in favour of personal opportunities.[15] As a consequence, territorial mobility within nations facilitates the exit option from regional identity, while the boundedness of nations inhibits the exit option from national identity. Therefore, in modern societies there are no sanctions for leaving the region and nor is one expected to pass tests or to be resident for a certain period of time in order to become a citizen. There is, however, one caveat relating to the European Union. It can be argued that the EU member states show less inclination to enforce loyalty on their citizens because Europeanisation, particularly the internal market, makes the borders of the member states to some extent permeable. However, even though the internal market has increased the movement of capital considerably, the labour market is still nationally fragmented.[16] On the one hand, numerous exit options decrease the potential for loyalty in the region, while this potential is greater regarding the nation. On the other hand, there is higher potential for solidarity in the region, as the semi-abstract community can further stronger ties among individuals.

However, regional solidarity is unlikely to replace the national appeal for loyalty and solidarity. Even though there are arguments suggesting that national solidarity is showing cracks as a result of globalisation and Europeanisation, and that we might expect a shift of solidarity to subnational arrangements, it is the nation-state (with the community component of the nation) that is likely to remain the primary target of solidarity expectations. It still possesses most of the instruments for enforcing solidarity and loyalty such as the power of taxation and revenue spending as well as the monopoly of violence. However, a division of solidarity between the national community and the regional ones is possible. As the experimental study of public solidarity suggests, a majority of individuals would choose a high tax rate in order to establish a national public pension system.[17] As a result, globalisation and Europeanisation individualisation appear not to modify citizens' preferences for public solidarity and we might therefore not expect a retreat to private solidarity but rather a reshuffling of the solidarity expectations along different levels of public space. Regions can establish mechanisms of solidarity in the form of regional tax schemes or by making regional funds more attractive. In fact, we are witnessing that many European countries have devolved fiscal authority and responsibility to subnational authorities.

Is regionalism a new nationalism?

Within regionalism, the relationship between regional and national identity is a contested arena of scholarly debate. As mentioned above, scholars define regionalism as a phenomenon both different from nationalism and somehow similar to it.[18] Furthermore, a rather radical position claims that nation-states have become inefficient entities in facing globalising forces, and that they are being replaced by their global and regional functional equivalents.[19] As a consequence, both the attachment to the nation and the ability of the nation-state to generate stable collective identity decrease. However, this position is difficult to sustain, as despite growing internationalisation, national identity still scores high in citizens' attitudes of loyalty and solidarity.[20]

A more balanced position would acknowledge that despite the rise of new regionalism, national identity is not becoming obsolete. Instead, a shift of significance between regional and national identity has emerged, establishing a tension between these two phenomena but without a clear functional replacement. Two variants of this argument are possible. In the first variant, regionalism becomes as significant as nationalism but with a new equilibrium in favour of regionalism. Here, we would be confronted with a sort of regional nationalism complemented by traditional nationalism. In the second variant, the tension between nation and region occurs with a shift towards regional identity but with national identity remaining a core identity.[21] These two variants can be conceptualised as scenarios for the further development of the relationship between nationalism and regionalism, particularly if we assume that this relationship is dynamic.

Traditional nationalism at the macro-level

We can distinguish several arguments rejecting regions as new nations on a smaller scale. First, the historical and macrosociological argument highlights the process of nation-building of the nineteenth and twentieth centuries, which occurred only to the detriment of regional identities. In the process, national integration was accompanied by a weakening of the regions in favour of the centre, making the vertically integrated nation-state the driving force of modernity. Since nation-building was associated mainly with the establishment of states as powerful agents of collective identity creation, national identity has become the dominant collective identity in modern human societies. It follows that even today regional identities are usually significantly less institutionalised and have a less statist character, even in federal states, compared with national identities. In this perspective, nationalism at the macro level, that is exercised by the central government, still remains the key factor in the political activity of states. Even though regions might be more capable of solidarity because of their semi-abstract communities, the redistributive mechanisms of the modern welfare state have been introduced precisely in the name of the nation, not in the name of the region. Against this backdrop, the nation-state possesses significantly more resources for mobilisation, since nobody wages wars in defence of regions and nobody expects individuals to sacrifice their own life for them: national ideology has a stronger mobilising potential than does regional ideology. In addition, central government pursues a policy of identity construction and reconstruction more strongly than do regions. As discussed previously, according to Ernest Gellner nation-states generate and promote collective identity through a communicative homogenisation, which occurs mainly through a process called 'exo-socialisation' and via standardised education systems. Since the standardisation of language has to be steered centrally, it gives the central government a powerful tool for identity construction.

Second, an extension of the argument above, pertaining to the political meaning of the nation, should be considered here. Since nations have been capable of developing a strong political identification in their respective population because of state-building, they still posses a quite effective and resilient institutional power both to generate national compliance from and to offer a comprehensive political framework for individuals. No comparable political rights and obligations exist at the regional level since national citizenship is established in the national range and does not vary regionally. Even though exceptions exist, for instance, with special group rights for indigenous people, such as in Canada, the USA and Australia, they do not question the validity of nations and their mass appeal.[22] Moreover, the effectiveness of citizenship can only be assured in the framework of the nation-state and against the background of a nation as the comprehensive community.[23] Whereas no substantial citizenship supports regional identity, for the majority of individuals it is difficult to assume a new national identity or to give up the old one, as citizenship has been fused with national identity and subject to primary socialisation.

Third, a further extension of the political argument points out that nations play a decisive role in legitimising political systems. As we have previously discussed, this legitimacy is nurtured from two sources. On the one hand it is legitimacy by output: the quality of the results of the political process. On the other hand it is the participation of citizens in the process of political decision-making. Regarding both sources of legitimacy, the nation retains relevant tasks that cannot be replaced at the regional level. The output of the political system can only be guaranteed if the nation provides for the stability of the entire political order. Hence, the legal, political and cultural claims of the inhabitants of regions rely heavily on the effectiveness of the national rule of law as well as on the capability of the nation-state to fulfil its tasks, such as the production of collective goods (for instance, monetary and fiscal policy). However, the greatest challenge for the nation-state in this field is globalisation, rather than regionalism, as internationalisation processes set limits to national effectiveness.[24]

Concerning the input source of legitimacy, that is citizens' participation, nations remain the most important system of reference.

Even in highly federalised states, citizens deem national elections to be more significant than regional or European elections, since the key channels of political participation such as the political parties are organised at the national level. In this context, the nation remains responsible for legitimising the collectively binding decisions relating to the entire society, and not only to its regional fragments. Therefore, nations, at least in their democratic variation, are more likely to guarantee an integrated public discourse necessary for democratic legitimacy.

Fourth, we can formulate an argument in favour of nations based on the self-esteem-oriented perspective, also previously discussed in the section on the effects of nations. In this view, regional identity is likely to be prone to rational and instrumental construction because of its own permeability and the existence of national identity as the framework identity. As collective identity can be individually manipulated, although not necessarily consciously, group members virtually exercise 'image management' of their groups, maintaining the same level of perceived group attractiveness despite evidence to the contrary. Only if the image management does not function do individuals tend to select a more attractive group membership and leave the old one. Although in the case of nations image management is ubiquitous because of the constrained opportunities of the exit option, regions can be more easily deserted. One can be an actor of regionalism without being born in the region, and one can leave the region without being called a traitor or unpatriotic.[25]

Regional nationalism at the meso level

An alternative version of the new relationship between nationalism and regionalism pertains to regional nationalism, in which the region is subject to relative strengthening. This strengthening can be associated with three arguments relating to structural development in the regions. The first refers to economic globalisation or internationalisation, which is expected to promote regional activity of the actors. In this view, the markets expand beyond the nation-state and become increasingly deregulated; this is accompanied by an erosion of economic control of nation-states in favour of the regions.[26] In the process regionally active economic actors become less dependent on the national market and the national capital.

As a result of globalisation/internationalisation, we can observe not only a rise in direct foreign investment in the regions, but also new possibilities to receive bank loans from foreign banks. Hence, regional actors can develop new incentives to become attractive in order to attract international capital. In this perspective, regional actors cease to rely exclusively on subsidies from their nation-states and can become more independent.[27] On the one hand regions are, as a rule, large enough to provide sufficient infrastructure for capital accumulation. On the other hand, regions tend to assume increasingly more significance for the wellbeing of their population, particularly if there is a further retreat of the welfare state at the national level due to the global economic crisis.[28] The retreat of the welfare state and the growing competition among the regions regarding investments can entail a shift of citizens' loyalties back to the regional level, thus promoting regional nationalism.[29]

Second, regionalism appears to profit from change in the capitalist mode of production and change in the regulation of the economic system. Therefore, regional nationalism can be conceptualised in the context of the transition from modern Fordist production to so-called post-Fordism. This economic perspective corresponds with the functionalist understanding of nations as epiphenomena of modern capitalism and specifically industrialisation offered by Ernest Gellner and presented in Chapter 1. When the mode of production changes, we should also expect a modification in the nature of nations. Common features of modern capitalist economy include mass production of homogeneous goods, their extensive storage, regulated work time and homogeneous labour markets, as well as functional and spatial hierarchies of production. In contrast, post-Fordist capitalist economies tend to be characterised by flexible production of homogeneous goods in smaller numbers, limited storage, flexible work time, interregionally segmented labour markets, and regional clusters and networks of production.[30] With these changes a transformation in the functionality of nations might also ensue, generating pressure towards smaller functional units such as regions.

Furthermore, these changes engender an already visible shift in social norms and social bonds.[31] The change in the structure of production goes hand in hand with heterogeneous patterns of consumption, heterogeneous lifestyles, a variety of cultures, and flexible time structures and households (singles, temporary partnerships), while Fordism developed along the lines of mass consumption, homogeneous lifestyles and a fixed time regime (working, shopping, sleeping).[32] In this view, post-Fordism becomes increasingly associated with the regional variety of consumption cultures and lifestyles and the regionalised structure of production, thus promoting regional heterogeneity as opposed to the homogenising effects of Fordism.[33] If this holds true, the changes in the economic structure will further regional nationalism as a collective identity, rather than integrating effects of nations.

Third, the European Union seems to be an additional factor responsible for the increasing relevance of regionalism in Europe. This is associated first and foremost with the EU's structural policy and its institutional support for regional, rather than national, ties. On the one hand the regions in the member states of the EU are transmission belts for European structural funds, which represent the second-greatest expenditure of the EU and constitute one of the most relevant aspects of the EU's redistribution policy.[34] On the other hand, the EU has been searching for a rationale for its existence beyond economic gains. Therefore, support for the regions in Europe belongs to the realm of the organisation's self-legitimising activities.[35] In this context, regions function as agents for the EU's policy to re-establish its legitimacy after the occurrence of the 'Post-Maastricht blues', or at least symbolise the EU's closeness to citizens.[36] For this purpose, the EU supports projects and finances initiatives at the regional level even in traditionally unitary states such as Sweden, Great Britain and Poland. Additionally, it encourages an intermediary level of political decision-making by offering numerous European programmes and cooperation initiatives to the regions and stimulates regional representation in Brussels, around which regional identities can crystallise.[37] In this sense, we could argue that the EU supports regional nationalism at the meso level. Some authors even suggest that 'Brussels' supports European regions much more efficiently and to a higher degree than the nation-states, which would point to diverging politics of macro nationalism of central governments and the politics of meso-nationalism supported by the EU.[38] In the process the EU becomes a political point of crystallisation for regional policies and interest representation and perhaps even regional identities. The aggregate resources devoted by subnational governments to representation in the EU are comparable to those committed by national governments.[39]

Furthermore, regions are crucial for the complex political

system of the EU, which in recent years has been described as a 'multilevel system' with 'multilevel governance'.[40] Multilevel governance integrates a plurality of actors, including the regions that negotiate with each other and with other actors such as the European Commission in various political arenas.[41] As a result of the rise of new regional actors in European policymaking and the resulting pressure for regional participation and integration new elements of interlacing and interlocking politics in the EU have been introduced. Against this backdrop, the autonomisation of regions ensues, as national governments no longer play the role of intermediaries between regions at international or European level. Therefore, regions are no longer politically anchored exclusively within national states; they increasingly create their own structures of influence with supranational actors, mainly the European Commission, and with other regional actors in different states.[42] This suggests that regions are becoming more powerful in institutional terms and able to bundle individuals' political attention, activities and loyalties. Thus, they support new dynamics of regional identity creation as well as regional nationalism.

Types of regional nationalism

As regional nationalism is situated at the meso level, it includes various narratives referring to regional interests and ideas and their construction, as well as conflicts between contending visions of these narratives, as different political and societal groups at the intermediary level disseminate them between the individual and the central government.[43]

Even if regional nationalism is supported by the structural developments described in the previous section, it can assume the form of an ideology or policy that perpetuates the differentiation between the regional self and the regional and national other. Consequently, regional nationalism promotes an exclusion of the environment, which is defined as not belonging to the region, as well as an internal integration within the space, defined as regional. Hence, regional nationalism attempts to construct or strengthen regional identity, and thus it can acquire various forms.

We stated previously that two basic types of nationalist discourse at the meso level are instrumental and ideological nationalism. Against this background, we can identify several forms of regional nationalism, including the rationalist form of regional nationalism, more ideological political regionalism as well as regionalism as a component of multiple identities. The rationalist form of regional identity is based on utility: actors realise their interests and attain goals by using their economic resources as well as political influence channels. This type of regional nationalism can be drawn from the feeling of success in prospering regions. It can also be promoted by an ideology that tries to enhance the economic attractiveness of the regions in order to increase the welfare of the regional population. In this case we can deal with a deliberate construction of regions with the goal of, for instance, attaining financial resources from EU funds. This type of rational regional identity can be illustrated by Scotland, Wales or Bavaria, which profit on the one hand from the globalised capital markets and on the other from European financial support, thus circumventing central governments, at least to some extent.[44] Globalisation and Europeanisation make the national markets less attractive, and the regions can additionally represent their interests via Brussels, without an official break from Great Britain or the Federal Republic of Germany. However, the rationalist regional nationalism can also acquire a form of welfare chauvinism, which is directed against poorer regions. This can engender separatist tendencies, as in the case of Lombardy (the example of the Lega Nord), or protests against the financial or social compensation of poorer regions by the richer ones, as in the case of German federalism (the example of Bavaria).[45] Even though the core of welfare chauvinism is not political, it can still use populist politics as an instrument for its aims, and thus carries political implications. This can be called fragmentation of the political community, as wealthy regions want to separate themselves from poorer ones by arguing that they constitute a different political community, not ready to espouse solidarity within the region, rather than within the nation. In this sense, regional actors strive for a fragmentation of the nation or for the exclusion of other regions from the solidarity-based national community. In the latter case, the region becomes the new smaller nation.

The authors who regard regional nationalism's tendency to fragment nations as a collateral effect of globalisation highlight the ideological type of regional nationalism. They argue that globalisation not only gives more power and resources to regions but also produces winners and losers because of the social change induced by globalisation.[46] Both losers and winners can easily become targets of populist ideologies of political fragmentation. Regional winners of globalisation tend toward welfare chauvinism, whereas the losers of globalisation act against 'alien' competition and 'over-foreignisation'. They also want to fragment the political community – not in the territorial manner, however, but rather via the social exclusion of foreigners by supporting 'social regionalism'. Welfare chauvinism sometimes finds its defiant counterpart in the regional nationalism of poor and unsuccessful regions. Hartmut Häussermann and Claus Offe describe this phenomenon in the following terms: 'We might not be successful, but not least because of that, we are even more distinctive ourselves.'[47]

It is not always easy to discern whether we are dealing with rationalist regional nationalism or ideological regional nationalism. Even regional actors subscribing to political regionalism seldom seek full independence from central government, as their motives can be both economic and political. Even though demand for political self-determination can have an ethnic background, it often remains a project of regional social harmony, which is connected to the utopian ideal of a perfect society existing on the periphery of society, rather than an ethnic project.[48] These ideological projects of regional nationalism can have three variations. The first is the autonomist variation that claims to defend the region against political interventions from the central government, seen as the illegitimate one. Second, we can identify the federalist variation with its claim of independent policies, but with the goal of influencing the national level and of reconstructing the nation according to the rule of subsidiarity. Here, the nation assumes a pluralist form, rather than a unified one, resembling the differentiation proposed by Liah Greenfeld between the pluralistic and the collectivistic nation, discussed earlier in the book. Third, we can distinguish the separatist variation, which combines the exit option with the region's ambition to create its own polity or to join another in the form of a 'greater something'.

Since the majority of political regionalisms show no separatist tendencies, some authors argue that we are dealing here with new nationalism in a regionalist form as opposed to old nationalism.[49] Old nationalism covers ethnonationalistic movements that relate to politics of identity and symbolic reproduction, often cultivating separatist sentiments and using political pressure and violence.[50] In this sense, it was old nationalism that exploded in the 1990s in multinational states such as Yugoslavia or the Soviet Union. In contrast, new regional nationalism does not necessarily strive for its own state-building, nor does it need to aspire to a national territory. For instance, the nationalism of ethnic minorities only wants to be respected by the political centre in the form of autonomy; it does not automatically seek to establish its own state, as in the case of Transylvania in Romania. According to Rogers Brubaker, nationalism is nationalism not because it has an ethnic character but because it somehow relates to statehood. He believes that Transylvania is rather a case of transborder regional nationalism, which enjoys the political and economic support of a third state with the same ethnic definition.[51] This nationalism rests on a state doctrine, according to which ethnically related people who are citizens of different countries should be integrated to some extent, even if not necessarily into one single nation-state. In the case of Transylvania, this state doctrine is being followed by the Hungarian government (the macro level of nationalism), which supported Romanian EU membership in order to reunite Hungarians beyond the nation-state. Therefore, the difference between macro nationalism and meso nationalism (regional nationalism) rests on their relation to statehood, not primarily ethnicity, even though an ethnic principle of national integration can be applied.[52]

In addition to the rationalist and ideological forms of regional nationalism, we can distinguish regional identity as a layer of multiple identities integrated in a nation of more complex collective identities.[53] This position follows the claim that individuals increasingly tend to hold multiple collective identities, pointing to a simultaneous sense of belonging to the region, the nation-state and the European Union, without having to choose their primary attachment. This notion implies that instead of one dominating national identity, individuals are likely to develop multiple identities as a result of globalising and individualising processes.[54] Different layers of identity offer varying frames of orientation in this complex age of mobility and flux, and these do not necessarily stand in a conflictive relationship to each other. In other words, strong regional identity could be perfectly compatible with strong national identity. Nonetheless, the binding potential of each identity layer differs. The supranational and European layers of identity are likely to be the weakest, since for the majority of individuals they are the least salient and are therefore not capable of establishing visible boundaries between 'us' and 'them'. In contrast, regional and local identities offer stronger binding forces since they are based on common specific experiences. Those different layers of a multiple identity can relate to each other in various configurations. For instance, Thomas Risse argues that identities can be nested, crosscutting, or resemble a marble cake. Nesting suggests some hierarchy between the layers of individuals' sense of belonging, whereby Europe forms the outer boundary, and regions or nation-states constitute the core.[55] In crosscutting identities, members of one collectivity are also members of another identity group, even though conflictive relationships between the group identities are not excluded. Finally, in the marble cake model, the various layers or components of identity cannot be clearly separated, but rather blend into one another.[56] In this case, depending on the salience of a given social situation, individual citizens tend to change between their identity layers.

In the sections above we argued that the scholarly discourse on regionalism includes nationalism as its semantic system of reference, and European integration as a causal framework for the so-called new regionalism in Europe. In many cases regionalism and nationalism mesh into each other so that it remains uncertain whether we are dealing with new phenomena of regional nationalism or minority nationalism, or are able to distinguish in a traditional manner between regionalism and nationalism. Regardless of the conceptual confusion, regional nationalism or new nationalism is increasingly occurring against the background of European integration, which appears to be a relevant aspect of the new perspective on nationalism.

Euro-nationalism: is there 'supranational nationalism' in Europe?

The bulk of the research on nationalism deals with nation-states for the obvious reason that nationalism has been and still is associated with the activities of nation-states. In this context, the European Union has frequently been viewed as a circumvention of nationalism, rather than its rescue or repetition at a higher level. As long as the EU was a more of a traditional international organisation focusing on economic integration, the issue of EU nationalism was not subject to any serious debate. Only at the beginning of the 1990s did a progressing political institutionalisation of the EU, in terms of both its institutional deepening and the extension of its activity scope, ignite a debate on the need for a collective identity in the EU, which was supposed to alleviate its growing legitimacy deficit.

In this section, we will focus on the issue of collective identity in the EU as a marker of European nationalism, since the EU is at pains to construct collective identity in a way that emulates the integrative logic of nationalism. In this sense, it is attempting to generate a national sense of belonging in a non-nation-state environment. It is a particular case of nationalism, even though most EU scholars negate the nation-state character of the EU, either by using neologisms such as 'mixed polity', 'consortio', 'condominio' and 'proto-federation'[57], thus denying the state character of the EU.[58] Various versions of the arguments supporting nation-oriented EU identity and nation-like EU community can be found in the debate on European identity, in particular in the context of the EU's democratic deficit. One of the reasons for the democratic deficit is believed to be because the EU lacks the collective feelings of mutual trust and belonging to the same political community which are necessary to underpin the majority decisions it makes.

This diagnosis has been accompanied by scepticism about the EU's ability to reproduce national identity at a higher level, coming mainly from scholars of nationalism. For instance, Anthony D. Smith argues that the search for European identity arises from the flawed assumptions made about the end of the nation-states; these assumptions are unsubstantiated as they ignore the perseverance of nation-states as long-term historic phenomena and therefore the rootedness of national identities. In accordance with his ethnosymbolic perspective, Smith argues that Europe lacks a common ethnic base with a reliable and visible set of common historical memories, myths, symbols and values, since abstract allegiances lead to strong and stable identities.[59] A further sceptic, David Miller, rejects the idea of European nationalism on the grounds of a lack of trust between European citizens. According to Miller, the EU must justify material redistribution beyond self-interest, which requires obligations between compatriots. Such obligations are justifiable only against the background of reciprocity and trust, which in turn can be provided only by a national community, since this community embodies continuity between generations and holds up the virtues of the ancestors by encouraging citizens to live up to them. However, the EU is unable to generate an equal level of trust and to justify these obligations; the prospect for a national community at EU level is therefore unrealistic.[60]

Regardless of this scepticism, the EU does apply identity technologies towards its citizens with the goal of constructing a collective European identity, albeit in a more subtle manner than the EU member states can do by reverting to nationalism. The 'nationalism light' of the EU either uses selected identity technologies of nationalism or uses the technologies at a more subtle level, as the EU cannot emulate nationalism with regard to its aggressiveness and sacrificial expectations.[61]

In the next two sections, we will discuss the identity technologies of European nationalism by focusing on the manipulation of symbols by the EU and the generation of positive self-images of the EU. The final section will offer a juxtaposition of European patriotism and European nationalism.

The EU identity and the manipulation of symbols

Two scenarios confront the EU concerning its Euro-nationalism.[62] First, the EU can induce a 'soft' collective identity by promoting a fluid and fragmented identity in an attempt to weaken national bonds in the member states. As mentioned above, the European Union seems to be one of the most important factors responsible for the increasing relevance of regionalism in Europe. As the EU increasingly becomes a political point of crystallisation for regional policies and interest representation, institutions of national identity formation are circumvented, even if they are not rendered entirely obsolete. Second, from a sceptical viewpoint the EU might fail to establish any sense of broad collective identity at all. European cultural and political diversity is therefore viewed as undermining a solid sense of collective self and of social belonging. For instance, Gerard Delanty suggests that the EU cannot rest on any culturally stable grounds similar to a common language, a shared history, religion, an educational system and mass media. Even if sceptical, Delanty's position stresses the significance of cultural symbols for the construction and stability of European identity.[63] These cultural symbols are expected to pave the way for an emergence of collective identity based not only on the dichotomy of Europeanness and non-Europeanness, but also on identification allowing for a 'thicker' or more resilient collective identity.

Against this background, some authors believe that the EU engages in a manipulation of cultural symbols pertaining to collective identity. One such case is the introduction of the common currency in the EU.[64] The establishment of the tangible symbol of the euro and its iconography increases the salience of Europeanness without the necessity of homogenising European cultural diversity, since the euro allows for different iconographic connotations. Simultaneously, a common currency establishes a degree of commonality and therefore bolsters new Europe-wide and specific identity content.[65] This common currency is open to multiple interpretations, endowing the citizen with something with which to identify without having to surrender his or her own subjective vision of the European 'community'. This trend towards abstraction is also visible with regard to other collective symbols such as flags and anthems.[66] In the same vein, Thomas Risse stresses the significance of the euro for the development of collective identity in the European Union. Since money generally fulfils a role of a relevant symbolic marker in the processes of community-building, the euro is essential for the creation of collective European identity. Risse argues that the euro has had a substantial impact on citizens' identification with the EU and Europe, as the common currency enhances the 'realness' of Europe by providing a tangible link from the European level to the daily lives of the citizens.[67] Subsequently, the EU attempts to use cultural symbols that are tangible and sufficiently abstract at the same time. Symbols that are overly abstract are likely to be ignored by individuals as lacking connection to their daily social practices. Against this backdrop, the EU decided against a unique writing or pronunciation of the common currency – Greece and Bulgaria, for instance, use their national alphabets and pronunciation. This vernacular diversity of the euro helps the common currency to function as an 'identity signifier'.

Further cases of manipulation of cultural symbols pertain to the EU's cultural policy. This includes symbolic initiatives such as the European City of Culture, with the goal of raising the EU's visibility and identifiability. The EU increasingly promotes commonality symbols while attempting to respect the realm of national cultures.[68] It is thus attempting to enhance its salience via symbolic diffusion into the everyday life of citizens, but without surrendering symbolic ambiguity. This ambiguity does not, however, cause confusion, but rather is to be viewed as a response to European cultural diversity. In contrast to the aggregated view of cultural policy, Michael Bruter examines separate symbols and items pertaining to collective identity in Europe. According to his qualitative analysis of focus-group discussions in France, Great Britain and the Netherlands, he argues that the majority of the participants' perceptions of Europe and their self-assessment of their European identity referred to predominantly 'civic' images, whereas only a minority perceived the EU in 'cultural' terms. This classical vocabulary of ethnic (or cultural) and civic nationalism suggests that the images of Europe are not distant from the categories used in the nationalism research. The images of 'cultural' Europe held by the participants were associated with peace, harmony, the disappearance of historical divisions and cooperation between similar people. In contrast, the images of 'civic' Europe were linked to borderlessness, circulation of citizens and prosperity.[69]

In his further study, Bruter confirms his preliminary conclusions about civic and cultural images with regard to symbols. He highlights that the EU imitates nation-states by delivering proper national symbols in order to encourage a European political community. These include – besides euro notes and coins – a flag, an anthem, a national day and, until recently, an attempt to introduce a constitution.[70] As a result, one could argue that the EU manipulates cultural symbols to construct European mass identity by emulating technologies of national identity.[71] One could further argue that attempts to personify the EU, for instance through the establishment of the office of Foreign Minister, High Representative for Foreign Policy or President of the Council (as a result of the Lisbon Treaty), point in the same direction as the manipulation of symbols.[72] Personification techniques are frequently used by the nation-state elites to stimulate collective identity and hence the loyalty of their citizens. Since nation-states represent abstract or imagined communities, they necessitate a more concrete embodiment for the mass population to conceive of them and develop a shared identity. This embodiment can occur as personification, in which a polity becomes associated with the most salient figures in the political system. Recent studies in political psychology confirm the hypothesis that the personification of political systems facilitates 'stronger' attitudes and hence may be decisive in the formation of collective identities.[73] In contrast to personification, embodying the political system as a parliamentary institution is likely to produce weaker attitudes, which leads to the conclusion that a widespread practice of personification of the political system has potentially far-reaching attitudinal consequences. In the context of the EU, it suggests that the proposals made in the Lisbon Treaty suggesting personification techniques would be more effective in terms of collective identity than public visibility of the European Parliament.

In sum, we can argue that the EU applies a mixed strategy of identity construction. On the one hand, it attempts to preserve and even promote cultural diversity to weaken the national bonds within the member-states. In this respect, it employs a balanced and 'soft' strategy that combines tangibility with the abstraction of identity symbols. On the other hand, it also uses more traditional technologies borrowed from nationalism, from both its civic and cultural versions. In addition, the EU seems to apply personification techniques, known from the context of the nation-state.

Positive self-images of the EU as the markers of Euro-nationalism

When the EU applies identity technologies to foster a collective European identity, we are confronted with Euro-nationalism and are dealing with a case of nationalism at the macro level.[74] Even though the EU is not a nation-state, its Euro-nationalism resembles the more traditional forms of nationalism. It includes the discursive legitimisation of political action through commitment to Euro-national interests, be it the welfare of the European community or examples of European integration such as the idea of a particular European identity or the grandness of the EU.

We mentioned in Chapter 2 that individuals tend to acquire a positive image from membership of a social group, and that this logic can be applied to explain the self-esteem booster effect of national identity. Comparing oneself favourably to the out-group creates motivation for positive social identity.[75] Consequently, if one identifies with a negatively valued group, the self-stereotyping will have a negative impact on one's current level of self-esteem. Since the underlying motivation for membership in groups is the enhancement of self-esteem, psychological gains are achieved only through identification with a favourably evaluated group.[76] Therefore, the production and diffusion of positive self-images can be an efficient instrument of generation of collective identity without the necessity to resort to symbols of commonality. This is also the case with the EU.

The first type of positive imagery used to construct Euro-nationalism is 'cosmopolitan Europe'.[77] Here, the EU utilises the academic discourse ascribing specific cosmopolitan qualities to it, within which one of the most ardent proponents of cosmopolitan Europe has been the influential German philosopher Jürgen Habermas. Habermas believes that the European Union can create a collective identity stemming from a set of universalistic principles such as human rights, but evolving and thickening into a 'European constitutional patriotism'. This sort of European civic nationalism is expected to replace the ethnic ties of individual European nations.[78]

In this context, the EU should represent a 'post-national constellation' based on universalistic principles, in which European citizens will develop a sense of loyalty and solidarity 'among strangers' with regard to each other by abstracting from their particular national identities. Rather than reflecting the specific institutional set-up of the EU, 'cosmopolitan Europe' is induced by the process of European constitution-making, associated with a constitution anchored in a shared culture of universal and liberal values.[79] Even though 'cosmopolitan Europe' is supposed to offer a relatively open and inclusive identity, this self-image of Europe shows normative boundaries which distinguish Europe mainly from the United States as Europe's 'significant Other'. Habermas regards the historical and institutional peculiarities of Europe, including secularisation, the priority of the state over the market, the primacy of social solidarity over achievement, rejection of the law of the stronger and the commitment to peace, as a normative boundary mechanism.[80]

Other scholars also relate the cosmopolitan collective identity in Europe to its 'constitutional' distinctiveness. Here too, the US remains the major 'Other', while the EU constructs its European identity along the lines of both cosmopolitan and particularistic features.[81] Accordingly, a set of constitutional identity distinctions between the EU and the United States serves as a template for constructing and strengthening a European collective identity. This civic or constitutional nationalism of the EU shows the EU in a more favourable light by pointing to a much more positive conception of the state. In contrast to US constitutionalism, the European constitutional tradition involves the creation of justice and protection of citizens against misfortunes stemming from the inequalities and irrationalities of the market.[82] A further fundamental difference pertains to minority rights, since European constitutional identity exhibits less faith in the positive effects of individualistic liberal principles, in particular when they are linked to prejudices and discrimination of minorities.[83] In contrast, American constitutionalism can be viewed as hostile to minority rights, since it is based on the liberal approach to the American immigrant society, where the main concern of new minorities is to enjoy the same rights as the older population. Moreover, there is a crucial difference between American and European constitutional identity with regard to the secularity of the state. Since in the United States the constitutional doctrine protects a separation of state and religion, many practices in European states (such as the German state's tax-collecting for the church, or favouring certain churches as in the case of the Church of England) would be deemed unconstitutional.[84] At the same time, the political culture in Europe is likely to be less tolerant of frequent references to God and religion in the public discourse, which is apparently a feature of the American political culture. Although European civic nationalism is expected to be ingrained in universalistic principles, the differences between the US and the European constitutional identities function in the cosmopolitan image as a 'difference engine', thus fostering European common identity.[85]

In addition, the cosmopolitan image of the EU is expected to rest on the EU's transformed concept of power politics in international relations, according to which the EU exports the rule of law, democracy and human rights worldwide, rather than merely maximising its economic or military potential. Erik Oddvar Eriksen argues that the criteria for the EU's missionary activities can be derived from cosmopolitanism, suggesting that the EU subordinates its external policies to a higher-ranking law. The readiness of the EU to act out of a sense of justice or moral duty renders it different from and morally superior to other actors in international politics, perpetuating the maximising of interests. Consequently, infringements of human rights by other actors become sanctioned, whereby the EU increasingly fulfils the role of the forerunner of the new ethical international order.[86] Not only does the EU carry out a projection of its cosmopolitan image externally, but it also attempts to enhance the consistency of the positive image between the externally projected and the internally applied standards. The

EU Charter of Fundamental Rights is believed to be the indicator of these attempts. The EU's construction of a positive image via differentiation from the United States and its missionary cosmopolitanism espouses an ethical supremacy vis-à-vis other actors in international politics and thus can become a source of enhanced self-esteem for European citizens.

A further positive image utilised by the EU to construct a collective identity pertains to the notion of civilian power.[87] This issue has raised significant interest in recent years, since it gives the EU an additional feature to distinguish itself from other global powers, such as the United States. The notion of civilian power refers to the methods of international politics rather than the substance.[88] The EU is believed to pursue its ethically orientated goals by using methods of normative change rather than force. According to this self-image, the civilian power Europe acts primarily in tune with values and not military or economic strength like the US, Russia or China. In this sense, the EU's actions are believed to be humanitarian and civilising, which corresponds to the conviction that the EU is a progressive, post-Westphalian political system, rather than a traditional one. In this perspective, the EU's external policies result from the 'post-modern', 'post-sovereign' and 'post-national' nature of the political system of the EU.[89] One of the tenets of civilian power Europe is believed to be multiculturalism, which is a form of self-binding by law. In this view, the EU's objective is to promote the development of an international society according to the rule-based international order of multilateral institutionalism. The EU therefore fosters the power of international institutions and regional organisations, which allows for the extensive coordination and cooperation of actors in international politics. The goal is the creation of institutionalised and global governance capable of solving international collective problems. As opposed to the US, which defines its civilising mission more internally, EU member states revert to deliberative and institutionalised cooperation mechanisms among themselves.[90] As a result, even in an uncertain political environment, member states are likely to remain attached to deliberation and cooperation, which is an indicator of a basic trust between them that points to the bonds of community or civic nation.[91] Even though the sceptical scholars of nationalism, like Anthony D. Smith or David Miller, question the ability of the EU to develop such trust, it is precisely this moral resource that is expected to play a significant role in European identity construction, as opposed to the anarchy of brute power outside the EU.[92]

The third self-image of European identity refers to the EU as a normative power, which is directly linked to the cosmopolitan and civilising image and sometimes blurs with both of them. Here, too, the EU stresses its progressive stance in promoting and implementing human rights and environmental policies, and by so doing it asserts its leading role and depicts the US as a laggard. In other words, the EU promotes its positive image as the forerunner in advocating human rights worldwide and in the fight against climate change, thus claiming its moral supremacy.[93] Concurrently, the EU represents the policies and concerns of the United States as illegitimate and over-attached to state sovereignty as well as to economic and security interests.[94] Consequently, the EU uses the vanguard-laggard dichotomy in order to describe its own identity in contrast to the US, as is the case with the cosmopolitan image. However, here the EU uses differentiation techniques associated with the construction of the inferiority of the others with the aim of establishing and perpetuating its own positive image.[95] The image of the EU as a normative power is applied to, among other things, its ability to transform border conflicts and to promote selfless environmental politics. Since borders are socially constructed institutions, they rely on discursive processes of constructing a shared understanding among participants. Normative power in Europe is expected to be capable of bringing about conflict transformation through the desecuritisation of conflicts.[96]

It is still difficult to assess how effective the positive self-images of the EU as 'identity markers' will be and whether the EU can develop a consistent set of identity politics based on images of moral superiority. For instance, Robert Falkner argues that the EU's policies, especially in the field of environmental protection, do not result simply from normative orientation but from domestic economic conflicts. For example, in the debate on genetically modified (GM) food, the EU offered international leadership only after strong anti-GM sentiments appeared among the public. Prior to this, the EU attached little importance to the bio-safety talks. However, even after it claimed international leadership in that field, it sought to export its own domestic regulatory model, which would ensure that international rules would not damage its economic interests in medical biotechnology.[97] In addition, it is increasingly argued that there is nothing altruistic or value-orientated about the EU's external policies. For instance, Sandra Lavenex demonstrates that the 'Europeanisation' of some policy fields such as immigration control does not necessarily follow merely humanitarian considerations, since the shift 'outwards' can be regarded as a strategy to increase the autonomy of national ministers towards political, normative and institutional constraints on democratic policy-making in the member states. If this holds true then, paradoxically, the civilian image of the EU would rely on the attempts of executive actors to free themselves from democratic control.

To summarise, we could argue that the EU's 'nationalism light' poses certain problems. On the one hand, the positive self-images generated by the EU exhibit cracks in consistency, which may inhibit their capacity to construct identity. On the other hand, the self-images can be regarded as propaganda instruments with the goal of manipulating the EU population, as they are not entirely mirrored in social reality and espouse double standards. This can have negative implications for the legitimacy of the EU. In addition, we can point to the 'dark side' of collective identity formation. The dark feature of collective identity can be traced back to contestation and even conflict between in-group and out-group. In this context, one can argue that collective identities are not necessarily based on aversion to others, because strangers do not have to be enemies. Nevertheless, the in-group/out-group antagonism is a latent phenomenon which can be activated under certain circumstances, such as the insiders' perception that outsiders pose a threat to the in-group. In this situation, insiders will react with discrimination against outsiders in order to protect the collective self from perceived or real, substantial or symbolic 'attacks' of the obvious others.[98]

European patriotism or European nationalism?

Regardless of the methods by which European collective identity is created, there is a debate on its 'thickness' leading directly to the notion of Euro-nationalism. As discussed above, some authors would like to reproduce the strength and resilience of the national bond in the EU by establishing a sort of European civic nationalism. In this context, the concept of constitutional patriotism proposed for the EU by Jürgen Habermas can be interpreted as a form of civic nationalism grounded in a devotion to the liberal and democratic principles of a European political community.[99] Even if constitutional patriotism rests on cosmopolitan values, it requires contextualisation with regard to a specific territory and a concrete community and thus supersedes pre-political identities of citizens such as the ethnical or the national ones. In this view, not only could European constitutional patriotism supersede collective identities of nation-states, but it could also induce a European identity based on rational moral and political bonds.[100]

Nonetheless, constitutional patriotism does not have to be interpreted as circumventing nationalism, but rather as close to the notion of civic nationalism, since both concepts exhibit communitarian features.[101] It remains controversial whether Habermas himself is a proponent of constitutional patriotism or rather an advocate of civic nationalism, as he speaks of a supportive political culture which would stabilise allegiance to the legal principles of a political community.[102] In this reading, Habermas's constitutional patriotism would still be a form of Euro-nationalism, similar to the collective identity he wished to stimulate in postwar Germany. Craig Calhoun argues that constitutional patriotism should be supplemented by a stronger approach to social solidarity, which would include the creation and reproduction of social institutions and the reconfiguration of social relations, as it is too weak to generate sustainable collective identity.[103] Consequently, he proposes a European form of civic nationalism that embraces both constitutionalism and social solidarity. However, it implies that the more constitutional patriotism shifts away from civic nationalism, the less collective and cohesive an identity it can create. Whenever the cosmopolitan element in constitutional patriotism becomes dominant, it will lead to more inclusiveness, but it will also entail weaker collective bonds. In the same vein, Philippe Schmitter and Michael W. Bauer argue in favour of expanding social citizenship in the European Union, which would entail stronger and more numerous redistributive measures in the EU.[104] This would shift the EU again in the direction of a welfare state with nation-like bonding. Schmitter and Bauer want to enhance the visibility of the EU by bringing it closer to European citizens, thus making it a part of their everyday lives.

Beyond the problem of the 'thickness' of European nationalism, there are some other methodological dilemmas voiced by, for instance, Rogers Brubaker in his studies on nationalism. As discussed in previous chapters, Brubaker questions the dichotomy between civic and ethnic nationalism on methodological and normative grounds. Regarding the criteria of 'thickness', civic nationalism does not have to be distinct from its ethnic variant, as civic communities are a culmination of a long past of common endeavours, sacrifice and devotion, which are stabilised by institutions, customs, historical memories and common values. In this sense, even civic nationalism or constitutional patriotism are not merely chosen but are also given, since they are incapable of generating collective identity without the back-up of the common culture and collective memory.[105] In addition, Brubaker questions the normative assumption of civic nationalism as being inclusive, since it is based on citizenship and not on ascriptive features or descent. He argues that civic nationalism is also exclusive, but in a different way from ethnic nationalism. Civic and ethnic nationalism manage access to the nation differently, but they are both devices of social closure and exclusion.[106] The exclusionary aspects of the EU are currently apparent, even without the internal bonds denoted as civic nationalism.[107]

Anita Böcker and Tetty Havinga, for instance, argue that statistics on asylum applications in the EU have been deliberately used in the debates on refugees and asylum policies in a highly selective manner to justify restrictive measures. Consequently, even with its dedication to cosmopolitism and civility, the EU establishes and uses mechanisms of social closure and exclusion.[108] In addition, Peo Hansen argues that the concept of European identity envisaged by the European Community has given the citizen/non-citizen of the EU categories increasingly ethnocultural underpinning, with implications for European identity. As a result of ethnocultural articulation, European citizenship became an instrument of exclusion towards the EU's non-white and non-Christian populations, thus fostering a collective identity in essentialist terms.[109] In other words, we could argue that European integration with its inclusive developments has strongly relied on the continued exclusion of outsiders, which renders the EU by no means a post-Westphalian polity, but rather territorial and replicating the identity-making mechanisms of the nation-state.[110] Even though the EU is perceived as endorsing multicultural values and attitudes, we could argue in accordance with Brubaker that civic and multicultural European identity (in the sense of European nationalism) could be associated with intolerance towards non-members. Laurent Licata and Olivier

Klein argue that even the mere creation of the status of 'Citizen of the Union' in Maastricht may promote intolerance towards resident foreigners, thus questioning the normative validity of collective identity. In this case, a paradoxical situation could emerge, as a degree of tolerance exercised by citizens towards foreigners would contradict the values propagated by the EU.[111]

In contrast, for Habermas it is neither possible nor desirable to melt down the national identities of the member states into a European nation.[112] Therefore, a new form of (post-conventional and post-national) identity is supposed to rest on a community other than the nation-state. For this purpose, a shared political and social space (for instance in the form of European civil society) should be promoted in order to generate new emotional attachments (or redirect the emotional energy of national identities towards the EU) which would lie at the heart of European identity. Others argue that European identity cannot be easily produced, as most Europeans are still strongly attached to their nations.[113] For instance, Mathieu Deflem and Fred C. Pampel suggest that European citizens' concern with the interests of their own countries implies the persistence of national identity at the expense of post-national identity. They conclude that there exists a myth of post-national identity, which does not reflect the reality of the European Union.[114]

Beyond the debate on European nationalism in terms of civic and ethnic categories, there is a turn towards a narrative understanding of European identity in which nationalism becomes intertwined with Europeanism, as the EU interlocks both the political sphere of the nation-state and the European Union. In this perspective, even nations are not 'given', but are constructed in discourse, which establishes both uniqueness of the self and the differences towards the outer world.[115] In this vein, one could argue that the sense of European identity can be found in political actors' discursive commitment to the fundamental values of the EU, such as solidarity, parity and equality between member states, which echoes European constitutional patriotism.[116] Discursive narratives reveal actors' reasoning and motives with regard to the historically developed identities.[117] Against this background, European identity might be understood as a set of narratives by which political actors regard themselves profoundly and enduringly as constituents of the EU as a political entity. The commitment to the EU can be discovered by examining arguments used to justify the transfer of main nation-state functions onto the European level. Merely supporting the sovereignty transfer does not denote the sense of European identity, as their support could be motivated by national interests, for example to enhance the efficiency of political decisions, to stimulate economic growth or to guarantee external and legal security.[118] In this case, actors are inclined to maintain or improve nation-state functions via the European Union, but they do not necessarily exhibit any real commitment to European values. In this perspective, the values of solidarity, equality and parity take into account other member states. This would have implications for European identity. First, we deal with contextualised European identity, since both political actors and citizens can develop commitment to European values to a varying degree depending on the political issue at hand. Consequently, European identity might be viewed as an issue-dependent phenomenon rather than as a territorial or holistic concept.

Second, one can point to a necessary decoupling of support for the EU and European identity. This is because support for EU institutions (and therefore for the transfer of sovereignty) may occur on the basis of national narrative – in other words, in the name of nationalism. Conversely, actors rejecting sovereignty transfer onto the European level can exhibit stronger European identity than its advocates.

Summing up the entire chapter, there are two implications for collective identity in the post-national context from the perspective of theories of nationalism. First, we might identify national identity as historically non-coincidental. In this case, national identity cannot be replaced or superseded at the post-national level. Although there might be collective identities beyond the nation-state, they will never assume a resilience and durability comparable to national identity. In this perspective, the nation-state represents the end of history in terms of nationalism.

Second, there might be post-national identities with similar strengths and stability as national identity. However, the construction of such an identity would need to follow the same path of state-building as nation-states. In other words, we would be dealing with a new nation-state at a higher level, which would spawn a European nation. The development of a European nation would occur to the detriment of national identities, which would be diluted in the process. In addition, a European nation would be associated with European nationalism, involving its sinister side in the form of discrimination and even oppression, mostly with regard to non-European minorities. Even if European nationalism exhibited a weaker discriminatory potential than its nation-state protoplast, it would be based on exclusion and boundary-making.

Notwithstanding the controversies on the possibility and necessity of European identity as European nationalism, the mainstream debate argues that the emergence of a collective European identity is central for the viability of the EU. It is expected to compensate for the lack of direct interactions among citizens, thus creating a symbolic illusion of unity in a space without social interaction. However, the concept of European nationalism is linked to technologies of collective identity departing from the analytical and methodological template of the nation-state. Therefore, European nationalism, precisely because it has no certain roots, is associated with a danger – or even a necessity – of the EU elites engaging in propaganda actions and strategic socialisation with the aim of changing the attitudes of European citizens, even if it occurs in a more subtle form of 'nationalism light'. The manipulation of symbols and the generation of positive self-images are methods thereof. When we consider that state nationalism developed in Europe largely under non-democratic circumstances of elite-driven mobilisation, it could imply that any European nationalism (as an ideology of the EU and identity technology practised by the EU) would shift the focus within European citizenship more strongly from active citizen towards compliant subject, which would be disastrous for the democratic deficit of the EU and the EU's legitimacy problems.

Notes

1. See Ireneusz Paweł Karolewski and Andrzej Marcin Suszycki (eds), *Nationalism and European Integration: The Need for New Theoretical and Empirical Insights* (New York: Continuum, 2007); Lars-Erik Cederman, 'Nationalism and bounded integration: what it would take to construct a European demos', *European Journal of International Relations* 7, 2 (2001), pp. 139–74.
2. See Ireneusz Paweł Karolewski, 'Regionalism, nationalism, Europeanization', in Karolewski and Suszycki (eds), *Nationalism and European Integration*, pp. 8–31.
3. Among others, Mathias Albert and Brock Lothar, 'Debordering the world of states: new spaces in international relations', *New Political Science* 35 (1996), pp. 69–106; Andrew Church and Peter Reid, 'Urban power, international networks, and competition: the example of cross-order cooperation', *Urban Studies* 33, 8 (1996), pp. 1,297–318.
4. Björn Hettne and Frederik Söderbaum, 'Theorising the rise of "regionness"', *New Political Economy* 5, 3 (2000), pp. 457–73.

5. Fredrik Söderbaum and Luk van Langenhove (eds), 'The EU as a global actor: the role of interregionalism', *Journal of European Integration* 27, 3 (special edition) (2005).
6. Anthony D. Smith, *National Identity* (Harmondsworth: Penguin Books, 1991).
7. Björn Hettne and Fredrik Söderbaum, 'The new regionalism approach', *Politeia* 17, 3 (1998), pp. 6–21.
8. Björn Hettne, 'Globalization and the new regionalism: the second great transformation', in Björn Hettne, András Inotai and Osvaldo Sunkel (eds), *Globalism and the New Regionalism* (New York: St. Martin's Press, 1999).
9. Fredrik Söderbaum, 'The international political economy of regionalism', in Nicola Phillips (ed.), *Globalizing International Political Economy* (Basingstoke: Palgrave, 2005), pp. 221–45.
10. Björn Hettne, 'Neo-mercantilism: The pursuit of regionness', *Cooperation and Conflict* 28, 3 (1993), pp. 211–32.
11. Hettne and Söderbaum, 'Theorising', p. 12; Alberta Sbragia, 'Review article: Comparative regionalism: what might it be?', *Journal of Common Market Studies* 46, Annual Review (2008), pp. 29–49.
12. See Ireneusz Paweł Karolewski and Viktoria Kaina, 'European identity: preliminary conclusions and open questions', in Ireneusz Paweł Karolewski and Viktoria Kaina (eds), *European Identity: Theoretical Perspectives and Empirical Insights* (Hamburg: LIT-Verlag, 2006).
13. Anna Olsson, 'Theorizing regional minority nationalism', in Ireneusz Paweł Karolewski and Andrzej Marcin Suszycki (eds), *Multiplicity of Nationalism in Contemporary Europe* (Lanham, MD: Lexington Books, 2009), pp. 107–31.
14. Jonathon W. Moses, 'Exit, vote and sovereignty: migration, states and globalization', *Review of International Political Economy* 12, 1 (2005), pp. 53–77.
15. Naomi Ellemers, Ad van Knippenberg, Nanne de Vries and Henk Wilke, 'Social identification and permeability of group boundaries', *European Journal of Social Psychology* 18 (1988), pp. 497–513.
16. Bill Dunn, 'Capital mobility and the embeddedness of Labour', *Global Society* 18, 2 (2004), pp. 127–43.
17. Werner Güth, Matthias Sutter, Harrie Verbon and Hannelore Weck-Hannemann, 'Family versus public solidarity theory and experiment', Discussion Paper 86 (Tilburg University: Center for Economic Research, 2001).
18. Hettne et al., *Globalism and the New Regionalism*.
19. Kenichi Ohmae, *The End of the Nation State: The Rise of Regional Economies* (New York: Free Press, 1995).
20. Nicola Buecker, 'Protective nationalism in today's Poland: theoretical considerations and empirical findings', in Karolewski and Suszycki (eds), *Nationalism and European Integration*, pp. 116–32.
21. See Gary Marks, 'Territorial identities in the European Union', in Jeffrey J. Anderson (ed.), *Regional Integration and Democracy: Expanding on the European Experience* (Boulder, CO: Rowman & Littlefield, 1999), pp. 69–91.
22. Daniel Beland and Andre Lecours, 'Sub-state nationalism and the welfare state: Quebec and Canadian federalism', *Nations and Nationalism* 12, 1 (2006), pp. 77–96; Elke Winter, 'Trajectories of multiculturalism in Germany, the Netherlands and Canada: in search of common patterns', *Government and Opposition* 45, 2 (2010), pp. 166–86; Will Kymlicka, *Multicultural Citizenship* (Oxford: Oxford University Press, 1995).
23. Thomas H. Marshall, *Citizenship and Social Class* (1950; repr. London: Pluto, 1992).
24. Michael Zürn, 'Global governance and legitimacy problems', *Government and Opposition* 39, 2 (2004), pp. 260–87; S. N. Eisenstadt, 'The reconstitution of collective identities and inter-civilizational relations in the age of globalization', *Canadian Journal of Sociology* 21, 1 (2007), pp. 113–26.
25. See Nick Stevenson, 'Globalization, national cultures and cultural citizenship', *Sociological Quarterly* 38, 1 (1997), pp. 41–66; Jean L. Cohen, 'Rethinking human

rights, democracy, and sovereignty in the age of globalization', *Political Theory* 36, 4 (2008), pp. 578–606.

26. Adam Lupel, 'Regionalism and globalization: post-nation or extended nation?', *Polity* 36, 2 (2004), pp. 153–74; Peter Evans, 'The eclipse of the state? Reflections on stateness in an era of globalization', *World Politics* 50, 1 (fiftieth anniversary special issue) (1997), pp. 62–87; Stein Tonnesson, 'Globalising national states', *Nations and Nationalism* 10, 1/2 (2004), pp. 179–94.

27. David Brady, Jason Beckfield and Martin Seeleib-Kaiser, 'Economic globalization and the welfare state in affluent democracies, 1975–2001', *American Sociological Review* 70 (2005), pp. 421–48; Brion Burgoon, 'Globalization and welfare compensation: disentangling the ties that bind', *International Organization* 55, 3 (2001), pp. 509–51.

28. See Christoffer Green-Pedersen, 'Welfare-state retrenchment in Denmark and the Netherlands, 1982–1998: the role of party competition and party consensus', *Comparative Political Studies* 34, 9 (2001), pp. 963–85; Samuel Krislov, 'Can the welfare state survive in a globalized legal order?', *The Annals of the American Academy of Political and Social Science* 603 (2006), pp. 54–79.

29. Suzanne Berger, 'Globalization and politics', *Annual Review of Political Science* 3 (2000), pp. 43–62.

30. Frederic Vandenberghe, 'Deluzian capitalism', *Philosophy & Social Criticism* 34, 8 (2008), pp. 877–903; Sean O Rian, 'States and markets in an era of globalization', *Annual Review of Sociology* 26 (2000), pp. 187–213.

31. Richard Devetak and Richard Higgott, 'Justice unbound? Globalization, states and the transformation of the social bond', *International Affairs* 75, 3 (1999), pp. 483–98.

32. See Heidi Gottfried, 'Developing neo-Fordism: a comparative perspective', *Critical Sociology* 21 (1995), pp. 39–70; Erik Swyngedouw, 'Globalisation or glocalisation? Networks, territories and rescaling', *Cambridge Review of International Affairs* 17, 1 (2004), pp. 25–48.

33. See Jamie Peck and Nik Theodore, 'Variegated capitalism', *Progress in Human Geography* 31, 6 (2007), pp. 731–72.

34. See Fritz W. Scharpf, 'The European social model: coping with the challenges of diversity', *Journal of Common Market Studies* 40, 4 (2002), pp. 645–70; Michael Baun, 'EU regional policy and the candidate states: Poland and the Czech Republic', *Journal of European Integration* 24, 3 (2002), pp. 261–80.

35. Fritz Scharpf, *Governing in Europe: Effective and Democratic?* (Oxford: Oxford University Press, 1999); Svein S. Andersen and Kjell A. Eliassen (eds), *The European Union: How Democratic is it?* (London: Sage, 1996); Giandomenico Majone, 'Transaction-cost efficiency and the democratic deficit', *Journal of European Public Policy* 17, 2 (2010), pp. 150–75.

36. Richard C. Eichenberg and Russell J. Dalton, 'Post-Maastricht blues: the transformation of citizen support for European integration, 1973–2004', *Acta Politica* 42, 2 (2007), pp. 128–52.

37. Chris Ansell, 'The networked polity: regional development in Western Europe', *Governance: An International Journal of Policy and Administration* 13, 3 (2000), pp. 303–33.

38. See Tanja A. Börzel, *States and Regions in the European Union. Institutional Adaptation in Germany and Spain* (Cambridge: Cambridge University Press, 2002); Charlie Jeffery, 'Regional information offices in Brussels and multi-level governance in the EU: a UK-German comparison', *Regional and Federal Studies* 6, 2 (1996), pp. 183–203.

39. See Gary Marks, Richard Haesly and Heather A. D. Mbaye, 'What do subnational offices think they are doing in Brussels?' *Regional and Federal Studies* 12, 3 (2002), pp. 1–23; François Nielsen and Jane Salk, 'The ecology of collective action and regional representation in the European Union', *European Sociological Review* 14, 3 (1998), pp. 231–54.

40. Beate Kohler-Koch and Rainer Eising (eds), *The Transformation of Governance in*

the European Union (London: Routledge, 1999); Liesbet Hooghe and Gary Marks, *Multi-level Governance and European Integration* (Boulder, CO: Rowman & Littlefield, 2001).

41. Liesbet Hooghe and Gary Marks, 'European Union?', *West European Politics* 31, 1/2 (2008), pp. 108–29; Liesbet Hooghe, Gary Marks and Kermit Blank, 'European integration from the 1980s: state-centric versus multi-level governance,' *Journal of Common Market Studies* 34, 3 (1996), pp. 341–78.

42. Lisbet Hooghe and Gary Marks, 'Channels of regional representation in the European Union', *The Journal of Federalism* 26, 1 (1996), pp. 73–91; Gary Marks, François Nielsen, Leonard Ray and Jane Salk, 'Competencies, cracks, and conflicts: Regional mobilization in the European Union', *Comparative Political Studies* 29, 2 (1996), pp. 164–92.

43. See Michael Keating, *State and Regional Nationalism. Territorial Politics and the European State* (New York: Wheatsheaf, 1988).

44. See Michael Keating, 'Rescaling Europe', *Perspectives on European Politics and Society* 10, 1 (2009), pp. 32–48; Michael Keating, 'Scottish independence', *Scottish Affairs* 69 (2009), pp. 95–112; Michael Keating, 'Thirty years of territorial politics', *West European Politics* 31, 1/2 (2008), pp. 60–81.

45. See Benito Giordano, 'A place called Padania? The Lega Nord and the political representation of Northern Italy', *European Urban and Regional Studies* 6, 3 (1999), pp. 215–30; Benito Giordano, 'The continuing transformation of Italian politics and the contradictory fortunes of the Lega Nord', *Journal of Modern Italian Studies* 8, 2 (2003), pp. 216–30; Eve Hepburn, 'The neglected nation: the CSU and the territorial cleavage in Bavarian party politics', *German Politics* 17, 2 (2008), pp. 184–202.

46. See Michael Zürn and Stephan Leibfried, 'A new perspective on the state: reconfiguring the national constellation', *European Review* 13, 1 (2005), pp. 1–36.

47. Hartmut Häussermann and Claus Offe, 'Projekt-Idee: Kultur und wirtschaftliche Entwicklung', unpublished manuscript (1990), p. 2.

48. See Liesbeth Hooghe and Gary Marks, 'Europe with regions: channels of regional representations in the European Union', *Publius: The Journal of Federalism* 26, 1 (1996), pp. 73–91.

49. Fredrik Soederbaum and Timothy M. Shaw (eds), *Theories of New Regionalism: A Palgrave Reader* (New York: Palgrave Macmillan, 2003); Michael Keating, *The New Regionalism in Western Europe. Territorial Restructuring and Political Change* (Aldershot: Edward Elgar, 1998).

50. Raimo Vaeyrynen, 'Regionalism: old and new', *International Studies Review* 5 (2003), pp. 25–51.

51. Rogers Brubaker, 'Myths and misconceptions in the study of nationalism', in John Hall (ed.), *The State of the Nation: Ernest Gellner and the Theory of Nationalism* (Cambridge: Cambridge University Press, 1998), pp. 272–306; Rogers Brubaker, 'In the name of the nation: reflections on nationalism and patriotism', *Citizenship Studies* 8, 2 (2004), pp. 115–27.

52. Rogers Brubaker, 'Ethnicity without groups', *Archives Européennes de Sociologie* XLIII, 2 (2002), pp. 163–89.

53. Thomas Risse, 'Nationalism and collective identities: Europe versus the nation-state?', in Paul Heywood, Eric Jones and Martin Rhodes (eds), *Developments in West European Politics* (Basingstoke: Palgrave, 2nd edn, 2002), pp. 77–93.

54. Michael Zürn, 'What has changed in Europe? The challenge of globalization and individualization', in Hans-Henrik Holm and Georg Sørensen (eds), *Whose World Order? Uneven Globalization and the End of the Cold War* (Boulder, CO: University Press of Colorado, 1995), pp. 137–63.

55. Thomas Risse, *A Community of Europeans? Transnational Identities and Public Spheres* (Ithaca, NY: Cornell University Press, 2010).

56. Matthias L. Maier and Thomas Risse (eds), 'Europeanization, collective identities and public discourses', Final Report (Robert Schuman Centre for Advanced Studies,

European University Institute, Florence, 2003); Rogers Brubaker, 'Ethnicity, race, and nationalism', *Annual Review of Sociology* 35 (2009), pp. 21–42.

57. Philippe C. Schmitter, 'Representation and the future Euro-polity', *Staatswissenschaften und Staatspraxis* 3, 3 (1992), pp. 379–405; Markus Jachtenfuchs, Thomas Diez and Sabine Jung, 'Which Europe? Conflicting models of legitimate European political order', *European Journal of International Relations* 4, 4 (1998), pp. 409–45.

58. Markus Jachtenfuchs, 'Theoretical perspectives on European governance', *European Law Journal* 1 (1995), pp. 115–33; Ben Rosamond, 'Conceptualizing the EU model of governance in world politics', *European Foreign Affairs Review* 10, 4 (2005), pp. 463–78; Thomas Risse-Kappen, 'Exploring the nature of the beast: international relations theory and comparative policy analysis meet the European Union', *Journal of Common Market Studies* 34 (1996), pp. 53–80.

59. Anthony D. Smith, 'A Europe of nations or the nation of Europe?', *Journal of Peace Research* 30, 2 (1993), pp. 129–35; Anthony D. Smith, *Nations and Nationalism in a Global Era* (Cambridge: Polity Press, 1995).

60. David Miller, *On Nationality* (Oxford: Oxford University Press, 1995), p. 36.

61. See Viktoria Kaina and Ireneusz Paweł Karolewski, 'EU governance and European identity', *Living Reviews in European Governance* 4, 2 (2009), available at www.living reviews.org/lreg-2009-2 (accessed on 14 February 2011); Ireneusz Paweł Karolewski, 'Regionalism, nationalism, and European integration', in Karolewski and Suszycki (eds), *Nationalism and European Integration*, pp. 9–32.

62. Ireneusz Paweł Karolewski, *Citizenship and Collective Identity in Europe* (London: Routledge, 2010).

63. Gerard Delanty, *Citizenship in a Global Age: Society, Culture, Politics* (Buckingham: Open University Press, 2000), p. 114ff.; see also Gerard Delanty, *Inventing Europe: Idea, Identity, Reality* (London: Palgrave, 1995).

64. See Eva Jonas, Immo Fritsche and Jeff Greenberg, 'Currencies as cultural symbols: an existential psychological perspective on reactions of Germans towards the euro', *Journal of Economic Psychology* 26, 1 (2005), pp. 129–46.

65. Jacques E. C. Hymans, 'The changing colour of money: European currency iconography and collective identity', *European Journal of International Relations* 10, 1 (2004), pp. 5–31; see also Thomas Risse, Daniela Engelmann-Martin, Hans-Joachim Knopf and Klaus Roscher, 'To euro or not to euro? The EMU and identity politics in the European Union', *European Journal of International Relations* 5, 2 (1999), pp. 147–87; Matthias Kaelberer, 'The Euro and European identity: symbols, power and the politics of European Monetary Union', *Review of International Studies* 30 (2004), pp. 161–78.

66. See Karen A. Cerulo, *Identity Designs: The Sights and Sounds of a Nation* (New Brunswick, NJ: Rutgers University Press, 1995).

67. Thomas Risse, 'The Euro between national and European identity', *Journal of European Public Policy* 10, 4 (2003), pp. 487–505; see also Anke Müller-Peters, 'The significance of national pride and national identity to the attitude toward the single European currency: a Europe-wide comparison', *Journal of Economic Psychology* 19, 6 (1998), pp. 701–19.

68. Monica Sassatelli, 'Imagined Europe: the shaping of a European cultural identity through EU cultural policy', *European Journal of Social Theory* 5, 4 (2002), pp. 435–51.

69. Michael Bruter, 'On what citizens mean by feeling European: Perceptions of news, symbols and borderless-ness', *Journal of Ethnic and Migration Studies* 30, 1 (2004), pp. 21–39; Michael Bruter, 'Time bomb? The dynamic effect of news and symbols on the political identity of European citizens', *Comparative Political Studies* 42, 12 (2009), pp. 1,498–536.

70. See also Carol Clark, 'Forging identity: Beethoven's ode as European anthem', *Critical Inquiry* 23, 4 (1997), pp. 789–807; Sophie Duchesne, 'Waiting for a European identity: reflections on the process of identification with Europe', *Perspectives on European Politics and Society* 9, 4 (2008), pp. 397–410.

71. Michael Bruter, 'Winning hearts and minds for Europe: the impact of news and symbols on civic and cultural European identity', *Comparative Political Studies* 36, 10 (2003), pp. 1,148–79; Michael Bruter, *Citizens of Europe? The Emergence of a Mass European Identity* (Basingstoke: Palgrave, 2005).

72. See Spyros Blavoukos, Dimitris Bourantonis and George Pagoulatos, 'A President for the European Union: a new actor in town?', *Journal of Common Market Studies* 45, 2 (2007), pp. 231–52.

73. Kathleen M. McGraw and Thomas M. Dolan, 'Personifying the state: consequences for attitude formation', *Political Psychology* 28, 3 (2007), pp. 299–327.

74. Ireneusz Paweł Karolewski, *Citizenship and Collective Identity in Europe* (London: Routledge, 2010); Kaina and Karolewski, 'EU governance and European identity'.

75. Rupert Brown, 'Social Identity Theory: past achievements, current problems and future challenges', *European Journal of Social Psychology* 30, 6 (2000), pp. 745–78.

76. See Riia Luhtanen and Jennifer Crocker, 'A collective self-esteem scale: self-evaluation of one's social identity', *Personality and Social Psychology Bulletin* 18, 3 (1992), pp. 302–18.

77. See Gerard Delanty, 'The idea of a cosmopolitan Europe: on the cultural significance of Europeanization', *International Review of Sociology* 15, 3 (2005), pp. 405–21; Ulrich Beck and Edgar Grande, 'Cosmopolitanism: Europe's way out of crisis', *European Journal of Social Theory* 10, 1 (2007), pp. 67–85; see also Ulrich Beck and Natan Sznaider, 'Unpacking cosmopolitanism for the social sciences: a research agenda', *British Journal of Sociology* 57, 1 (2006), pp. 1–23.

78. Jürgen Habermas, 'Toward a cosmopolitan Europe', *Journal of Democracy* 14, 4, (2003), pp. 86–100; see also Heidrun Friese and Peter Wagner, 'The nascent political philosophy of European polity', *Journal of Political Philosophy* 10, 3 (2002), pp. 341–64.

79. See Omid Payrow Shabani, 'Constitutional patriotism as a model of postnational political association: the case of the EU', *Philosophy and Social Criticism* 32, 6 (2006), pp. 699–718; Justine Lacroix, 'For a European constitutional patriotism', *Political Studies* 50, 5 (2002), pp. 944–58.

80. Jürgen Habermas and Jacques Derrida, 'February 15, or what binds Europeans together: a plea for a common foreign policy, beginning in the core of Europe', *Constellations* 10, 3 (2003), pp. 291–7.

81. Wojciech Sadurski, *European Constitutional Identity?*, EUI Working Papers, Law No. 2006/33, p. 9ff.; Michel Rosenfeld, 'American constitutionalism confronts Denninger's new constitutional paradigm', *Constellations* 7, 4 (2002), pp. 529–48.

82. Sadurski, *European Constitutional Identity?*, p. 13ff. For a view on European constitutionalism as 'responsible and inclusive', see Jo Shaw, 'Process, responsibility and inclusion in the EU constitutionalism', *European Law Journal* 9, 1 (2003), pp. 45–68; Jo Shaw, 'Postnational constitutionalism in the European Union', *Journal of European Public Policy* 6, 4 (1999), pp. 579–97.

83. See Wojeciech Sadurski, 'Europe and its values', *Polish Foreign Affairs Digest* 4, 17 (2005), pp. 59–64.

84. See Kenneth D. Wald and Allison Calhoun-Brown, *Religion and Politics in the United States* (Lanham, MD: Rowman & Littlefield, 2007).

85. See Judith Squires, 'Liberal constitutionalism, identity and difference', in Richard Bellamy and Dario Castiglione (eds), *Constitutionalism in Transformation: European and Theoretical Perspectives* (Oxford: Blackwell, 1996), pp. 208–22.

86. Erik Oddvar Eriksen, 'The EU – a cosmopolitan polity?', *Journal of European Public Policy* 13, 2 (2006), pp. 252–69.

87. See Björn Hettne and Fredrik Söderbaum, 'Civilian power or soft imperialism? The EU as a global actor and the role of interregionalism', *European Foreign Affairs Review* 10, 4 (2005), pp. 535–52.

88. Jan Orbie offers a review of this debate, 'Civilian power Europe: review of the original and current debates', *Cooperation and Conflict* 41, 1 (2006), pp. 123–8.

89. See Karen E. Smith, 'The European Union: a distinctive actor in international

relations', *Brown Journal of World Affairs* 9, 2 (2003), pp. 103–13; Christian Freres, 'The European Union as a global civilian power: development cooperation in EU-Latin American relations', *Journal of Interamerican Studies and World Affairs* 42, 2 (2000), pp. 63–85.

90. See, for example, Sandra Lavenex, 'Shifting up and out: the foreign policy of immigration control', *West European Politics* 29, 2 (2006), pp. 329–50.

91. Jennifer Mitzen, 'Anchoring Europe's civilizing identity: habits, capabilities and ontological security', *Journal of European Public Policy* 13, 2 (2006), pp. 270–85; Federica Bicchi, 'Our size fits all: normative power Europe and the Mediterranean', *Journal of European Public Policy* 12, 2 (2006), pp. 286–303.

92. See Andreas Føllesdal, 'Union citizenship: unpacking the beast of burden', *Law and Philosophy* 20, 3 (2001), pp. 313–43; Jonathan Mercer, 'Anarchy and identity', *International Organization* 49, 2 (1995), pp. 229–51.

93. See Adrian Hyde-Price, 'Normative power Europe: a realist critique', *Journal of European Public Policy* 13, 2 (2006), pp. 217–34.

94. Sibylle Scheipers and Daniela Sicurelli, 'Normative power Europe: a credible Utopia?', *Journal of Common Market Studies* 45, 2 (2007), pp. 435–57; Ian Manners, 'Normative power Europe reconsidered: beyond the crossroads', *Journal of European Public Policy* 13, 2 (2006), pp. 182–99.

95. Ian Manners and Richard Whitman, 'The difference engine: constructing and representing the international identity of the European Union', *Journal of European Public Policy* 10, 3 (2003), pp. 380–404; Thomas Diez, 'Constructing the self and changing others: reconsidering normative power Europe', *Millennium: Journal of International Studies* 33, 3 (2005), pp. 613–36.

96. Ole Wæver, 'European security identities', *Journal of Common Market Studies* 34, 1 (1996), pp. 103–32; Tuomas Forsberg, 'Explaining territorial disputes: from power politics to normative reasons', *Journal of Peace Research* 33, 4 (1996), pp. 433–49.

97. Robert Falkner, 'The political economy of normative power Europe: EU environmental leadership in international biotechnology regulation', *Journal of European Public Policy* 14, 4 (2007), pp. 507–26.

98. Kaina and Karolewski, 'EU governance and European identity'.

99. See Patchen Markell, 'Contesting consensus: Rereading Habermas on the public sphere', *Constellations* 3, 3 (1997), pp. 377–400.

100. Patchen Markell, 'Making affect safe for democracy: on constitutional patriotism?', *Political Theory* 28, 1 (2000), pp. 38–63 (p. 39).

101. See Lacroix, 'For a European constitutional patriotism', pp. 944–58 (p. 945ff.); Richard Bellamy and Dario Castiglione, 'Lacroix's European constitutional patriotism: A response', *Political Studies* 52, 1 (2004), pp. 187–93.

102. Lacroix, 'For a European constitutional patriotism', p. 955.

103. Craig Calhoun, 'Constitutional patriotism and the public sphere: interests, identity, and solidarity in the integration of Europe', *International Journal of Politics, Culture and Society* 18, 3/4 (2005), pp. 257–80.

104. Philippe C. Schmitter and Michael W. Bauer, 'A (modest) proposal for expanding social citizenship in the European Union', *Journal of European Social Policy* 11, 1 (2001), pp. 55–65.

105. Rogers Brubaker, 'The Manichean myth: rethinking the distinction between civic and ethnic nationalism', in Hanspeter Kriesi, Klaus Armingeon, Hannes Siegrist and Andreas Wimmer (eds), *Nation and National Identity: The European Experience in Perspective* (Zurich: Rüegger, 1999), pp. 55–71 (p. 62).

106. Ibid. p. 65.

107. See Theodora Kostakopoulou, 'The protective union: change and continuity in migration law and policy in post-Amsterdam Europe', *Journal of Common Market Studies* 38, 3 (2000), pp. 497–518.

108. Anita Böcker and Tetty Havinga, 'Asylum applications in the European Union: patterns and trends and the effects of policy measures', *Journal of Refugee Studies* 11, 3 (1998), pp. 245–66.

109. Peo Hansen, 'European citizenship, or where neoliberalism meets ethno-culturalism', *European Societies* 2, 2 (2000), pp. 139–65.
110. Else Kveinen, 'Citizenship in a post-Westphalian community: beyond external exclusion?', *Citizenship Studies* 6, 1 (2002), pp. 21–35.
111. Laurent Licata and Olivier Klein, 'Does European citizenship breed xenophobia? European identification as a predictor of intolerance towards immigrants', *Journal of Community and Applied Social Psychology* 12, 5 (2002), pp. 323–37.
112. See Dominique Schnapper, 'Citizenship and national identity in Europe', *Nations and Nationalism* 8, 1 (2002), pp. 1–14.
113. Markell, 'Making affect safe for democracy', pp. 38–63 (p. 39).
114. Mathieu Deflem and Fred C. Pampel, 'The myth of postnational identity: popular support for European unification', *Social Forces* 75, 1 (1996), pp. 119–43.
115. See Rudolf de Cillia, Martin Reisigl and Ruth Wodak, 'The discursive construction of national identities', *Discourse & Society* 10, 2 (1999), pp. 149–73.
116. Andrzej Marcin Suszycki, 'European identity in Sweden', in Karolewski and Kaina (eds), *European Identity*, pp. 179–207.
117. See Thomas Diez, 'Europe as a discursive battleground: discourse analysis and European integration studies', *Cooperation and Conflict* 31, 1 (2001), pp. 5–38; Thomas Diez, 'Speaking Europe: the politics of integration discourse', *Journal of European Public Policy* 6, 4 (1999), pp. 598–613.
118. See Andrew Moravcsik, 'Preference and power in the European Community: a liberal intergovernmentalist approach', *Journal of Common Market Studies* 31, 4 (1993), pp. 473–524; Andrew Moravcsik, *The Choice for Europe: Social Purpose and State Power from Messina to Maastricht* (Ithaca, NY: Cornell University Press, 1998).

CHAPTER EIGHT

Further Research Foci of Nationalism

As a complex phenomenon, nationalism can be studied from several perspectives. Besides the aforementioned research we can identity three additional foci of nationalism research: globalisation, religion and gender.

The first of the foci deals with nationalism in relation to globalisation processes.[1] In this context, we can differentiate three aspects: the decreasing relevance of the nation-state, the issue of national citizenship and the 'new nationalism'. First, the question of whether nationalism will vanish in a globalising world is the subject of a growing number of studies. However, much of this work tends to interpret the issue as a debate over the future of the nation-state, exploring whether the nation-state will continue to exist in its hitherto known form in an era of high mobility of capital, people and technology. The most commonly discussed challenges to the nation-state are transnational flows of global capital, the rise of global communications and the radically increasing density of time and space, which changes social interactions and relations.[2] Furthermore, large population flows are leading to a growth of permanent foreign residents in host societies, challenging the traditional membership of a particular nation-state. This position tends to subscribe to the scholarly literature on the 'impending crisis of the hyphen' in the concept of the nation-state.[3] In this reading, as a consequence of globalisation ever fewer societies can be described as nation-states.[4] As the global economic dynamics transcend national borders and become less controllable for national governments, the autonomy and effectiveness of the nation-state is increasingly being questioned.

This has implications for nationalism as a nation-state ideology, which regards autonomous and homogeneous national cultures represented by distinct states as natural and organic entities. As national identities increasingly erode, not least as a result of the new waves of transnational migration, we face a spread of global values and a simultaneous re-invention of culture on subnational levels. The new migration trend differs from historically similar phenomena in terms of quantities, global range and frequency. As a consequence, large numbers of migrants cannot be easily assimilated into the national population, since they come from increasingly distant regions and cultures.[5] Furthermore, as social structure is becoming transnationalised, an epistemological shift is required to become in tune with the ontological change.[6] New interdisciplinary transnational studies are expected to generate a shift in the focus of social inquiry replacing the nation-state as the basic unit of analysis with the transnational social structure as the new appropriate unit.

Second, some authors highlight the role of independent rights, which circumvent national citizenship and render it obsolete.[7] Arguments used in favour of this position are both empirical and normative. The former relate to the structural change in the global capitalist mode of production as well as to transnational migration, both of which put the nation-state and its territorial citizenship under increasing pressure. As a consequence, citizenship is transforming itself and finds a new form beyond the nation-state, liberating itself from the constraints of national identity.[8] Against the background of globalisation in particular, new approaches are developed that conceptualise citizenship without relating it to nation-states. For example, Seyla Benhabib pleads for a 'republican federalism', which is expected to enhance popular sovereignty by perpetuating cosmopolitan norms such as those pertaining to refugee, immigrant and asylum status across the local, national and global levels. At the same time, Benhabib acknowledges that these norms challenge the nation-state by escaping from its control.[9] Equally, in his account of European citizenship, Rainer Bauböck builds on a modification of Kant's model for a global confederation of republics, with a new form of transnational citizenship. He focuses on institutional aspects of the architecture of citizenship such as the differentiation of citizenship statuses in Europe, the allocation of voting rights to these categories and the rules for acquisition and loss of citizenship at various levels.[10] Against this background, scholars argue that processes of denationalisation can be conducive to the inclusiveness of citizenship, as the emergence of cosmopolitan norms such as those of universal human rights, crimes against humanity as well as refugee, immigrant and asylum status strengthens citizenship rather than undermining it. While citizenship finds itself in a process of reconstitution, it shifts from national citizenship towards a citizenship of residency, pertaining to the multiple ties to locality, to the region and to transnational institutions. In this respect, we are witnessing a universalistic extension of civil and social rights, and, in some cases, even of political participation rights (as in the context of the European Union).[11]

Third, contrary to the doubts about the further existence of the nation-state, some authors argue that it is precisely globalisation that has triggered the current wave of nationalism, rather than the enduring nature of the national idea. This argument rejects the well-known essentialist position of Anthony D. Smith, which relates nations and nationalism to ethnic cores resistant even to modernisation processes. For instance, Mary Kaldor elucidates the current wave of nationalism against the background of global changes in the division of labour and in communication processes.[12] The 'new nationalism' is to be found in places like Nagorno Karabakh or Bosnia-Herzegovina and develops under circumstances of insecurity, perpetuated by globalisation. The 'new nationalism' breeds violence and excludes 'others' of a different ethnicity (framed as nationality), and thus it shares a common aspiration with religious fundamentalism, as both insist on a rigid following of religious or national doctrines. As a consequence, it can be argued that there is a considerable overlap between militant nationalist and religious movements, not only because of the religiously dogmatic character of militant nationalism but also because many nations are defined in religious terms (Bosnian Muslims, Hindu nationalists) and many religions are described in nationalist terms (Judaism or Islam). Even though Kaldor's argument departs from the modernist paradigm, in which nationalism is associated with the structural conditions associated with modernity, she suggests that the conditions under which modern nationalism was spawned have changed considerably. The new IT-based economy has replaced industrialism and simultaneously requires a much more differentiated workforce.

While digital communication is currently becoming more important than print technology (essential for Anderson's concept of
imagined community), it gives rise to new horizontal or transborder cultural communities which perforate the traditional form
of nationalism.[13] Instead, new militant nationalist and religious
ideologies support novel forms of violence, whereas wars between
states become rather an anachronism. According to Kaldor, traditional nationalism gives way to new horizontal ideologies with an
exclusive and fundamentalist character, including sub-state and
transborder nationalism as well as global Islam.

Against the background of the 'new nationalism', a novel focus
has occurred with regard to the relationship between nationalism
and religion. For Michael Mann both nationalism and religion
belong to the same category of 'ideological network of power',
which is described as follows:

> It comprises of [sic] networks of persons bearing ideologies
> which cannot be proved true or false, couched at a sufficient
> level of generality to be able to give 'meaning' to a range of
> human actions in the world – as religion, socialism, or nation
> alism all do, for example. They also contain norms, rules of
> interpersonal conduct which are 'sacred,' strengthening con
> ceptions of collective interest and cooperation, reinforced, as
> Durkheim said, by rituals binding people together in repeated
> affirmations of their commonality. So those offering plausi
> ble ideologies can mobilize social movements, and wield a
> general power in human societies analogous to powers yielded
> by control over economic, military, and political power
> resources.[14]

Even though religion and nationalism are different ideologies,
varying in terms of their sources, composition and scope, they
can be regarded as similar in their response to social change. As
communications and migration render social borders permeable
to transcultural flows, social groups (both religious and nationalist) laying claim to ultimate meanings search for ways to maintain
a coherent worldview. One of the strategies of coping with the
culturally porous world is the organic and aggressive response of
launching a 'holy war' for society as a whole. The 'holy war' can
be waged on religiously or nationalistically dogmatic grounds,
both pertaining to the ultimate meanings and moral certitude. As

a consequence, the social group in question attempts to seize the state and with its instruments impose 'an organic unity on an inorganic social body', as Robert W. Hefner puts it.[15] Once the project of state seizure is perpetuated by a religious group, nationalism assumes religious traits and entails high costs for the entire society, including antagonising religious and ethnic minorities, frustrating nonconforming members of the faith and destroying the freedoms necessary for peaceful social order.

However, this religious nationalism is not the only possible outcome of the relationship between nationalism and religion. Uri Ram suggests four possible heuristic modules of ideology, which are composed of different blends of nationalism and 'religionism'. These modules are constructed by the crosscutting of two axes: the axis of nationalism, which shows a scale from weak to strong nationalism, and the axis of religionism, which shows weak to strong religion, whereby the extreme case of 'weak religion' implies secularism. The four modules are strong nationalism/weak religionism, strong nationalism/strong religionism, weak nationalism/weak religionism and weak nationalism/weak religionism. The module of strong nationalism/weak religionism implies a dominant and vigorous secular nationalism which treats religion as a competitor for political legitimacy. In contrast, strong nationalism/strong religionism is the case of a fusion between strong nationalism and strong religionism, which creates the aforementioned 'religious nationalism' as a indissoluble mesh of both ideologies feeding off each other in the quest for the organic unity of culturally diverse societies. The module of weak nationalism/weak religionism pertains in turn to strong constitutionally/contractually legitimised communities, where pre-political, primordial and religious identities are rather weak or play no role in political legitimacy. The fourth module of weak nationalism/strong religionism points to the pervasiveness of religion as a communal identity and weakness or even absence of nationalism, which can assume a form of a 'transnational religious fundamentalism', often attributed to Islamism.[16]

Even though the relationship between religion and nationalism is examined in different cultural contexts,[17] the role of Islam and Islamism has been increasingly prominent in the research.[18] In this context, some authors argue contrary to the common transnational view on Islam that it can be regarded as equivalent to nationalism. Even though it does not pertain to territory or state, it is constructed in the context of particular countries and their politics. While its appeal is pan-Islamic, its reality is often particular. The anti-colonial sentiments, proclaimed as hostilities towards Western powers and Israel, have a mainly political substance, even though they are conceived in terms of religious solidarities. In addition, forms of Islamic nationalism develop within the context of a globalised Islam, outside the framework of nation-states but empowered by the liberties and institutions of Western culture and polities, which are targeted as its antagonists.[19] However, this is not to say that Islam breeds nationalism and violence by its very nature. This simplistic claim is applied, for example, in Russia's state ideology in support of its own version of nationalism. Russian national ideology accuses Muslims of the Russian Federation of being potential Islamists, keen to support the Chechen separatist project of establishing an Islamic state in the Caucasus. Elise Giuliano challenges this claim, which assumes that Muslims in Russia form a coherent group based on common religious identity and thus represent a similar anti-state nationalism turned against the Russian state. She examines ethnic identity and politics in Dagestan and Chechnya, where there was the most radical surge in societal Islamisation, and demonstrates that the religious belief and practice of Islam does not correlate with anti-Moscow political mobilisation and it is the ethnicity, rather than the Muslim identity, that entails political mobilisation.[20] However, this mobilisation stems from the contextual factors of Russia's ethnic republics, rather than from religious motivation, since Muslims in Russia have largely opposed radical Islamic movements during the past fifteen years. Therefore, radical Islamic mobilisation in the West not only occurs to a larger extent than in the Russian Federation, but it also has a very different nature.

The last research focus on nationalism concerns its relationship with the gender *problématique*. The vast majority of classical approaches to nationalism either ignore the gender issue or argue (as do, for instance, Greenfeld and Anderson) that the rise of nationalism coincided with an expansion of women's rights. In the latter sense, nationalism is assumed to have had a gender-equalising function. However, other authors (for example, Carole Pateman and Susan Okin) suggest that nationalism has had mainly monogendered equality effects.[21] They point out that the nationalist myths of origin are mainly based on an ideology of brotherhood. Even though liberal variants of nationalism highlight the equality among the members of the national community by rejecting the traditional concept of patriarchalism (the 'rule of the fathers'), they maintain or even strengthen the ideology of fraternity (the masculine 'rule of the brothers and husbands').[22] As a consequence modern nationalism has inherently legitimised masculine patriarchalism, as until the twentieth century most of the nation-states refused to grant civil status and rights to women.[23] This gender bias has been echoed both in political practice and in legal status even in the twentieth and the twenty-first centuries, perpetuating discrimination between women and men with respect to national rights and responsibilities. The critics of 'gendered nationalism' argue that the connection between gender and nationalism is not accidental.[24] As membership of a nation bestows entitlements to the resource distribution by the state, the masculine bias in nationalism goes hand in hand with exclusion from rights and entitlements, enhancing their concentration in the masculine part of the citizenship. However, this questions the very nature of national citizenship as horizontal equality, which is bounded regarding the distinction between citizens and non-citizens, but internally integrated through an inter-unit equality.

In a similar vein, other authors such as Joane Nagel highlight a differently envisaged functionality of men and women in relation to the 'nation'. For instance, through the construction of patriotic manhood and exalted motherhood as icons of nationalist ideology 'gendered nationalism' designates 'gendered places' for men and women in national politics.[25] This gendered designation is subject to the domination of masculine interests and ideology in nationalist movements. Two features are characteristic for the masculine domination in nationalism. First, there is the interplay between masculine micro-cultures and nationalist ideology. It can be argued that both in the masculine micro-culture and nationalist ideology the mothers and daughters of the family and of the nation must be 'pure'. As a consequence, nationalists often have a special interest in the sexuality and sexual behaviour of women. While traditionalist men are defenders of the family's and the nation's honour, women embody both the shame of the family and the shame of the nation.[26] Second, modern nationalism is associated with sexualised militarism, which constructs simultaneously sexualised 'enemy' men and 'enemy' women. Modern military institutions as bearers of nationalism are sexualised centres for the depiction of the 'enemy' in conflicts. These institutions convey images of enemy men either as sexual demons, aiming to rape nationalist women, or as 'eunuchs', incapable of sexual virility. In contrast, enemy women are often characterised as sexually promiscuous and available, and thus legitimate targets of rape.[27]

A particularly interesting example of the relationship between gender and nationalism relates to religious nationalism. As mentioned above, religious nationalisms are responses to the cultural and territorial porousness of contemporary nations through the deployment of God in the service of the nation-state. This also has consequences for gender relations. Religious nationalism attempts to create an organic unity of religion and nation and by so doing it often seeks to confine women to a womanly place and to regulate sexuality in the context of the nation as a patriarchal family. As Roger Friedland argues, religious nationalists attempt to restore and revitalise the masculine gender of state. Therefore, controlling the reproductive forces of women and men is one essential element in the religiously based project of creating the nation as a collective subject of rule. As a consequence, religious nationalists discipline both female and male sexuality not only as a way to create social order, but also to construct a powerful state. Religious nationalists apply God as the ordering representation for the reconstruction of national collectivity.[28]

These three foci are likely to mark new research trends regarding nationalism. Their advantage is their interdisciplinary character. It allows the problem of a narrow, one-discipline perspective which has so far characterised many studies on nation and nationalism to be overcome. We believe that significant problems regarding the emergence and development of nationalism in Europe can be better addressed and explained by means of a larger analytical angle. An analysis going beyond the traditional one-discipline perspective can contribute to a better understanding of the phenomenon. Although this volume shows some deficits of research on nation and nationalism in Europe and offers a more systematic perspective on the topic (by differentiating between different levels of analysis of nationalism), we are aware of the fact that further research will be needed to cover the main conceptual, analytical and methodological problem regarding, for example, new forms of nationalism in old European nation-states, the dynamics of nationalism in newly independent states, the complex relationship between nationalism and regionalism or the causal link between nationalism and European integration.

This multiplicity of nationalism should be examined in more depth, at both the theoretical and the empirical level. The linearity of nationalism proposed by Anthony D. Smith and Ernest Gellner needs to be replaced with more complex approaches to contemporary nationalism, in particular regarding its dynamics. The multiplicity of nationalism suggests that there will be new research foci, which should be subject to further exploration. In this context, a promising possible theoretical development might attempt to relate these different forms of nationalism and shift the discourse beyond the traditional civic–ethnic divide.

Notes

1. Saskia Sassen, 'Globalization or denationalization?', *Review of International Political Economy* 10, 1 (2003), pp. 1–22; Stephen Castles and Alastair Davidson, *Citizenship and Migration: Globalization and the Politics of Belonging* (Basingstoke: Palgrave, 2000); Catarina Kinnvall, 'Globalization and religious nationalism: self, identity, and the search for ontological security', *Political Psychology* 25, 5 (2004), pp. 741–67.
2. Ana María Alonso, 'The politics of space, time and substance: state formation, nationalism and ethnicity', *Annual Review of Anthropology* 23 (1994), pp. 379–405; Douglas Kellner, 'Theorizing globalization', *Sociological Theory* 20, 3 (2002), pp. 285–305; Jonathon W. Moses, 'Exit, vote and sovereignty: migration, states and globalization', *Review of International Political Economy* 12, 1 (2005), pp. 53–77.
3. David McCrone and Richard Kiely, 'Nationalism and citizenship', *Sociology* 34, 1 (2000), pp. 19–34; Richard Falk, 'The decline of citizenship in an era of globalization', *Citizenship Studies* 4, 1 (2000), pp. 5–17; Björn Hettne, 'The fate of citizenship in post-Westphalia', *Citizenship Studies* 4, 1 (2000), pp. 35–46.
4. Gerard Delanty, *Citizenship in a Global Age: Society, Culture, Politics* (New York: Open University Press, 2000); Richard Münch, *Nation and Citizenship in the Global Age* (Basingstoke: Palgrave, 2001); for the EU, see Catherine Wihtol De Wenden, 'Post-Amsterdam migration policy and European citizenship', *European Journal of Migration and Law* 1 (1999), pp. 89–101; Michael Peter Smith, 'Transnationalism, the state, and the extraterritorial citizen', *Politics & Society* 31, 4 (2003), pp. 467–502.
5. Castles and Davidson, *Citizenship and Migration*; Lydia Morris, 'Globalization, migration and the nation-state: the path to a post-national Europe?', *British Journal of Sociology* 48, 2 (1997), pp. 192–209.
6. William I. Robinson, 'Beyond nation-state paradigms: globalization, sociology, and the challenge of transnational', *Sociological Forum* 13, 4 (1998), pp. 561–94; Fred W. Riggs, 'Globalization, ethnic diversity, and nationalism: the challenge for democracies', *Annals of the American Academy of Political and Social Science* 581 (2002), pp. 35–47.
7. This position is more than merely a critique of the first method of linking citizenship and collective identity. It takes it to a higher level of negating the relevance of the first method.
8. Trevor Purvis and Alan Hunt, 'Identity versus citizenship: transformations in the discourses and practices of citizenship', *Social & Legal Studies* 8, 4 (1999), pp. 457–82.
9. Seyla Benhabib, 'Twilight of sovereignty or the emergence of cosmopolitan norms? Rethinking citizenship in volatile times', *Citizenship Studies* 11, 1 (2007), p. 31; see also William Smith, 'Cosmopolitan citizenship', *European Journal of Social Theory* 10, 1 (2007), pp. 37–52.

10. Rainer Bauböck, 'Why European citizenship? Normative approaches to supranational union', *Theoretical Inquiries in Law* 8 (2007), pp. 439–74; see also Rainer Bauböck, *Transnational Citizenship: Membership Rights in International Migration* (Aldershot: Edward Elgar, 1994); Heinz Kleger (ed.), *Transnationale Staatsbürgerschaft* (Frankfurt: Campus, 1997). See also Heinz Kleger, 'Transnationale Staatsbürgerschaft oder: Lässt sich Staatsbürgerschaft entnationalisieren?', *Archiv für Rechts- und Sozialphilosophie* 62 (1995), pp. 85–99.

11. Seyla Benhabib, 'Twilight of sovereignty or the emergence of cosmopolitan norms?: Rethinking citizenship in volatile times', *Citizenship Studies* 11, 1 (2007), pp. 19–36; see also James Bohman, 'Republican cosmopolitanism', *Journal of Political Philosophy* 12, 3 (2004), pp. 336–52.

12. Mary Kaldor, 'Nationalism and globalization', *Nations and Nationalism* 10, 1/2 (2004), pp. 161–77; Mary Kaldor, *Old and New Wars: Organized Violence in a Global Era* (Cambridge: Polity Press, 1999).

13. See also Willfried Spohn, 'Multiple modernity, nationalism and religion: A global perspective', *Current Sociology* 51, 3–4 (2003), pp. 265–86.

14. Michael Mann, 'The sources of social power revisited: a response to criticism', in John A. Hall and Ralph Schroeder (eds), *An Anatomy of Power: The Social Theory of Michael Mann* (Cambridge: Cambridge University Press, 2006), pp. 343–96 (p. 346).

15. Robert W. Hefner, 'Multiple modernities: Christianity, Islam, and Hinduism in a globalizing age', *Annual Review of Anthropology* 27 (1998), pp. 83–104. See also Willfried Spohn, 'Political sociology: between civilizations and modernities. A multiple modernities perspective', *European Journal of Social Theory* 13, 1 (2010), pp. 49–66.

16. Uri Ram, 'Why secularism fails? Secular nationalism and religious revivalism in Israel', *International Journal of Politics, Culture and Society* 21 (2008), pp. 57–73.

17. See Willfried Spohn, 'Europeanization, religion and collective identities in an enlarging Europe: A multiple modernities perspective', *European Journal of Social Theory* 12, 3 (2009), pp. 358–74.

18. Roxanne L. Euben, 'Killing (for) politics: Jihad, martydom, and political action', *Political Theory* 30, 1 (2002), pp. 4–35; John A. Armstrong, 'Religious nationalism and collective violence', *Nations and Nationalism* 3, 4 (1997), pp. 597–606; Roger Friedland, 'When God walks in history: the institutional politics of religious nationalism', *International Sociology* 14, 3 (1999), pp. 301–19.

19. Sami Zubaida, 'Islam and nationalism: continuities and contradictions', *Nations and Nationalism* 10, 4 (2004), pp. 407–20.

20. Elise Giuliano, 'Islamic identity and political mobilization in Russia: Chechnya and Dagestan compared', *Nationalism and Ethnic Politics* 11 (2005), pp. 195–220; see also David G. Rowley, 'Imperial versus national discourse: the case of Russia', *Nations and Nationalism* 6, 1 (2000), pp. 23–42.

21. Carole Pateman, 'The fraternal social contract', in John Keane (ed.), *Civil Society and the State: New European Perspectives* (London: Verso, 1988), pp. 101–28; Susan Moller Okin, *Justice, Gender, and the Family* (New York: Basic Books, 1989).

22. Maureen Molloy, 'Imagining (the) difference: gender, ethnicity and metaphors of nation', *Feminist Review* 51 (1995), pp. 94–112.

23. Philip N. Cohen, 'Nationalism and suffrage: Gender struggle in nation-building America', *Signs* 21, 3 (1996), pp. 707–27.

24. See also Spike V. Peterson, 'Gendered Nationalism', *Peace Review* 6, 1 (1994), pp. 77–83; Mary Ann Tetreault and Haya al-Mughni, 'Gender, citizenship and nationalism in Kuwait', *British Journal of Middle Eastern Studies* 22, 1/2 (1995), pp. 64–80; Eileen McDonagh, 'Political citizenship and democratization: the gender paradox', *American Political Science Review* 96, 3 (2002), pp. 535–52.

25. Joane Nagel, 'Masculinity and nationalism: gender and sexuality in the making of nations', *Ethnic and Racial Studies* 21, 2 (1998), pp. 242–69; Anne McClintock, 'Family feuds: gender, nationalism and the family', *Feminist Review* 44 (1993), pp. 61–80.

26. Ibid. p. 254.

27. Ibid. p. 257.
28. Roger Friedland, 'Money, sex, and God: the erotic logic of religious nationalism', *Sociological Theory* 20, 3 (2002), pp. 381–425; Roger Friedland, 'Religious nationalism and the problem of collective representation', *Annual Review of Sociology* 27 (2001), pp. 125–52.

Index

0110 concerts, 119, 158n

Albania, 141–2
Anderson, Benedict, 18, 26–7, 33n, 37, 61, 82n, 171, 210, 212
anti-Semitism, 102
assimilation, 7, 12, 39–41, 48, 52n, 73, 122, 129

Banting, Keith, 75, 84n
Barry, Brian, 72, 83n
Belgian nation, 114n, 120–1
Belgian Royal House, 120
Belgium, 13, 16, 72, 114n, 115–21, 157–8n
belonging, 6, 25–6, 30, 35n, 44–6, 48, 70, 81, 93, 95, 114n, 122, 135, 139–40, 153, 156, 158n, 170–2, 180, 183–6, 215n
Berlusconi, Silvio, 143, 162n
Billig, Michael, 19, 33n, 52–3n, 97, 103n
Brubaker, Rogers, 7, 14n, 29, 33n, 35n, 52n, 94, 99, 101, 102–3n, 163n, 183, 195–6, 202–3n, 205n
Bulgaria, 13, 115, 121–5, 158–9n, 187

Calhoun, Craig, 20, 34n, 195, 204–5n
chauvinism, 6, 181–2
Chechnya, 149, 212, 216n
citizenship, 25, 33–5n, 44, 52–4n, 74–6, 83–4n, 93, 96, 101, 103n, 118, 128–9, 145–7, 156, 163n, 176, 195–6, 199, 200n, 202–6n, 207–9, 213, 215–16n
   European, 196, 199, 206n, 208, 215–16n
   national, 44, 176, 207–9, 213
   postnational, 35n
   transnational, 25, 35n, 208, 216n
communitarian, 8–9, 73–6, 116, 135, 195
constructivism, 10, 49, 79
'cosmopolitan Europe', 190, 204n
cosmopolitanism, 76–7, 83–4n, 94, 102n, 191–2, 204n, 216n
Czechoslovakia, 100, 151

deliberation, 46, 68, 72–3, 126, 159n, 192
democracy, 12, 18, 26, 33n, 35n, 54n, 57–8, 68–72, 74, 78, 83–4n, 94, 103n, 118, 153, 155, 164n, 191, 200–1n, 204–6n,